SPENSER STUDIES

IV

SPENSER
STUDIES
A Renaissance
Poetry Annual

IV

EDITED BY

Patrick Cullen AND *Thomas P. Roche, Jr.*

AMS PRESS, INC.
NEW YORK, N.Y.

SPENSER STUDIES:
A RENAISSANCE POETRY ANNUAL
edited by Patrick Cullen and Thomas P. Roche, Jr.

is published annually by AMS Press, Inc. as a forum for Spenser scholarship and criticism and related Renaissance subjects. Manuscripts ordinarily should be from 3,000 to 10,000 words in length, should include an abstract of 100–175 words, should conform to the *MLA Style Sheet,* and should be submitted *in duplicate.* They will be returned only if sufficient postage is enclosed (overseas contributors should enclose international reply coupons). Manuscripts and editorial correspondence should be addressed to Thomas P. Roche, Jr., Department of English, Princeton University, Princeton, N.J. 08544.

ISSN 0195-9468
Volume IV, ISBN 0-404-19204-1

Contents

Spenser's remarriage shortly after his fortieth birthday is made part of a series of biographical fictions which explore the conditions of poetic identity and personal survival. In *Amoretti* and *Epithalamion,* a midlife crisis conspicuously different from that of a Dante or a Petrarch is charged with anxieties more appropriate to the histories of Spenser's aristocratic fellow poets at court, who incurred the wrath of their queen when they ventured to marry an earthly Elizabeth. The poems published after 1590 trace Spenser's changing poetics by means of a series of alternative stories of poetic survival: Sir Arthur Gorges brooding on his wife's death; the dead shepherd, Sir Philip Sidney, transformed along with his Stella into the flowers of other poets' verse; Sir Walter Ralegh, the Shepherd of the Ocean, whose involvement at court exposes him to the stormy bouts of disfavor which Spenser eludes by keeping his distance and celebrating a private marriage in distant Ireland. Colin's attainment of his Irish home is made a condition for his precariously balanced love of all the Elizabeths in his life; like his neighbor Bregog he wins his love at the price of a more public name for himself. The story of Timias in the 1596 *Faerie Queene* is a contrasting one of irreconcilable conflicts: Belphoebe, Amoret, and Arthur make absolute and exclusive demands on his loyalty, and he can be true to one only by being false to the other two. His quandary is symptomatic of the disintegrating public world of Spenser's later poetry, and contrasts with the quest for a private, separate peace.

Instead of idealizing his contemporaries in his poetry, Spenser typically seizes on the problems that they raise—psychological, moral, or political. In order to analyze these problems, he often fragments the historical persons into several distinct fictional characters, each fictional figure embodying an aspect of its original. This fragmentation of historical characters leads to a typically Spenserian play with perspectives, a portrayal of character or situation from several points of view. The most elaborate instances of fragmentation and perspectivism appear in the allegory of Lust, Amoret, and Timias in *FQ* IV.vii.

Through the allegory of Timias and Belphoebe, which traverses the 1590 and 1596 editions of *The Faerie Queene,* Spenser comments on two phases of Sir Walter Ralegh's career in Elizabeth's service. In the first, Timias's conquest of the wicked "fosters" celebrates Ralegh's part in helping to crush the Desmond Rebellion of the early 1580s and his heroism upon being ambushed by rebels at a ford. Spenser then introduces Belphoebe, who simultaneously heals and wounds Timias, as an analogue for Queen Elizabeth in the period that Ralegh described as his "sorrowfull success," an era of mixed fortune, extending to 1592, during which his power was eroding under pressure from the queen's new favorite, the earl of Essex. In the second edition, Spenser alludes to Ralegh's first major disgrace, when the queen discovered that he had impregnated and then secretly married one of her maids-in-waiting, Elizabeth Throckmorton. Spenser's complex treatment of this event reveals his immense sympathy with both Elizabeth and Ralegh; he hints at Ralegh's culpability, but also shows him as a victim, more worthy of pity than of censure. Book IV centers on his rejection and posits a later reconciliation, while Book VI charges Ralegh's enemies at court with malice, even as it suggests that he is partly responsible for his own dilemma.

This essay is an attempt to deal with the interrelationships of the three stories told in the Despair canto: Arthur's narrative of his visitation by the fairy queen, Trevisan's narrative of Terwin's succumbing to Despair, and Redcross's encounter with Despair. It asks the question why Arthur's love vision should be included in the same canto as the Despair episode, and why Spenser had to mediate these two stories with the Trevisan-Terwin story, which I suggest is linked to the plight of the poet-lover of the sonnet sequence. In the English sequences the poet-lover almost always ends in a state of despair. Through an analysis of repeated rhyme words used in all three stories, I hypothesize another kind of linkage in cantos going beyond characterization and narrative technique to make sense of Spenser's inclusion of these incidents in this canto.

The nature and significance of Guyon's "faint" after his experience in the Cave of Mammon is complicated by the fact that Guyon is not merely described as unconscious but is discussed, by characters who know better, as though he were *dead*. The image of the man, self-consciously aware as Guyon is of his consummate good deeds (II.vii.2), who nevertheless is spiritually "dead," was well known to Spenser's English readers. The "Sermon on Good Workes" from the *Elizabethan Book of Homilies* identifies two forms of faith—a dead faith and a true and lively faith. Those morally good works done without a spiritual basis are sterile and "for a similitude . . . they which glister and shine in good workes without fayth in God, bee like dead men. . . . He that doeth good deedes, yet without faith he hath no life." A dead faith reveals itself as grounded in self-confidence, while a true and lively faith reveals confidence in God as man's support against temptation. This may be the one flaw in Guyon's otherwise admirable character: he professes what he does not ultimately believe, because he views the world essentially ethically but not spiritually, and he views himself as beyond the usual human predicament. With his acknowledgement of Arthur as the "Patrone of his life" (II.viii.55), however, Guyon acknowledges God as his necessary protector and defender—his patron.

"Fixt in heauens hight":
Spenser, Astronomy, and the Date of the *Cantos of Mutabilitie*
RUSSELL J. MEYER

Little attention has been given to Spenser's acquaintance with contemporary astronomers or his knowledge of the "new science" which developed so rapidly in his lifetime. Through Ralegh and his circle, as well as through Gabriel Harvey and his brother Richard, Spenser would have been familiar with the recent discoveries in astronomy which were challenging the Aristotelian and Ptolemaic views of the universe. These discoveries, in fact, appear to be at the heart of the *Cantos of Mutabilitie*, where Spenser describes a lunar eclipse. An awareness that Spenser is describing an actual event provides for a better understanding of the significance of the *Cantos*; but more importantly, a comparison of the details of that description with the actual celestial phenomena indicates that the date of the *Cantos* is after April 1595.

"Sometimes I . . . mask in myrth lyke to a Comedy":
Spenser's *Amoretti*
ELIZABETH BIEMAN

The uniqueness of the *Amoretti* in their occasion and their ending in throwing emphasis upon the autobiographical elements has had the unfortunate effect of deafening readers of the sequence to witty and frequently bawdy intricacies of language. Such effects may derive from a rhetoric of indirection prescribed in Ramist theory for circumstances in which the rhetorician cannot count on the ready assent of the object of his exercise in persuasion. When readers are prompted to

Contents

notice certain disguised attributions of sexuality to the lady they find her poetic configuration, appropriately, more similar to that of Britomart than to the conventional lady of the sonnet tradition.

Spenser's *Fowre Hymnes* form a unified narrative of the erotic and religious development of a fictional poet-lover, whose spiritual career follows one of the patterns recently described by Ana-Maria Rizzuto, a psychoanalyst who charts the evolution of the "god idea" from early infancy into adult life. The *Hymnes* are additionally unified by the relation of each to a "sense" of medieval exegesis and by their numerological symbolism ("four" was, for example, the Platonic number of "cosmic concord"). The dedication, also, which has seemed paradoxically to "recant" the first two hymns by way of an introduction to their reissue, can be better understood when "retractation" is read in its sixteenth-century sense of "revision" and when the dedication's numerological puns are deciphered.

SPENSER STUDIES

IV

DONALD CHENEY

Spenser's Fortieth Birthday
and Related Fictions

*A*T SOME point in the early 1590s, Edmund Spenser turned forty; it is his allusion to "those fourty" years in *Amoretti,* sonnet 60, alongside similarly generalized or riddling references to his marriage some two years later, on 11 June 1594, that constitutes our evidence for the traditional attribution of his birth date to 1552 or thereabouts.[1] Like others of his time and class, Spenser left a frustrating paucity of biographical information. Scholars assume that he was the Edmund Spenser who married Maccabaeus Chylde at St. Margaret's, Westminster, in 1579, simply because he must have been married about that time in order to have had a son old enough to take his widowed stepmother to court around 1602; but of the first Mrs. Spenser nothing is known other than that she must have existed, with or without benefit of Westminster clergy. Like so many women of her time, she is largely ignored by the public records; like other poets' wives, she is equally absent from her husband's verses.

At about the time of Spenser's fortieth birthday, however, these conditions of personal and spousal anonymity are altered dramatically, with important consequences for the tenor and implications of Spenser's later poetry. The subject of this essay is not the historical Edmund Spenser about whom so little is known, but the autobiographical fiction that becomes so conspicuous a part of his poetry after 1590, as well as analogous biographical fictions of his invention. I would suggest that the poetry written or at least published between the two installments of *The Faerie Queene* traces a pattern of related fictions which bear on the new directions given to the major poem in 1596. I take the instance of the poet's fortieth birthday—in itself no more than a glancing allusion—as a useful point of entry into a poetics dominated by a sense of time's urgency, of darkening shadows in private and public sectors alike. The death of one poet and his absorption into the flowers of poetry he leaves behind, the need for another to choose between the dead past and the limited and threatened though living present, move into the foreground of Spenser's vision as metaphors for alternative strategies of survival in the final years of the century and of an era.

A fortieth birthday, in literature as in life, is a potential invitation to personal retrospection. One may come to such a pass at thirty, fearing the shadow of the gallows like Villon or at least banishment from the circle of those who are certifiably young; or at thirty-three, the Christological year when mere survival becomes a paradoxical intimation that one is merely mortal; or at thirty-five, the midpoint of one's threescore years and ten and the starting point of Dante's drama of regeneration. Forty is, if anything, a bit late for a midlife crisis; one might expect Spenser's to run the more heavily toward weary musings on the transience of earthly delights and the desirability of eternal rest in the hereafter. Since readers usually find what they look for, this is the Spenser of common repute: the Spenser whose failure to satisfy earlier expectations is so frequently ascribed to exhaustion. Perhaps there are three main sources of this aspect of the poet's reputation. There is the extraordinary influence of C. S. Lewis in forming our notions of the orthodoxy of both Spenser and Milton; it was he who spoke of the "church-wardenly" Spenser and colored our sense of the poet's middle-aged romance by suggesting that it was doubtless more pleasant to experience than to read about.[2] Second, and more pernicious, is Milton's compliment to a "sage and serious" Spenser, "whom I *dare be known* to think a better teacher than Scotus or Aquinas"—with a courageous recommendation like that, Spenser has never needed detractors.[3] Finally, there is indeed some supporting evidence in Spenser's own later poems: the balancing and reformation of his hymns to love and beauty; the longing for a Sabbath's sight, so often cited; the invoking of spiritual priorities at various points in *Amoretti*.

But we must set against this theme of weary exhaustion and affirmation of values which extend beyond the grave other affirmations equally present in the later poetry, though insufficiently recognized. Spenser's fortieth birthday is productive not so much of a turning to God, or to a spiritualized object of desire, a Laura or Beatrice who will lead the poet thither, as it is of a new commitment to the things of this world. When he looks into his middle-aged heart he finds the *veteris vestigia flammae;* unlike Dido's, this flame is fanned by cupids—little loves, *amoretti*—of his own begetting. The resultant public image of the poet is far removed from that of a Dante or Petrarch, or even a Sidney: Spenser's *Vita Nuova* is a drama of survival, a revitalized acceptance of his old life. This fact brings with it serious problems of self-presentation. The remark of C. S. Lewis mentioned above indirectly illustrates as much: although God's law permits a widower to remarry, for increase or for mere companionship, the customs of mortals do not encourage the public celebration of remarriage. The only place on stage for such an impulse is as the butt of satire directed against those randy pantaloons whose untimely and unconvincing lusts threaten the proper and seasonable transfer of wealth. In the love of an older man for a younger woman, such economic concerns are associated with darker, incestuous reminiscences. The *senex* must be divested of both daughter and ducats if a healthy society is to renew itself.

THE ANXIETIES OF COURTSHIP

The fictionalized remarriage of the poet is enacted with a full awareness of such prejudices as these, with results that readers have recognized as characteristically Spenserian. Harry Berger has remarked that "the great minor poems present Spenser as both poet and man, faced with the problem of establishing the correct decorum between the urge to make poems and the urge to do anything else; these are by no means congenial urges, and he is often hard pressed to make each serve, rather than hinder, the other."[4] This remark applies with particular force to the tensions observable in *Amoretti* and *Epithalamion*, where a sonnet collection on the model of Petrarch's *canzoniere* experiences a series of anxious deviations from the norm. It seems that Spenser goes out of his way to avoid a simple, direct celebration of what in itself he must rightly have considered a perfectly blameless private courtship and marriage. Riddling and disjunctive hints of numerical or calendrical schemes tantalize the reader, as may be seen even in that sixtieth sonnet which alludes to the poet's age:

> They that in course of heauenly spheares are skild,
>   To euery planet point his sundry yeare:
>   in which her circles voyage is fulfild,
>   as Mars in three score yeares doth run his spheare.
> So since the winged God his planet cleare,
>   began in me to moue, one yeare is spent:
>   the which doth longer vnto me appeare,
>   then al those fourty which my life outwent.
> Then by that count, which louers books invent,
>   the spheare of Cupid fourty yeares containes:
>   which I haue wasted in long languishment,
>   that seemed the longer for my greater paines.
> But let my loues fayre Planet short her wayes
>   this yeare ensuing, or else short my dayes.
>
> (*Amoretti;* sonnet 60)

In the absence of a more full and coherent reading than I know how to give it, this sonnet seems to promise more in the way of structural codes

DONALD CHENEY

than it delivers. The octave and sestet contrast astronomical skills with "that count, which louers books inuent," a sixty-year orbit of Mars with a forty-year orbit of Cupid. Since both numbers seem comparably fanciful or arbitrary (Mars has either a seventy-nine-year "voyage" or one of just under two years),[5] the number sixty seems to allude to the number of the sonnet in this collection.[6] And it is true enough that the hoped-for short-cut or short-circuiting of the courtship does take place; Spenser is not required or permitted to write another sixty sonnets, or even forty, before the marriage day.

Yet a reader who has observed all this is left thirsty for more. Perhaps the calculations of "louers books" are to be sought elsewhere in the collection, and the poem will be seen to possess a consistent symmetry previously unnoticed. More likely, though, our awareness of such hints of patterning will remain insufficient to rend the veil of secrecy that cloaks these echoes of a private conversation.[7] We are never permitted to forget the atmosphere of hasty accidents that sets these poems apart from the completed calendrical models of the Petrarchan *canzoniere* or of Spenser's own *Calender*. It seems that a song of desire fulfilled has to be at odds with time; completed patterns belong to songs of loss and deferral. Though the *Epithalamion* itself would seem to be an exception to this rule, its very completeness as a "goodly ornament" is provisional and chancy; it is made "in lieu of" other, proper ornamentation, and by a poet acutely aware that he cannot be at the same moment singer and bridegroom as he tries to "resound" his "owne loues prayses":

> Ne let the same of any be enuide:
> So Orpheus did for his owne bride,
> So I vnto my selfe alone will sing,
> The woods shall to me answer and my Eccho ring.
>
> (*Ep* 15–18)

Orpheus seems an ominous figure of the poet-husband in such a poem as this; and we might wonder about Echo as well. Is the poet in danger of being swallowed up by his own verbal riches, reduced to a voice and its echo? Is the object of his desire likely to disappear like Amoret, behind such a mask of love? Is this a gaining or a regaining of his Eurydice? Can the poet, like Orpheus, win her only by some turning away of his gaze? How can he tell his love without being envied?

It is this dramatization of concern for the poem's various readers, an anxious sense of the pervasive dangers of envious misreading, of failed other lovers whose stories shadow his happier one, that I would emphasize as characteristic of the *Amoretti* and of the courtship the sonnets enact. In the eightieth sonnet, for example, the poet-lover apologizes for interrupting his long race through fairyland:

> After so long a race as I haue run
>   Through Faery land, which those six books compile,
>   giue leaue to rest me being halfe fordonne,
>   and gather to my selfe new breath awhile.
> Then as a steed refreshed after toyle,
>   out of my prison I will breake anew:
>   and stoutly will that second worke assoyle,
>   with strong endeuour and attention dew.
> Till then giue leaue to me in pleasant mew,
>   to sport my muse and sing my loues sweet praise:
>   the contemplation of whose heauenly hew,
>   my spirit to an higher pitch will rayse.
> But let her prayses yet be low and meane,
>   fit for the handmayd of the Faery Queene.
>
> (*Amoretti*; sonnet 80)

This sonnet doubtless serves in part as an advertisement for the next installment of *The Faerie Queene,* to be published the following year; and on the surface it seems to make a proper distinction between genres: the poet claims a brief and well-earned vacation at this midpoint in his epic labors, in order to refresh his energies for the remaining task; pastoral contemplation of his lady will give him the strength to return. Yet even here there are awkward inconsistencies and ominous overtones. Is the poet's erotic relaxation "in middest of his race" somehow comparable to that of Red Cross? The fact that his "pleasant mew" is also characterized as a prison underscores such a possibility; we may recall that four sonnets earlier his lady's bosom had been called "the bowre of blisse" in far from opprobrious tones. Furthermore, the poet is betrayed here into suggesting that the heavenly hue of Elizabeth Boyle will provide a model for his praises of Elizabeth the queen; he retreats hastily from such a suggestion in the retraction of his final couplet, promising to observe decorum in his praises if not, apparently, in his thoughts.

This eightieth sonnet, with its anxious attempt to measure the stylistic distance between queen and handmaiden, elaborates a problem hinted in the seventy-fourth:

Most happy letters fram'd by skilfull trade,
  with which that happy name was first desynd:
  the which three times thrise happy hath me made,
  with guifts of body, fortune and of mind.
The first my being to me gaue by kind,
  from mothers womb deriu'd by dew descent,
  the second is my souereign Queene most kind,
  that honour and large richesee to me lent.
The third my loue, my liues last ornament,
  by whom my spirit out of dust was raysed:
  to speake her prayse and glory excellent,
  of all alive most worthy to be praysed.
Ye three Elizabeths for euer liue,
  that three such graces did vnto me giue.

                    (*Amoretti*; sonnet 74)

The poet's life is given order and continuity by this trinity of Elizabeths; yet as they are unfolded in the chronological order of their various "gifts" to him, and presented diachronically in the enactment of the poem's words, the conceit seems strained and problematic. The poem does not quite work; it seems tasteless. We may object that the three gifts of these graces—body, fortune, and mind—do not quite suit the givers; or from a slightly different perspective, that Elizabeth the queen intrudes awkwardly, seeming to mediate or cast a censorious veil over the oedipal connection that links mother and wife. At the very least, we must feel a certain lèse-majesté in the enthusiasm with which the lover seems to give his mistress the place of honour: "of all alive most worthy to be praysed."[8] Though the senior Mrs. Spenser may well be dead, and so doubly unable to take offense at her son's remark, the irascible Belphoebe is very much alive. What is more, the image of the graces in this poem seems to hover midway between the explicit celebration of the queen as the fourth grace in the *Calender*, "April," and the equally explicit celebration of Colin's mistress as the fourth grace in *The Faerie Queene*, VI.x. Surely the poet is asking for trouble.

Such sonnets as these convey a tone of clumsy anxiety in their rhythm: a compliment is provisionally advanced and then hastily and apologetically revised; the speaker seems to become aware of addressing one mistress in a context where he risks being overheard and misunderstood by another, or perhaps understood all too well.[9] Spenser constructs an autobiographical fiction in which envy is omnipresent, both in the world surrounding the lovers and in their private and personal discourse. The "venemous toung" assailed by the speaker in sonnet 86 seems external to the lovers, like the personified Ate or Sclaunder in Book IV; yet it follows sequentially and half-logically from mention of the poet's own "glad mouth" in sonnet 85. Determined to utter his lady's praises while knowing the world cannot "deeme of worthy things," the poet courts—and in some sense becomes—a Blatant Beast.

This autobiographical fiction of the poet's private love affair is linked to other biographical fictions which intrude recurrently in Spenser's poetry of the 1590s. Although many of the specific instances of such intrusions are necessarily speculative and debatable as to precise references, a pattern of topical allusion seems undeniable. One of these fictions seems particularly pertinent here: Spenser's assertions of friendship and figurative kinship with Sir Walter Ralegh.[10] In *Amoretti* 74 perhaps, but more explicitly elsewhere in the later poetry, Spenser alludes to the disgrace of Ralegh's secret marriage to Elizabeth Throgmorton, one of the queen's maids of honour, and his subsequent imprisonment for several months in 1592.

As though eager to share in Ralegh's disgrace, Spenser cannot help dramatizing his own relationship to another Elizabeth in terms which stress fortuitous and gratuitous parallels. Elizabeth Throgmorton was literally a handmaid of the fairy queen: the discovery of her hidden pregnancy must have awakened the full wrath of a Diana who would have felt that this Callisto in her midst made a mockery of her court and her court's titles, even before she had to consider that the satyr responsible was her beloved favorite. Although critics have frequently tried to ascribe such echoes of awkward situations at court to Spenser's provincial isolation in Ireland, or to his carelessness or weariness, it seems more reasonable to see them as figuring the universality and variety of his poem's subject: the danger and yet the necessity of loving actively and directly in this world. Spenser's portrayal of himself in relation to his fellow courtier-poets returns over and over to various aspects of this theme. In the 1590s, it seems, to cling to the dream or the memory of a lost or inaccessible lover is to be held in thrall to a fairy queen who increasingly takes on the aspect of a *belle dame sans merci;* yet to seek fulfillment with her earthly sister is to risk the wrath of Belphoebe.

THE BEREAVED SWAIN

The importance of such biographical fictions to Spenser's revision of the *canzoniere* and epithalamion becomes clearer when one turns to his comparable revisions of complaint and pastoral during this period. William Oram has shown how *Daphnaida* initiates a new phase in Spenser's poetry, by means of its complex strategies of fictional "mirroring."[11] Oram describes the relation between the narrator and his protagonist Alcyon as contrasting patterns of grief. The narrator is able—like other singers of successful pastoral elegy—to end his lament at the end of day, and return home to his pastoral "cabinet"; but Alcyon's grief is unassuaged and he willfully, wildly is moving deeper into the savage wilderness when last seen.

Both Oram's study and a similarly valuable study by Duncan Harris and Nancy Steffen[12] suggest that the poem—or the poet, or the discriminating reader—ends by seeing Alcyon as a negative example of excessive grief. Certainly there is a contrast between civilization and wilderness, between acceptance of God's world and stubborn, dark brooding; and I would agree that if Arthur Gorges, Spenser's friend and the obvious model for the fictional Alcyon, were to have read the poem, he would doubtless have received a gently indirect message of encouragement to come back and rejoin his friends and family. One measure of the difference between this poem and its Chaucerian model is the greater distance between Spenser's Alcyon and the reader's sympathies. Yet, as Oram notes, the poem is dedicated not to Gorges himself but to Lady Helena, marquess of Northampton, the wife of Gorges's uncle; whatever message for Gorges the poem may contain is being delivered very obliquely. Similarly, the narrator is by no means explicitly the autobiographical Spenser, however tempting it may be to read back from the autobiographical fictions of remarriage a few years later to find here a grieving widower.[13] The melancholy of Spenser's narrator is left unexplained in the poem; and in this Spenser copies his Chaucerian model—and that model's models.[14]

Perhaps a fuller sense of the resonance of this curiously powerful poem can come from considering the names Spenser has given his fictional protagonists. Alcyon's name comes, of course, from the *Book of the Duchess:* Chaucer's narrator tells the first part of Ovid's story of Ceyx and Alcyone in connection with his own insomnia, before coming to his encounter with the man in black.[15] Yet Spenser was well acquainted with Ovid's treatment of the legend, and used it notably in his description of the house of Morpheus in Book I of *The Faerie Queene.* He would have known the ending of Ovid's story and would have observed that Chaucer conspicuously fails to complete his retelling of it: "Hyt were to longe for to dwelle." In breaking off his story, Chaucer seems concerned not only to save time but also to avoid a premature example of grief transcended and redeemed. Ovid does not simply (like Chaucer) tell us that Alcyone dies of grief when she learns in a dream that her husband has drowned. Rather, he tells that she goes to the seashore and finds his body on the waves. Running to meet him, she skims the water and finds herself changed to a bird, the halcyon or kingfisher:

> And through the pity of the gods, the husband
> Became a bird, and joined his wife. Together
> They suffered, and together loved; no parting
> Followed them in their new-found form as birds.
> They mate, have young, and in the winter season,
> For seven days of calm, Alcyone
> Broods over her nest on the surface of the waters
> While the sea-waves are quiet. Through this time
> Aeolus keeps his winds at home, and ocean
> Is smooth for his descendants' sake.[16]

Spenser's Alcyon, a male counterpart of the widowed Alcyone, carries in his name a highly charged figure of the paradoxical relationship between darkness and creativity. At the tragic pole of uncompromising grief, the gods take pity and transform one kind of brooding on the dark waves into another, more fertile one;[17] a story of death by water turns into one of renewed life in the depths of winter. One can see why a later poet, brooding on a drowned acquaintance, might have been thinking of this story of kingfishers when he gave Edward King the name of one of Sannazaro's fishermen, Lycidas. Perhaps, too, this story is echoed in the later work where God and poet alike create through brooding on the dark abyss; if so, one wonders what Milton may have made of the fact that Ceyx, in Ovid, is a son of Lucifer.[18]

Even without an awareness of what Milton has done to some of the language in and behind the poem, *Daphnaida* affords a suggestive variation on the pastoral complaint. Spenser apparently follows Gorges's own poetic precedent in giving Alcyon's lost wife the name of Daphne, the laurel tree, and thereby suggesting a specifically poetic context for the brooding. Perhaps the single-mindedness of Alcyon's vision points him toward the possibility of a different, Petrarchan form of poetic creativity that Spenser's narrator is unable or unwilling to attempt.[19] Chaucer's *Book of the Duchess* has provided a model for the sense of distance and awe that one feels in the presence of a person transformed by grief, "As if that death he in the face had seen, / Or hellish hags had met vpon the way." In both poems, the narrator opts for the normal human relationship to the diurnal cycle, as embodied in Una's advice to Red Cross: "Then with the Sunne take Sir, your timely rest, / And with new day new worke at once begin."(*FQ* I.i.33) In this contrast between sleeping and waking, Spenser adapts his Ovidian and Chaucerian models by including elements from his own earlier poetry, most notably the series of complaints in *FQ* III.iv, where Britomart and Chrysogone lament by the seashore, and Arthur wears out a sleepless night "In restlesse anguish and vnquiet paine." These laments, which one critic has described as providing a "lyric theodicy,"[20] achieve their cumulative effect and resolution in the reader's sense of the purpose-ful workings of a romance plot line: in the 1590 *Faerie Queene* it seems certain that all will end happily, that Britomart will get her Arthegall, Mari-nell will not die and will get his Florimel, Arthur will get Gloriana; all of them will recover their lost sleep. By the time of *Daphnaida,* however, there is no longer this controlling form to contain the complaint. The narrator cannot, finally, comprehend a figure like Alcyon, and loses sight of him: "But what of him became I cannot weene." To opt for sleep has be-come a career choice; one surrenders the capacity to imagine sleeplessness.

THE DEAD SHEPHERD

Whatever does happen to Alcyon? Oram's essay suggests that the ques-tion is finally for Alcyon's model, Arthur Gorges, to answer. Perhaps he will decide to come home again, to the things of this world.[21] Alterna-tively, one may address the question by considering the Ovidian imagery of the poem itself, and the attitude implied toward such metamorphosis as that imagery has suggested. Alcyon ignores his dying wife's plea to love their child, Ambrosia, "in lieu of me . . . so shall our loue for euer last." Ambrosia is in fact the actual name of the Gorges's child;[22] Spenser seems to have seized on it for the obvious irony in having ambrosia the gift of-fered the grieving husband rather than to the dead and transfigured wife. But Alcyon rejects both the celestial food and the role of mindful parent; instead he characterizes himself as bad shepherd:

> My little flocke, whom earst I lou'd so well,
> And wont to feede with finest grasse that grew,
> Feed ye henceforth on bitter *Astrofell,*
> And stinking Smallage, and vnsauerie Rew;
> And when your mawes are with those weeds corrupted,
> Be ye the pray of Wolues: ne will I rew,
> That with your carkasses wild beasts be glutted.
>
> (*Daphnaida* 344–50)

What is immediately striking about this passage is the arrival of a new plant in the Spenserian botany. The unsavory aspects of "bitter *Astrofell*" (its spelling may suggest a fallen star as well as a lethal or bitter quality) constitute a malign transformation of Sir Philip Sidney, an allusion to whom seems virtually inevitable here, especially in view of the elegy which Spenser was to publish four years later. There the pitying gods transform the pair of lovers—the gored Astrophel together with his beloved Stella who has died of grief—into a single flower:

> That hearbe of some, Starlight is cald by name,
> Of others *Penthia,* though not so well:
> But thou where euer thou doest find the same,
> From this day forth do call it *Astrophel.*
> And when so euer thou it vp doest take,
> Do pluck it softly for that shepheards sake.
>
> (*Astrophel* 193–98)

In this evocation of a flowery Ovidian metamorphosis, and in the elegiac delicacy of the stanza's conclusion, the tone is certainly far from the savage bitterness of Alcyon. Nevertheless, a comparison of *Astrophel*—poem, man, and flower—with comparable elements in the 1590 *Faerie Queene* will make clearer how the memory of dead lovers has come to turn sour. If surviving mortals cannot draw nourishment from Ambrosia, neither can they feed on unsavory rue without corrupting their maws.

In the gardens of Adonis, Spenser celebrates the miraculous revival of Adonis in terms which contrast the lover of Venus with other failed lovers of myth who have been turned into flowers. In Spenser's version of the myth, Adonis continues to act as father of forms, providing Venus with continuing pleasure; meanwhile, around the mount of Venus is found "euery sort of flowre, / To which sad louers were transformd of yore." The generative principle of the garden benignly subsumes these sad lovers—Narcissus the self-lover, stranded at the watery shore; Hyacinthus the hapless mortal minion of competing gods; Amaranthus the bereaved fiancé. All have their place, if not in the story at least close to the action. Spenser suppresses Adonis's own transformation into a flower, apparently in order to suggest a distinction between the active sexual reproduction available to human beings and the more limited, indirect, passive participation in a continuity of kind found among flowers—and among those human creatures who for one reason or another do not reproduce themselves. Since flowers are the product of these gardens in any case, there is little sense of second-class citizenship implied: sad lovers continue to be born, the story suggests, even though other sad lovers have not begotten or borne them.[23]

Not surprisingly, a pastoral elegy like *Astrophel* is concerned with other matters, and with making other distinctions. What *is* rather surprising, though, is that *Astrophel* invites comparison with Spenser's earlier treatment of the gardens of Adonis, in ways that shed light on the later poem's peculiarities. Spenser has seemed embarrassingly inept in his praise of Sidney: not only does he wait for nearly a decade before paying any substantial homage to the dead poet (meanwhile calling attention to his delinquency in his dedication of *The Ruines of Time*), but he also seems to have alluded to Sidney's ladies in the most ignorant or tasteless fashion imaginable. Scholars have suggested that Spenser, out of touch in Ireland and far from rumors of court, may have identified Stella with Sidney's wife rather than with Penelope Rich.[24] Even if he imagined her to have been yet a third woman, however, there would still remain an irreducible oddness to his behavior. He dedicates his collection of laments to Sidney's widow, now countess of Essex and remarried to Penelope Rich's brother, and then goes on to describe a Stella who dies of grief at her lover's death. Since both ladies are conspicuously alive (and sexually active), it seems that the Stella of Spenser's fiction has a more restricted identity than does the Astrophel. She is, one might say, quite simply the Stella of Sidney's sonnets; after the death of the maker of those sonnets, she continues to live only as he does, a part of the flowering of Sidney's poetic genius.

Even in the 1590 *Faerie Queene,* Sidney's world is associated with the limited or specialized kind of survival associated with such poetic flowerings as may be gathered in anthologies or florilegia. Of the three species of flowers representing sad lovers only one is both heterosexual and postclassical:

> Sad *Amaranthus,* made a flowre but late,
> Sad *Amaranthus,* in whose purple gore
> Me seemes I see *Amintas* wretched fate,
> To whom sweet Poets verse hath giuen endlesse date.
>
> (*FQ* III.vi.45)

The Amintas who becomes the amaranth is the creature not of Tasso but of Thomas Watson and Abraham Fraunce; his story is one of a shepherd who dies of grief (after a protracted series of complaints) when his betrothed dies abruptly before their wedding day. Fraunce dedicates his translation of Watson's Latin poem to the countess of Pembroke in 1587; it is subsequently republished in 1591 as the second part of *The Countesse of Pembrokes Yuychurch* and made the pretext for an annual poetic gathering under Pembroke auspices, to be known as "Amintas Dale" in honor of the dead shepherd. Whether or not the dead Sidney is already figured behind this 1590 allusion to Amintas, it seems clear that Spenser is invoking the contemporary vogue for pastoral elegy as well as the poetic patronage represented by Sidney's sister.[25]

By the time he publishes *Astrophel,* he is able to invent a fable that combines elements in the antique tale of Adonis and the modern one of Amintas. The shepherd is gored like Adonis; the loving pair expire together in a *liebestod* like that of Amintas and his Phillis. As in both stories, a flowery metamorphosis occurs; but Spenser is able to improve on both by inventing a flower which contains both lovers, a star at the center of the blossom "Resembling *Stella* in her freshest yeares" (189), perhaps in reference to the fact that Sidney's poetic names, both Philisides and Astrophel, contain such a star within themselves. The alternative name for Spenser's flower, Penthia, like the similarly named figure in Ford's *The Broken Heart*,[26] may be another contemporary name for Stella/Penelope; but it also suggests sorrow, mourning, like the name of the Pentheus who defied Dionysus and was destroyed. In common with other writers of the later Elizabethan period, Spenser seems to be hinting at a common nemesis for all those who deny love, for whatever reason. They become the stuff of poetry, while the world and the court belong to the survivors.

Such a contrast between the quick and the dead is provided by the two halves of the book Spenser published in 1595 under a title that announced a tale of poetic survival and return, *Colin Clouts Come Home Againe.* The contrasting fictions of Spenser and Sidney, Colin and Astrophel, may be seen the more clearly if one considers their common relationship, along with that of *Daphnaida,* to Spenser's initial collection of eclogues, *The Shepheardes Calender,* presented to the world in 1579 under a dedication to the still-living Sidney. The figure of Colin in the earlier poem is at odds with the themes of seasonal renewal and containment of suffering which are implicit in the calendrical and pastoral formats. As Paul Alpers has noted, the *Calender* lacks a single, unifying voice to express such containment.[27] Colin is largely alienated from the poem's present world, his old songs rehearsed or recalled in his absence; he seems willfully to be courting the fate of an Amintas or a Narcissus.

In the later poems, the story of Colin is refracted into three different scenarios. Some shepherds may continue to mourn, and given an adequate theme may achieve greatness by that route. Such was the case with the greater calendar of Petrarch's *Rime;* such may still be the case with Alcyon, who is in this sense a projection of the earlier Colin's refusal to deny his pain and frustration. The jury is still out in the case of Alcyon, both at the end of *Daphnaida* when the narrator comes home from the darkness and loses sight of him, and in *Colin Clouts Come Home Againe* when the returned Colin pays him tribute from a similar distance:

> And there is sad *Alcyon* bent to mourne,
> Though fit to frame an euerlasting dittie,

Whose gentle sprite for *Daphnes* death doth tourn
Sweet layes of loue to endlesse plaints of pittie.
Ah pensiue boy pursue that braue conceipt,
In thy sweet Eglantine of *Meriflure,*
Lift vp thy notes vnto their wonted height,
That may thy *Muse* and mates to mirth allure.

(CCCHA 384–91)

Although Colin envisions a happy conclusion to Alcyon's poem, he seems to see it as proceeding from that same "braue conceipt" that now preoccupies him.[28] Perhaps Alcyon may still work through his grief to some higher form of achievement and poetic return.

Alternatively, some shepherds do die young (as Colin has imagined himself doing), and become an object of meditation for other poets: their lives are subsumed into the poetry of others. This is the case of Astrophel. The somewhat curious organization of Spenser's elegy seems a simplification of an analogous quality in the *Calender,* whereby a figure of the poet is variously present and absent, thereby undermining the more straightforward dramatic personification of the singer in earlier eclogue books. In *Astrophel* a narrator begins by singing a lament of his own composing; then he "rehearses" a lament attributed to Astrophel's sister Clorinda; then he abandons the field to poems which are in fact wholly the production of others. An eclogue book thus turns by degrees into a pastoral anthology. *Astrophel* may be seen, therefore, as a projection of Colin's absence from the *Calender,* whereas *Daphnaida* had been a projection of his complaining presence in that earlier poem.

THE WORLD OF WATERS: COURTSHIP AND THE COURT

Finally, there is the possibility of poetic survival and return. The 1595 *Colin Clout* volume balances the passing of Sidney or Astrophel into the lamenting voices of his survivors against the return of Spenser's pastoral persona into full control over his own songs. The confusion of voices in the *Calender,* which had been a measure of Colin's alienation, gives way to a single continuous, syncretic viewpoint expressed by the confident inheritor of Vergilian pastoral celebration:

The shepheards boy (best knowen by that name)
That after *Tityrus* first sung his lay,
Laies of sweet loue, without rebuke or blame,
Sate (as his custome was) vpon a day,
Charming his oaten pipe vnto his peres. (CCCHA 1–5)

Of the numerous strategies by which the poet achieves his pastoral odyssey, returning to a point of vantage where he can sing blamelessly and comprehensively of love, three in particular have bearing on Spenser's biographical fictions: Colin's syncretic infolding of the objects of his desire; his assertions of friendship with Ralegh, the Shepherd of the Ocean; and his story of Bregog and Mulla, whose marriage may be seen as defining mythologically the object of Colin's wanderings. Readers have sometimes been puzzled by the fact that Colin is prepared to assert a total, exclusive, and undying commitment to what seem to be several distinct ladies; at the very least the Rosalind praised in the closing lines seems other than the lady at the center of the poem.[29] In a poem which seems so topical and autobiographical in other respects, Colin's readiness to sing mutually exclusive celebrations of this sort suggests an advertisement of poetic versatility more than a revelation of deeply felt emotions. Yet if one recalls the comparable sonnet from *Amoretti,* in which the poet unfolds his beloved Elizabeth into the three figures of mistress, mother, and queen, one may sense that something like a complementary pattern is being traced here. Colin is now celebrating love in all its forms and denying that one must choose among them. All are subsumed into a singleness of purpose, without explicit identification of its object. Yet there are hints that Colin's love for an earthly lass leads him to attribute to her qualities that his queen would see as her royal prerogative. Consider the lines which constitute the precise midpoint of the poem:

> And I hers euer onely, euer one:
> One euer I all vowed hers to bee,
> One euer I, and others never none.
>
> (*CCCHA* 477-79)

Here Colin is ringing changes on Elizabeth's personal motto, *Semper eadem,* and taking from the queen the royal title of oneness that Spenser had given to the goodly maiden queen of Book I, Una. Perhaps one may feel that in the context of such mystical syncretism as is provided by Colin's talk about love, there is little risk of offense to the public Elizabeth; Colin is at worst equivocal in his references to his role as vassal to various kinds of mistresses, royal and domestic. The threat of royal envy is present even in this poem, however, most obviously in connection with the portrayal of Ralegh, the Shepherd of the Ocean, who accompanies Colin on his visit to court and presides over the "world of waters" which lies between the Irish countryside and the public world of England.

Colin's exchange of songs with the Shepherd of the Ocean provides a pair of contrasting myths which express erotic quests in watery terms. The

story of the marriage of Bregog and Mulla, like that of Fanchin and Molanna in the *Mutabilitie Cantos,* entails an underground disappearance which
permits sexual fulfillment and survival, but at the cost of losing one's name.
Such stories recall that of Alpheus and Arethusa, and serve as Spenser's myth
of the translation of pastoral from England across the sea to Ireland. At
the same time, Bregog's name (meaning "deceitful") and his loss of that
name as the price of his survival recall the wily homecoming of Odysseus.
The marriage of rivers is presented not merely as the outwitting of the
bride's possessive father, in the manner of New Comedy, but as a form
of incest forbidden to human beings but natural to gods, or to landscape,
or in some measure to those royal figures who share some of the qualities
of both.[30] It is the most natural thing in the world that brother and sister
streams, born of the same mountain Mole, should couple as they fall toward the plain, intensifying their forces and enclosing territory thereby.
It is almost as natural, *mutatis mutandis,* that a middle-aged poet and land-
holder should dream of marrying a distant cousin living downstream from
him at the mouth of the Blackwater, to which his Mulla or Awbeg is tribu-
tary.[31] Yet there are grander claimants to this territory, the local mountain
or the more distant but no less jealous queen. Spenser's celebration of his
Irish countryside hints at an eroticized landscape which the poet dreams
of possessing in secure anonymity, far from the envious court where Elizabeth views her courtiers' marriages as threats to her sovereignty.

Colin's hopeful identification with the watery fluidity of "my river
Bregog" is set against the experience of the Shepherd of the Ocean whose
relationship with Cynthia is deeply troubled, as the chaste but ever changing moon exerts her power over the waves. Ralegh's title links him to
Proteus; not only is he master mariner in his role as explorer but he also
participates in the instability of the medium he controls; "Water" is in fact
a pet name of Elizabeth for her Walter, and one reminiscent of his regional
origin. The extensive description of the "world of waters" (196 ff.) is at
once a comic portrayal of a rude shepherd's rough crossing over the chan-
nel to England, and a metaphor for Walter's world, the emotional strains
of service to Cynthia. The storm-tossed Colin celebrates his completion
of a round trip to and from the courtier's world, choosing a provincial pastoral life on terra firma over the stormier life led by his more adventurous
friend.[32]

COLIN'S HOMECOMING

These poems published during the years between the 1590 and 1596 installments of *The Faerie Queene,* with their revisions of Spenser's lyric modes

under the pressures of these evolving biographical fictions, provide a useful introduction to the altered poetics of Spenser's epic. Whatever finally happened to Amoret? or more precisely, what happens to Scudamoret, the hermaphroditic coupling of Scudamour and Amoret which was removed from the ending of Book III in 1596?[33] In an emerging contrast between public and private fictions, this couple linked by AMOR disappears, goes underground, is refracted into the innumerable stories of young lovers in the later books. Meanwhile the central public action is occupied by the problematic relationship of Spenser's similarly hermaphroditic pair, Britomartegall. With their shared commitment to MARS and ART, violence and cunning, they live in the fallen realm of British history, and their union in Books IV and V is notoriously unsatisfactory—unromantic—denying the spectator the gratifying emblem of erotic closure afforded earlier by Scudamoret. If one looks for the "squire of love," Scudamour, and his "little love," Amoret, one finds glimpses of them, echoes of their names, in the secondary actions. Spenser's poem now becomes, in fact, a tale of many such squires, the poet included.[34] I want to comment on two of these: Chaucer's Squire, who provides a source and model for Spenser's revised poetics; and Timias, whose story illustrates most clearly perhaps the pressure of Spenser's biographical fictions on the poem's changing attitude toward fairyland.

The originating myth of the earlier books, Arthur's dream encounter with Gloriana, had been derived (with whatever mixture of piety and wit) from Chaucer's tale of Sir Thopas's quest for his "elf-queene"; Spenser seemed to be undertaking to complete the tale that Chaucer the pilgrim had been forced to interrupt.[35] The plot of the poem, according to this myth and according to the design outlined in Spenser's letter to Ralegh in 1590, seemed to point toward Arthur's union with Gloriana, the joining of British and fairy kingdoms, a twelfth-book marriage for which the betrothal of Red Cross and Una was paradigm and prefiguration. But with the second installment, Arthur's role becomes less prominent and more problematic; increasingly he seems to give way to a surrogate, his half-brother Artegall, for much of the action;[36] and the homage to Chaucer is reformulated and made more explicit in Book IV, as a proposal to complete Chaucer's other unfinished venture into romance, the *Squire's Tale.*

In his continuation of Chaucer, Spenser invents the resolution of a symmetrical marriage quaternio of two pairs of brothers and sisters.[37] At the end of Chaucer's fragment, the Squire had been promising to

> speke of Cambalo,
> That faught in lystes with the bretheren two
> For Canacee er that he myghte hire wynne.[38]

Since it had already been established that Cambalo was the brother of Canacee, this promise would seem to entail an incestuous denouement. Perhaps this was part of some oriental source for the tale, as critics have suggested; perhaps, too, its forbidden nature accounts for the tale's unfinished state, as a result of censorship by the poet or conceivably by one of the Canterbury pilgrims (in modern editions the Franklin congratulates the Squire before going on with his own optimistic and moral revision of romance, in which a squire demonstrates *gentilesse* by suppressing his lust). In any case, both Chaucer and Spenser would have known the name of Canace from *Heroides* 11 and other sources, as that of a daughter of Aeolus who fell in love with her brother.[39] Yet when Spenser chooses this single element out of many left unresolved by the Squire, he invents a conclusion that neatly avoids incest. When Campbell has killed Priamond and Diamond and seems about to kill the triple-lived Triamond, there appears on the scene a new character, Cambina, sister of the three brothers, bearing a cup of nepenthe to calm Cambell's wrath. This crucial fourth character permits the simultaneous resolution of warfare by the exchange of wives, and the avoidance of incest by marrying a friend's sister and not one's own.

Spenser succeeds in capturing some of the naive discontinuity that characterizes Chaucer's fragment. One recent critic has remarked of the Squire's announced intention that it "suggests a composite romance of the scope of a *Faerie Queene,* and it is hard to believe that Chaucer ever seriously considered including anything on this scale in the *Canterbury Tales.* It seems more likely that the exuberance of the project is intended to match the exuberance of the Squire's youth and experience."[40] It is tempting to imagine that Spenser might have seen the Squire as proposing to write *The Faerie Queene;* indeed, since he is proposing not to complete an unfinished tale but to rewrite, "trace" a lost work, Spenser does in fact credit Chaucer with the tale he is rehearsing in Book IV, if not with the entire poem. One is reminded of Alastair Fowler's comparable suggestion, that when Arthur awakens from his (Chaucerian) dream in Book I, "he goes on to enact the epic Gloriana recited to him in his vision."[41] In both cases, Spenser's poem is presented as a rehearsal, a reenactment or remembering of a prior text.[42] In his relation now to Chaucer, Spenser laments time's erosion of Chaucer's poem:

> Then pardon, O most sacred happie spirit,
>   That I thy labours lost may thus reuise,
>   And steale from thee the meede of thy due merit,
>   That none durst euer whilest thou wast aliue,
>   And being dead in vaine yet many striue:

> Ne dare I like, but through infusion sweete
> Of thine owne spirit, which doth in me surviue,
> I follow here the footing of thy feete,
> That with thy meaning so I may the rather meete.

(FQ IV.ii.34)

This "infusion" of Chaucer's spirit into the surviving Spenser seems strikingly close to the passage of life from brother to brother in the story; in both cases a continuity from past to present seems adumbrated, as is true also of the history of fairyland read by Guyon with its echoing cast of characters. Perhaps the poet himself is in some sense merely the latest of poetic "brethren" to confront the sister-loving Campbell; like a later Franklin, or a more benevolent "old Mole" he seeks to divert the young man from his forbidden course.

Chaucer's Squire as storyteller is a figure of the youthful poet, bursting with energies and enthusiasm, filled with stories of magical power which imperfectly mask his own frustrated ambition. He can dream but he cannot act; carving before his father at table, he is like Hamlet in being unable to carve for himself. As a squire, a *scudarius* or shield-bearer, he carries a name that he does not yet fully possess. His tale breaks off when its protagonist is incautiously revealed as proposing a marriage forbidden to mortals, replicating as it does the precise identity of the parents, and thereby representing a threat of supplantation.[43] Spenser extricates the Squire from his difficulty by providing a crucial fourth character, and with her a supernatural drug which calms wrath and permits friendship and intermarriage. Nepenthe, the denial of *penthos,* suffering, is just such a drug as poetry provides, according to Plato; appropriately, it is borne by Spenser's contribution to the story, Cambina.

The pattern described above is obscure and elusive at best. The story of Campbell and Triamond may possibly carry such meanings far below its surface, in its relationships to earlier texts, obscure and heavily censored intimations of generational rivalry and forbidden unions; but what is immediately striking about Spenser's tale is just its opposite quality: its bland, perfunctory disposition of characters whose motives are never examined. It seems far removed from the strains and misunderstandings of everyday life; it is what might popularly be termed a fairy tale. By contrast, the story of Timias in the later books is more typical of life as found both inside and outside Spenser's poem. Since Timias has been generally recognized as a figuring of Ralegh in the poem, he may be taken as a final example of Spenser's adaptation of biographical fictions.

In the earlier books, Timias is presented as loyal and serviceable to his master, Prince Arthur, and also (though not usually at the same time) devoutly committed to a platonic courtship of Belphoebe. From the beginning, however, Spenser makes clear that he is intensely vulnerable. In Book I, Duessa needs only to sprinkle her poison lightly on his "weaker partes" and he is instantly "dismayd" and rendered subject to Orgoglio: in one stanza she accomplishes what has taken her half a book with Red Cross. When last seen in Book VI he is still being treated for festering wounds, this time from the Blatant Beast. No character in the poem has a lengthier medical history. Presumably his youth makes him susceptible both to lust and to the suspicion of lust; in this he is not unlike other squires in Spenser's poem, including the one whom Red Cross imagines he sees in Una's arms at the end of the first canto. Repeatedly referred to as a lovely or goodly "boy," he seems akin to Adonis or Cupid at times. As such, he can only experience intense frustration in his relationship to the ferociously chaste Belphoebe, who is wholly defined by her virginity. Other lovers in the poem may follow circuitous and painful routes to their beloved; but for Timias there is no place to go.

Condemned to the total continence of a Guyon without showing any of Guyon's natural talent in that direction, Timias encounters Lust in Book IV, together with the twin sister of Belphoebe. Since the villain uses Amoret as his shield, Timias cannot avoid wounding her as he strikes at the enemy. Finally (if one can trust any single reading of Spenser's ambiguous pronouns) Timias does deal Lust a telling blow:

> Yet he his hand so carefully did beare,
> That at the last he did himselfe attaine,
> And therein left the pike head of his speare.
> A streame of coleblacke bloud thence gusht amaine,
> That all her silken garments did with bloud bestaine.
>
> (*FQ* IV.vii.27)

At this point the villain flees, to be killed shortly thereafter by Belphoebe in his cave, where she finds the still intact Aemylia alongside a vile hag who has been performing the friendly service of satisfying the villain's lust in Aemylia's place. Moved by sympathy for Aemylia and loathing for the Hag (and by no apparent interest in the book's concern with friendship), Belphoebe returns to Timias:

> There she him found by that new louely mate,
> Who lay the whiles in swoune, full sadly set,
> From her faire eyes wiping the deawy wet,

Which softly stild, and kissing them atweene,
And handling soft the hurts, which she did get.
For of that Carle she sorely bruz'd had beene,
Als of his owne rash hand one wound was to be seene.

(*FQ* IV.vii.35)

In a sequence of events which recalls Red Cross's vision of Una in the arms
of that Squire in Book I, Belphoebe is filled with wrath, considers killing
the pair "With that selfe arrow, which the Carle had kild," but contents
herself finally with rebuking the Squire and fleeing the scene.

One may variously describe what has been happening in this episode.
From the viewpoint of Belphoebe's story, her reaction to the figures in Lust's
den shows that she makes an absolute distinction between chaste and unchaste women, as her education under Diana might have led us to expect.
Furthermore, although she does not know this, the apparently wanton girl
in her lover's arms is in fact her twin sister; a twinning process, so to speak,
is explicitly and literally at work here. By this logic, one may read this
as a story of Belphoebe's "misdeeming," projecting her own divided feelings as Red Cross had done earlier in Archimago's house. As Una had been
loyal in fact, so in fact is Timias here; he is merely attending to Amoret's
wounds and there is no more actual, culpable eroticism in the scene than
had been the case (for instance) with Britomart and Amoret in their shared
bed in canto i of Book IV—another scene parallel to that of I.i in giving
rise to misdeeming and slander. Since the aftermath of this present episode
shows Timias pining away alone in the wilderness, with no further involvement with Amoret, the barest outline of the narrative seems to support
this interpretation.

From this viewpoint there emerges a coherent analysis of Belphoebe's
ability to "overcome lust": her easy victory over the monstrous embodiment of lust is in fact (like the victory of Red Cross over the monster Error)
a sign of her unreadiness to confront lust as an internal, personal quality;
and it automatically produces a twin sister of herself as the projected object
of Timias's passion. She immediately finds Timias and Amoret in a posture
which recapitulates the scene in III.v where she had ministered lovingly
but chastely to a wounded Timias. By an ironic reversal, Belphoebe is unable this time to believe that Timias is capable of ministering as chastely
to Amoret's wounds; her parting words ("Is this the faith?") are tellingly
ironic, for this is indeed the faith which had earlier characterized their
own relationship.

But there are complicating factors to so one-sided an interpretation. For
one thing, the argument to canto vii says openly of Amoret that "The Squire

her loues." For another, this is a story of two encounters with Lust, that of Timias as well as that of Belphoebe. The imagery, together with the parallel seventh-canto encounters with figures of lust in Books I and III, encourages the reader to consider that Timias is wrestling with lust in a far more internal, psychological sense than has been true of Belphoebe. Furthermore, we have the long critical tradition by which the episode alludes to Ralegh's marriage to Elizabeth Throgmorton and his consequent fall from grace in Elizabeth's court. Such factors point to an alternative reading: that Belphoebe's invincible chastity has caused *Timias* to conjure up a twin sister of Belphoebe trained in womanhood rather than virginity. In the case of this putative identification with Ralegh's personal history, the maiden in question shares a Christian name with the inaccessible mistress if not a common parentage.[44] From opposed or complementary motives, therefore, two distinct dreamers have invented an identical vision.

One may also note the ways in which Timias's history invites comparison with its source in the *Orlando Furioso.* Belphoebe's initial cherishing of the wounded Timias in Book III recalled the scene in Ariosto where Angelica tended the wounded Medoro and the two became lovers, with the consequence of Orlando's madness. Such a comparison is made more nearly complete by this pendant episode in Book IV, which variously enacts a fulfillment of love and a jealous fury. As he completes the allusion, however, Spenser refracts almost indefinitely Ariosto's love triangle. Belphoebe is the one who seems destined now for the role of Orlando, furious at this evidence of her lover's infidelity; but it is Timias, bereft of her affection, who enacts Orlando's savage alienation. In the Spenserian fiction, Ralegh's inability to have both Elizabeths at once becomes a figure of his fury, his divided self.[45]

Timias seems to combine two meanings in his name, the English *time* and the Greek *timé,* honor; and it is time which restores him to honor at court, as it did (much later) Ralegh. But time has seriously encroached on the fabric of Spenser's fiction. In the more orderly narrative of Book I, Red Cross is united with Una after he has experienced the consequences of his error; he wanders to a full understanding of himself and is made whole at the House of Holiness and in Una's arms. Belphoebe's error, if it is that, is never corrected; she merely abates her rage. Whatever may be the cause of Amoret's disappearance from the poem, as Timias's lover in this episode, it is certainly not that Belphoebe has assimilated her values into herself. Timias is reunited with the same chaste figure he had known previously, and on the same terms. When Spenser describes this reunion he rather surprisingly suggests that Timias's service to Belphoebe is radically incompatible, now, with service to his master:

In which he long time afterwards did lead
  An happie life with grace and good accord,
  Fearlesse of fortunes chaunge or enuies dread,
  And eke all mindlesse of his owne deare Lord
  The noble Prince.   (*FQ* IV.viii.18)

"Happie . . . grace . . . good accord": Timias's bliss is described in strongly
positive terms in the first three lines of this stanza; yet the fourth line, with
its delayed identification of "his owne deare Lord," provides an equally
powerful sense of his indifference to the rest of the world as a virtual apos-
tasy. In fact, the following stanza indicates that it is for Arthur now to
complete the rescue of Aemylia and Amoret. Perhaps by 1596 Spenser has
come to see Elizabeth's court, like Belphoebe's,[46] as a place of sterile dalliance not far removed from Phaedria's or Acrasia's bowers. Restored to
grace, Timias/Ralegh seems here to resemble that negative view of Adonis,
Verdant in the Bowre of Bliss, his armor rusty from long disuse. He is to
Belphoebe, now, as Hippolytus was to Diana or Adonis to Venus: all are
mortals in the throes of commitment to a jealous and partial goddess. Unable to worship both Diana and Venus at once, they are less than whole.

  I think it is no coincidence, then, that Spenser characterizes his own
erotic impulses, and the poems that express them, as "little cupids" or "little
loves," *amoretti.* This association with his figure of goodly womanhood,
Amoretta, links him to the Ralegh/Timias story of earthly love and royal
envy; it affirms a need to embrace the feminine in physical love as well
as in maternal and matriarchal patterns of honor and worship; and finally,
it becomes part of a strategy by which guile and self-effacement can enable
a middle-aged poet to return to a vital manhood and cheat time as well
as the envious censor, going underground as need be in order to come home
to that forbidden dream of completeness which seems essential to his continued fertility as both man and poet.

  Spenser's imagery, and his mythic vocabulary as seen in his relation to
earlier texts, develop a sense of the dynamics of this midlife pastoral of revision, revival, remarriage. One has a sense in the later Spenser that the
Elizabethan younger generation is itself turning middle-aged, chafing like
Theseus at the slow waning of the dying moon, "Long withering out a
young man's revenue." The sixth book of *The Faerie Queene* provides one
climax to Spenser's subversive drama when it shows Colin Clout himself
conjuring up his private lady in the midst of the poem's public landscape.
Calidore's intrusion on such a scene disperses it instantly, for it is inherently and literally obscene, not meant for others' eyes. Perhaps a similar
sense of the incompatibility of public and personal worlds causes the poet

of 1596 to banish the vision of Scudamoret at the end of Book III: loving unions cannot bear observation, even by the half-envious Britomart.

We leave the poem, finally, with a prayer for a spectacle that will not vanish. At the end of the *Cantos of Mutabilitie,* Spenser dreams in what seems a totally different mood of a time when there shall be no more change, no more Titans with their titanic energies:

> But thence-forth all shall rest eternally,
> With Him that is the God of Sabbaoth hight:
> O that great Sabbaoth God, graunt me that Sabaoths sight.
> *FQ* VII.viii.2)

Yet even here, for those Elizabethans who know their Hebrew, the difference is more apparent than real; for in seeking those various Elizabeths unfolded in *Amoretti* 74 according to their several graces, the poet is finally seeking the radical first design of those happy letters framed by skillful trade: Eli-sabbath, Elizabeth's divine anagram, the Alpha and Omega to her Beta.[47]

In point of biographical fact, the adventure of Spenser's remarriage was not to be a midlife experience after all. Aside from the *Mutabilitie Cantos,* the second half of his great poem remained unwritten, and he was granted his sabbath sight before the decade was out. And Elizabeth Spenser, like other poets' widows, was to outlive two more husbands, bearing children to each, before going to her own rest. We may feel that this is not part of Spenser's story; but I think that a careful reading of his fictions suggests otherwise. Balancing his version of survival against other models for confronting mutability, Spenser places his fortieth birthday, and the motives surrounding it, in the context of other squires, other Elizabeths, and other Sabbaths.

University of Massachusetts, Amherst

Notes

1. Alexander C. Judson, in *The Works of Edmund Spenser: A Variorum Edition,* ed. Edwin Greenlaw et al. (Baltimore: Johns Hopkins Press, 1932–57), vol. 11, pp. 62–63, 166–75.
2. C. S. Lewis, *The Allegory of Love* (Oxford: Oxford University Press, 1936), p. 321; and *English Literature in the Sixteenth Century Excluding Drama* (Oxford: Clarendon Press, 1954), p. 372.

3. John Milton, *Areopagitica,* in *Complete Poems and Major Prose,* ed. Merritt Y. Hughes (New York: Odyssey Press, 1957), pp. 728–29, emphasis added.

4. Harry Berger, Jr., "The Prospect of Imagination: Spenser and the Limits of Poetry," *SEL* 1 (1961), 109.

5. See the remarks of Jortin and Dodge, *Var.* 8.440; and A. Kent Hieatt, "A Numerical Key for Spenser's *Amoretti* and Guyon in the House of Mammon," *YES* 3 (1973), 14–27.

6. Compare the possible similar wordplay in *Amoretti* 4: "New yeare forth looking out of Ianus gate."

7. See Hieatt, "A Numerical Key"; Alexander Dunlop, "The Unity of Spenser's *Amoretti,*" in *Silent Poetry,* ed. Alastair Fowler (London: Routledge and Kegan Paul, 1970), pp. 153–69, and "The Drama of *Amoretti,*" *Spenser Studies* 1, ed. Patrick Cullen and Thomas P. Roche, Jr. (Pittsburgh: University of Pittsburgh Press, 1980), pp. 107–20; James Nohrnberg, *The Analogy of "The Faerie Queene"* (Princeton, N.J.: Princeton University Press, 1976), pp. 68–71. The fragmentary and discontinuous nature of such patterns has been attributed to the discordant dramatic perspectives evoked by the story of the courtship: see O. B. Hardison, Jr., "*Amoretti* and the *Dolce Stil Novo,*" *ELR* 2 (1972), 208–16. I would suggest as well a possibly deliberate presentation of the sonnets as fragmentary, cut off by the same "hastie accidents" as those cited in *Epithalamion* and published (as Ponsonby notes in his dedication) in the poet's absence. See Thomas P. Roche, Jr., "The Calendrical Structure of Petrarch's *Canzoniere,*" *SP* 71 (1974), 152–70.

8. Possibly this third quatrain is trying to say something more akin to the argument of *Amoretti* 80, and refers to the queen in lines 11–12: my private love affair has restored my spirits and enabled me to speak (once again) my queen's praises. Such a reading is obviously strained, however, working backward, as it were, from the assumption that it must be the queen who is "most worthy."

9. In his study of Book IV, Jonathan Goldberg (*Endlesse Worke: Spenser and the Structures of Discourse* [Baltimore: Johns Hopkins University Press, 1981], esp. pp. 35–36) adopts Jacques Lacan's concept of *méconnaissance,* an act of misunderstanding, misidentification, or "misreading" which is simultaneously false, because willful and subjective, and yet true because it creates a *stade du miroir* in which the subject can identify itself, and thereby imposes a new meaning on the text. Though I shall try to describe this syndrome more comprehensively in the case of Belphoebe's misdeeming of Timias, where the willfulness of the interpretation is more obvious, it seems equally operative in the nervous self-consciousness of the narrator of *Amoretti.*

10. See Walter Oakeshott, *The Queen and the Poet* (London: Faber and Faber, 1960), pp. 81–99; Allan H. Gilbert, "Belphoebe's Misdeeming of Timias," *PMLA* 62 (1947), 622–43; H. M. English, Jr., "Spenser's Accommodation of Allegory to History in the Story of Timias and Belphoebe," *JEGP* 59 (1960), 417–29; Stephen J. Greenblatt, *Sir Walter Ralegh: The Renaissance Man and His Roles* (New Haven, Conn.: Yale University Press, 1973), esp. pp. 60–62; and the essay by James P. Bednarz in this volume.

11. William Oram, "*Daphnaida* and Spenser's Later Poetry," *Spenser Studies* 2 (1981), 141–58.

12. Duncan Harris and Nancy Steffen, "The Other Side of the Garden: An Interpretive Comparison of Chaucer's *Book of the Duchess* and Spenser's *Daphnaida,*" *JMRS* 8 (1978), 17–36.

13. Oram, "*Daphnaida,*" p. 158, n. 21. I am not trying to disavow the suggestion attributed to me here, but to underscore Oram's own caution in giving it qualified acceptance. The autobiographical fiction hinted in the narrator's grief is here obscured by the conventions of the complaint tradition. The unspecified nature of the narrator's grief, and

its imitation of the similarly unspecified (but perhaps more conventionally lovelorn) woe of Chaucer's narrator,may hint that the sleeplessness of a solitary lover (like the "old flame" of the widow Dido) does not clearly distinguish between past and present or future objects of desire.

14. Critical debate about the *Book of the Duchess* resembles that raised by Spenser's poem: it questions the source of the narrator's grief, his relation to the widowed protagonist, and the poem's problematic "consolation"; see Robert B. Burlin, *Chaucerian Fiction* (Princeton, N.J.: Princeton University Press, 1977), pp. 59–74; Barbara Nolan, "The Art of Expropriation: Chaucer's Narrator in *The Book of the Duchess*," in *New Perspectives in Chaucer Criticism,* ed. Donald M. Rose (Norman, Okla.: Pilgrim Books, 1981), pp. 203–22; Helen Phillips, "Structure and Consolation in the *Book of the Duchess*," *Chaucer Review* 16 (1982), 108–18; R. A. Shoaf, "'Mutatio Amoris': 'Penitentia' and the Form of *The Book of the Duchess*," *Genre* 14 (1981), 163–89. James Wimsatt has described in great detail Chaucer's relation to his predecessors; see *Chaucer and the French Love Poets: The Literary Background of "The Book of the Duchess"* (Chapel Hill: University of North Carolina Press, 1968); and "The Sources of Chaucer's 'Seys and Alcyone,'" *Medium Aevum* 36 (1967), 231–41.

15. Wimsatt, "Sources," argues for the relative importance of Guillaume de Machaut's *Dit de la fonteinne amoreuse.* Ovid would be well known to Spenser and his audience as providing the fullest version of the Alcyone story; but since Machaut too describes the transformation of the lovers (lines 689 ff.), Chaucer abridges his source in either case.

16. Ovid, *Metamorphoses,* trans. Rolfe Humphries (Bloomington: Indiana University Press, 1961), xi. 741–48.

17. For Ovid's sources, see Brooks Otis, *Ovid as an Epic Poet* (Cambridge: Cambridge University Press, 1966), esp. pp. 392–94. Ovid suppresses elements in the tale that would make the metamorphosis of Ceyx and Alcyone a punishment for their having compared themselves to Zeus and Hera. In contrast to the avian transformations just preceding and following their story, those of Ceyx's brother Daedalion and of Priam's son Aesacus, they are indeed a pattern of unbroken love: Ovid provides an applauding elderly spectator thereto (*spectat et ad finem servatos laudat amores* [he watches and praises their love, true to the end], *Met.* xi. 750). But it should be noted that Alcyone is characterized by Ovid as a worried and possessive wife. The daughter of Aeolus and Aegiale ("seashore"), she fears the worst when her husband sets sail; she might be taken as a prototype of Chaucer's Dorigen. In fact, the Man of Law refers to Alcyone as belonging to the same class in which the Franklin places Dorigen because of her similar lament: "thise noble wyves" (Intro. to *MLT* 59; *FrankT* 918). All references to Chaucer are to F. N. Robinson, ed., *The Works of Geoffrey Chaucer,* 2nd ed. (Boston: Houghton Mifflin, 1957).

18. The adjacent stories of Daedalion and Aesacus describe suicidally vindictive and despairing figures; Daedalion in particular may be noted as the complementary son of Lucifer, transformed to a hawk: "With charity to none, for, having suffered, / He must make others suffer." (*Met.* xi.344–45).

19. See *The Poems of Sir Arthur Gorges,* ed. Helen Estabrook Sandison (Oxford: Clarendon Press, 1953); poems 94 and 98 cite a mistress named Daphne; 44 invokes the myth of Daphne's transformation. Otis, *Ovid,* pp. 269–77, describes the long stretch of amatory incidents in the *Metamorphoses* which he treats as expressive of "the pathos of love"; they begin with the "divine comedy" of Daphne in book i, where a passive female mortal is pursued by a god, and conclude with the story of Ceyx and Alcyone in book xi where mutual human love is finally recognized by the gods. The story of Aesacus at the end of book xi introduces the stories of Troy and Rome with which the poem concludes.

20. Georgia Ronan Crampton, "Spenser's Lyric Theodicy: The Complaints of *The Faerie*

Queene III.iv.," *ELH* 44 (1977), 205–21; Hugh Maclean, "'Restlesse anguish and unquiet paine': Spenser and the Complaint, 1579–90," in *The Practical Vision: Essays in English Literature in Honour of Flora Roy,* ed. James Campbell and James Doyle (Waterloo, Ontario: Wilfrid Laurier University Press, 1978), pp. 29–47.

21. See Helen Estabrook Sandison, "Arthur Gorges, Spenser's Alcyon and Ralegh's Friend," *PMLA* 43 (1928), 645–74; and her summary of Gorges's career in *The Poems,* pp. xiii–xxvii. Gorges did remarry in 1597, and was briefly banished the court for *his* marriage to an Elizabeth. Sandison's biography provides a useful corrective to the totally estranged and alienated individual suggested by Spenser's fiction.

22. Sandison, "Arthur Gorges," pp. 649–50; the name may be explained by the presence of Ambrose, earl of Warwick, at the christening.

23. Donald Cheney, *Spenser's Image of Nature* (New Haven, Conn.: Yale University Press, 1966), pp. 132–35.

24. Michael O'Connell, *"Astrophel:* Spenser's Double Elegy," *SEL* 11 (1971), 27–35.

25. *Thomas Watson's Latin Amyntas (1585),* ed. Walter F. Staton, Jr., and *Abraham Fraunce's Translation The Lamentations of Amyntas (1587),* ed. Franklin M. Dickey (Chicago: University of Chicago Press, 1967); Abraham Fraunce, *The Third Part of the Countesse of Pembrokes Yuychurch, Entitled Amintas Dale,* ed. Gerald Snare (Northridge: California State University Press, 1975).

26. Stuart Sherman, "Stella and *The Broken Heart,*" *PMLA* 24 (1909), 274–84; O'Connell, *"Astrophel,"* p. 33, notes that the word *péntheos* appears in the first line of Moschus's lament for Bion, which is modeled on Bion's lament for Adonis; Spenser's *Astrophel* is similarly modeled on Ronsard's *Adonis.*

27. Paul Alpers, "The Eclogue Tradition and the Nature of Pastoral," *College English* 34 (1972), 353–71.

28. Possibly "that braue conceipt" refers to "euerlasting dittie" or "Eglantine of *Meriflure.*" In 1940 the British Museum announced its acquisition of Egerton MS. 3165 containing Gorges's "lost poems"; these include what seems to be the Eglantine of Meriflure to which Colin alludes. A fragment of 36 lines entitled "A Pastorall unfynyshed," it appears as item 100 in Sandison's edition; her notes attempt to show several distinct stages of its development under the encouragement of Spenser: the opening stanzas identify the eglantine with the still-living Douglas, but later it is adapted to the queen (Douglas's royal kin) with a promise of showing the strife between "the redd rose and the whyte / apeasde in thys brave Eglantyne." In the process (and presumably after an initial reading by Spenser), Gorges adapts the description of Belphoebe's "Rose" (*FQ* III.v.52) to provide an origin for his Eglantine. Though Malone had seen "Meriflure" as a double anagram of *rime* and *fleur* (*Var.* 7.467), a generalized term like "florilegium," Sandison (*Poems,* p. 226) suggests a connection with Florimel, whom Spenser had compared to Daphne (*FQ* III.vii.26).

29. Raymond Jenkins, "Rosalind in *Colin Clouts Come Home Againe,*" *MLN* 67 (1952), 1–5; Charles E. Mounts, "Two Rosalinds in 'Colin Clouts Come Home Againe,'" *N&Q* n.s. 2 (1955), 283–84; David W. Burchmore, "The Image of the Centre in *Colin Clouts Come Home Againe,*" *RES* n.s. 28 (1977), 393–406.

30. This is of course an absurdly oversimplified definition or characterization of incest; see Claude Lévi-Strauss, *The Elementary Structures of Kinship,* rev. ed., trans. J. H. Bell and J. R. von Sturmer (London: Eyre and Spottiswood, 1969), pp. 12–25. Myths involving brother-sister incest, and less frequently (as with Myrrha and Adonis) father-daughter, figure pervasively in the fictions under discussion; they suggest a network of impulses to consolidate and preserve identity, and as such provoke envy in prior figures of authority. See notes 39, 43.

31. *Var.* 11, 168–69.

32. Ralegh's self-characterization is discussed by Greenblatt, *Ralegh,* esp. pp. 22–56; Oakeshott, *Queen and the Poet.*

33. Judith H. Anderson, "Whatever Happened to Amoret? The Poet's Role in Book IV of *The Faerie Queene,*" *Criticism* 13 (1971), 180–200; Nohrnberg, *Analogy,* p. 607.

34. Goldberg, *Endlesse Worke,* pp. 44–49, and passim, describes the ways in which Spenser's narrative dissolves the distinctions among characters' voices, so that one squire seems frequently to meld into another, and in an unpublished essay, Pamela Steiner argues that the squire Timias is a figure of the poet.

35. See A. Bartlett Giamatti, *Play of Double Senses: Spenser's "Faerie Queene"* (Englewood Cliffs, NJ: Prentice-Hall, 1975), pp. 47–52; the extent of Spenser's use of *Sir Thopas* has never been explored. Spenser borrows the name of Olifant for the male half of the brother-sister pair of lustful figures in III.vii, figures related to such other seventh-canto personifications of lust as Orgoglio in Book I and the elephantine villain in Book IV; Olifant was also the name of Roland's ivory horn. It may be of some significance, therefore, that Sir Thopas meets Olifant while seeking his elf-queen; one of the few substantive changes made in the 1596 version of Books I–III (beside the dropping of the hermaphroditic ending) is the alteration of III.vii.48, line 4, which had claimed that "Chylde *Thopas*" had brought Ollyphant to confusion. In 1596 Thopas's victory is cancelled, and a new elephantine image of lust appears in Book IV. The boundaries between Chaucer's two unfinished tales are unclear; it seems that the *Squire's Tale* assimilates rather than replaces *Sir Thopas* as model in 1596.

36. See Carrie A. Harper, *The Sources of the British Chronicle History in Spenser's "Faerie Queene"* (Philadelphia: John C. Winston, 1910); Edmund Spenser, *The Faerie Queene,* ed. A. C. Hamilton (London and New York: Longman, 1977), p. 330. The chronicle in II.x ends with the succession of Uther Pendragon, who was transformed by Merlin into the likeness of Ygrayne's (in Geoffrey of Monmouth, Ygerna's) husband Gorlois, so that he might lie with her and beget Arthur; after Gorlois's death Uther marries Ygerna and begets Arthur's sister, Anna. Geoffrey describes two lines descending from Ygerna: a prior legitimate one from Gorlois to Cador and Constantius, the other from Uther. The crown passes from Uther to Arthur to Constantius, then to Mordred's son Conan and his descendants. Spenser invents another son of Gorlois, Artegall (equal of Arthur; a Welsh Arthur), whose son receives the crown from Constantius and passes it to the remaining line of British kings. Gloriana's role as fairy queen may suggest an association with Anna, or with Morgan le Fay; has a Mordred already been gotten, betwixt sleeping and waking? In his study of Spenser's names, Joel Belson notes that Argante is a variant of Morgan: "In Layamon's *Brut,* for example (28610 ff.), Argante, not Morgan le Fay, is the queen of Avalon to whom Arthur is taken after the battle of Camelford." "The Names in *The Faerie Queene*" (Ph.D. diss., Columbia University, 1964), pp. 35–37. A darkening view of Arthur's quest, in the 1596 poem, seems to go hand in hand with increasingly frequent hints of such associations between Gloriana and the watery morgans of legend.

37. A. Kent Hieatt, *Chaucer, Spenser, Milton: Mythopoeic Continuities and Transformations* (Montreal: McGill–Queen's University Press, 1975), pp. 75–94; Nohrnberg, *Analogy,* pp. 622–23.

38. *SqT*667–69; Robinson (p. 721) notes that editors have tried to suggest that there are two distinct Cambalo/us figures, one the brother and the other the successful suitor; or alternatively, that "wynne" means "marry (to someone else)."

39. Ovid's presentation of Canace's soliloquy stresses the daughter's sense of divided loyalties (in terms that anticipate Britomart's guilty feelings, *FQ* III.ii), and her fear of a

father who rules the winds but cannot control his wrath (*Her.* xi.15). The most explicit reference in Chaucer to the story of the incestuous Canace appears, curiously, in the introduction to the *Man of Law's Tale* (78–79), where the Man of Law praises Chaucer for *not* having written "Of thilke wikke ensample of Canacee, / That loved hir owene brother synfully." He has just praised Chaucer for having written of a series of good women, starting with Alcyone—who is (by the Man of Law's standards) a good daughter of Aeolus. See note 43.

40. P. M. Kean, *Chaucer and the Making of English Poetry* (London: Routledge and Kegan Paul, 1972), vol. 2, p. 64.

41. Alastair Fowler, "Emanations of Glory: Neoplatonic Order in Spenser's *Faerie Queene*," in *A Theatre for Spenserians,* ed. Judith M. Kennedy and James A. Reither (Toronto: University of Toronto Press, 1973), p. 74.

42. See Goldberg, *Endlesse Worke.*

43. The anger of Aeolus in Ovid's version of the Canace story is matched by the disdain of Chaucer's Man of Law ("Of swiche cursed stories I sey fy!"), as befits someone with a professional concern for property rights: "Al was fee symple to hym in effect." His remarks have been taken as Chaucer's mischievous allusion to his friend and contemporary Gower, whose treatment of Canace (*Confessio Amantis* 3.143–360) is a warning against wrath; Gower is as sympathetic as Ovid had been to the plight of the lovers. Furthermore, the treatment of Lust in the final, eighth book of the *Confessio* is explicitly directed against incest, which is defined as an act that is not inherently or naturally immoral, since it was obviously necessary that the children of Adam and Eve should marry one another. Rather, incest was later forbidden by the "lex positiva" of the church. G. C. Macauley, *The Complete Works of John Gower* (Oxford: Clarendon Press, 1901), vol. 2, p. 493 (note on "lawe positif," 3.172). Chaucer may have recognized in Gower's text a certain "softness" on the subject of incest that he could encourage his Man of Law to misread. (In the *General Prologue,* a skill at verbal composition—"he koude . . . endite"—provides an unlikely but suggestive link between the Squire and the Man of Law.)

44. Michael O'Connell, *Mirror and Veil: The Historical Dimension of Spenser's "Faerie Queene"* (Chapel Hill: University of North Carolina Press, 1977), pp. 114–24; English, "Spenser's Accommodation," pp. 427–29.

45. Sandison, "Arthur Gorges," pp. 657–58, describes an incident in which the imprisoned Ralegh is so stimulated by the queen's passage in a barge outside the Tower that he struggles with his jailers to be allowed a glimpse. Gorges, who witnessed the scene, writes to Cecil of his "feare S.r W. Rawly; wyll shortely growe [to be] Orlando furioso; If the bryght Angelyca perseuer agaynst [hyme] a l[y]tt[le] lon[ger.]" As Greenblatt notes, *Ralegh,* p. 77, "The language of the letter nicely captures the self-consciously 'literary' quality of Ralegh Furioso." Ralegh, through Gorges, seems to anticipate, or at least collaborate with Spenser in developing the Ariostan parallel to his case.

46. See Judith H. Anderson, "'In liuing colours and right hew': The Queen of Spenser's Central Books," in *Poetic Traditions of the English Renaissance,* ed. Maynard Mack and George deForest Lord (New Haven, Conn.: Yale University Press, 1982), pp. 47–66; Hamilton, *Faerie Queene,* p. 482, notes that Timias's address to Belphoebe in IV.viii.17, "O dearest dred," echoes Spenser's to Elizabeth in I Pr. 4.9.

47. Nohrnberg, *Analogy,* p. 83; A. C. Hamilton, "Our New Poet: Spenser, 'well of English undefyld,'" in Kennedy and Reither, eds., *Theatre,* p. 110.

WILLIAM A. ORAM

Elizabethan Fact and Spenserian Fiction

D ONALD CHENEY'S discussion of Spenser's not-so-strangely-neglected minor poems of the 1590s suggests how much the work of the past twenty years has changed our view of the relation between Spenser's fictions and their historical background. In 1961 when Paul McLane published his study of *The Shepheardes Calender* he looked to it for historical material in a way which did not differ in essentials from Judson's treatment of historical reference in the poetry when he wrote Spenser's biography.[1] McLane was acting as critic, Judson as biographer, but they shared the assumption that when biographical or historical material gets into the fiction the interpreter's job is to get it out again. Both try to dig beneath the resistant surface of the poetry to discover the hidden truth of a historical reference. They find the poet's meaning by getting rid of his dark conceits, and assume that this meaning is to be found in the poet's description of what has happened or ought to happen in sixteenth-century Europe.[2] Thus Judson treats Colin's relation to the Shepheard of the Ocean in *Colin Clouts Come Home Againe* as evidence for what Spenser said and did when he saw Ralegh in 1589, and McLane argues that the allegory of *The Shepheardes Calender* is merely a thin disguise enabling the poet to comment on contemporary affairs without, like John Stubbs, losing a hand for his audacity.[3]

By contrast, recent criticism of Spenser's work has been concerned, by and large, less to retrieve the historical material from the poem than to find out how that material has been shaped in it. The allegory does not simply disguise an historical reference: it analyzes and universalizes it. The change in assumption and emphasis follows in part from our increased awareness of Renaissance attitudes toward fiction and of the complex relation between the imagined "second world" of the poem, as Harry Berger, Jr., calls it, and the primary world of history.[4] When Spenser gives his historical material fictional form, he gives it meaning. It is re-presented to the world as a version, a limited and clarified image, of what has happened or might happen. Thus in writing a poem about his trip to London in 1589–90, Spenser renames most of the historical figures, so that he is replaced by Colin Clout, Ralegh by the Shepheard of the Ocean, Elizabeth by Cynthia, and so on. By this pastoral disguising he frees himself from the demands of factual precision, and more importantly, from the need to assume—to represent himself as holding—any single attitude. He is free to present several different views of the court world. The meaning of the poem thus lies not in the historical facts that the work transforms or even in any single, consistent opinion, but in the play of many—at times contradictory—attitudes toward his subject. Kathleen Williams comments that in the poem "Cynthia the Queen and Rosalind are both cruel and kind, the English court is both ideal and corrupt, English poets are both fine and base, Ireland is both lovely and wretched, according to where one stands at the moment and where they stand at the moment. The complications of feeling, of judgment, of understanding and communicating with one's fellows or with the world at large, are nowhere simplified."[5]

Spenserian Portraiture

Such fictional shaping characterizes Spenser's treatment of his contemporaries throughout his work. Yet while Spenser's fictive self-portraits have received much attention, much less has been given to the thematically shaped portraits of others. One kind of fictional distortion, is of course, a Renaissance commonplace: epideictic poets may praise their subjects beyond their actual deserts, painting them as they ought to be rather than as they are.[6] But this is not the way Spenser usually works, outside of his proems and his dedications. Rather, he seizes on the problematic, questionable aspects of the historical figures he portrays. Queen Elizabeth, to take Spenser's most illustrious subject, appears in *The Faerie Queene* as Gloriana, Belphoebe, Mercilla. But Gloriana is a frustrating object of desire who remains absent from the poem, Belphoebe is usually seen making mistakes, however well intentioned, and Mercilla is represented in Book V, canto ix as unable to make the necessary, cruel decision to execute the Duessa who threatens the safety of her realm.[7] Spenser uses these portraits to investigate a series of connected problems: the difficult balance between a ruler's "private" and "public" selves; the proper relation between the queen and her courtiers; the attractions and risks of life at court.

Cheney's essay argues that Spenser uses his portraits of Ralegh, Sidney, and Gorges similarly to investigate his own situation as poet. This use appears most convincingly in his brilliant discussion of how Sir Walter Ralegh functions as foil to Spenser, in both *Colin Clout* and *The Faerie Queene*. Ralegh as Shepheard of the Ocean presents, as Cheney points out, an image of the courtier as an uneasy navigator on the troubled waters of the court. Indeed, one might add that the dangers of the court world are moral as well as emotional. In describing the ocean, Colin remarks that only

someone who loathes life and longs to behold death should venture on it.
He adds:

> And yet as ghastly dreadfull, as it seemes,
> Bold men presuming life for gaine to sell,
> Dare tempt that gulf, and in those wandring stremes
> Seek waies unknowne, waies leading down to hell.[8]

At first reading, this seems an epic reference—bold men like Aeneas and
Odysseus tempt the gulf and seek knowledge from the underworld. But
the passage stresses less the quest for heroic knowledge than the desire for
money: bold men presume to sell life "for gaine" and the wandering streams,
like the proverbial broad road, lead not to Hades, but hell. In becoming
a Shepheard of the Ocean one risks one's soul. Cheney's analysis of Ralegh-
as-Timias further suggests how the frustrations of court life reappear in the
pastoral world of Books III and IV of *The Faerie Queene*. Timias becomes
a figure of the public person unable to forge a private identity, committed
to an absorbing but fruitless life with Belphoebe.

Spenser's portrait of Ralegh joins those of other poets who appear in
the minor poems, Gorges in *Daphnaida* and Sidney in the *Astrophel* sequence.
Here in each case a complex individual is reduced to a foil for Colin himself. Cheney argues that Spenser published the *Astrophel* elegies with *Colin
Clout* to suggest an antithetical relationship: Colin lives and prospers while
Astrophel survives only in his work and that of his fellows. His thesis casts
light on both poems and begins to make sense of one of Spenser's most
perplexing minor works. Yet here he uncovers a vein without mining it:
we still need an extended analysis of how Astrophel's stellification informs
the very peculiar pastoral elegy we have.

Finally, Cheney's discussion of Spenser's portraiture illuminates his self-
portrait in this later period. His stress on a poet anxiously aware of the
split between private vision and public service is not new, but much of
his material is. One striking example is his treatment of Spenser's "clumsy
anxiety" in the sonnets of the *Amoretti* which attempt to reconcile love
of lady with love of queen by asserting an uneasy hierarchy of loyalties.
The discussion recalls Thomas Cain's discussion of the moment in the sixth
canto of *The Faerie Queene* when Spenser breaks off Colin's description of
the Graces to address Gloriana and beg pardon for praising a mistress in
terms which might befit a queen.[9] In each case the attempt to *settle* a
problem—to assert that the queen need not be envious—in fact *raises* it
for the audience, an audience whose intimate knowledge of the queen's jeal-
ousies would make the implicit characterization unmistakable. One wants

to ask old-fashioned unanswerable questions about whether Spenser intended such extraordinary awkwardnesses, but one's only answers are that he had the poems printed, and that the clumsiness is not necessary. What other author of an Elizabethan sonnet cycle apologizes to the queen for his love?

The subtlety and strength of Cheney's essay lies in its alertness to the thematic implications of Spenser's fictional reshaping; its occasional weakness comes from a tendency to find more meaning in such reshaping than the text provides. This tendency appears particularly when he relies on the evidence of names. Renaming is, as I stressed earlier, an obvious mark of fictional re-signifying, and the fictional shape appears more obvious when the name seems to carry an allegorical suggestion. But in Spenser names rarely fix the natures of characters precisely, as they do, say, in *Everyman*: rather they suggest the contexts in which to consider them. One instance of this tendency to overstress the importance of names appears in the brief treatment of *Daphnaida*.

Cheney argues that Alcyon, the mourner of the poem, carries in his name "a highly compressed figure of the relationship between darkness and creativity"—between the destructiveness of grief and its capacity to deepen a poet's understanding of the world and his art. There is, however, little evidence for such a reading. Cheney calls our attention to (1) Daphne's name, which suggests "a specifically poetic realm of the poet's brooding," (2) Alcyon's name, which recalls its Ovidian original in which the drowned Ceyx is revived and transformed into a kingfisher, and (3) a passage in *Colin Clout* in which Colin may be telling Alcyon to work though his sorrow to some "higher form of achievement." While the association of Daphne's name with the poetic laural does seem to me significant, it cannot alone point us to the complex interpretation suggested above.[10] The other evidence is more critical, and more suspect.

The argument from Alcyon's name depends on a reading of the Ovidian myth in which the metamorphosis of Ceyx and Alcyone appears as an image of transcendence. But we have no evidence that sixteenth-century writers understood Ovid's story in this way. Equally important, this reading of the myth distorts the emphasis of Ovid's text. The Ceyx story is the major set-piece of the eleventh book of the *Metamorphoses* with a parting, a storm, a dream, and several laments. Its major concern is with human helplessness and the final metamorphoses are comparatively unimportant. Further, these metamorphoses are not instances of self-transcendence. The intense pressure of her grief reduces Alcyone, Alcyon's namesake, to a kingfisher: such downward transformations occur often in Ovid when mortals feel more passion than they can bear. Ceyx, her husband, does, of course, rise reborn from the waves but even this comfort is muted. Both husband

and wife have become birds, and the calm with which the myth ends comes from the limitation of feeling proper to birds. As this couple and their descendants follow their seasonal pattern of acts and migrations, they are released from both the suffering and the wonder that is part of being human. They never become more than they were. To look to Alcyon's name for evidence that he will transcend himself through his grief is to ask for more than it will give.

The evidence of the passage in *Colin Clout* also seems to me unpersuasive. After mentioning that Alcyon's grief has turned "Sweet layes of love to endlesse plaints of pittie," Colin addresses the griever:

> Ah pensive boy pursue that brave conceipt,
> In thy sweet Eglantine of Meriflure
> Lift up thy notes unto their wonted height,
> That may thy Muse and mates to mirth allure.
>
> *(CCCH 387–91)*

·"That brave conceipt" may refer to "endlesse plaints of pittie," as Cheney suggests, or to "thy Sweet Eglantine of Meriflure" as I have always assumed. But in the parallel urging which follows Colin asks Alcyon to lift up his lays "unto their *wonted* height" (emphasis added), that is, to recover what he has lost, not to become more than he was before.

On balance, then, the evidence suggests that Alcyon's sorrow is an interruption, not a means of growth. Such a reading is made more likely by the portrait of the griever in the poem—boorish, self-centered, self-pitying, and as Cheney points out, a bad shepherd; he is the butt of a good deal of gentle irony. Of such poets Miltonic bards are not made. Some of the same tendency to rely on names without sufficient analysis of context appears in the discussions of the Cambell-Cambina episode. But while the speculation in this section raises more problems than it solves, it raises them admirably. The comments on the recurrent incest theme, the Chaucer-Spenser relation, the curiously pat, formulatic ending to the episode point to material which needs investigation.

FRAGMENTATION

Psychological allegory usually works by analysis, picturing the complex movements of the inner life as the interactions between simpler and more clearly defined characters. Thus the lady of *The Romance of the Rose* appears to the dreamer as many figures, each a fragment of her total personality. Similarly in Spenser the rounder characters of Redcrosse, Britomart and

Artegal are unfolded in the multitude of minor figures that surround them. Britomart may not meet herself as Redcrosse does when he meets Sans Joy or Despair, but she exists in a world peopled largely by fragmentary personalities, clarified and simplified versions of the drives present in herself and the other major characters of the poem. Cheney's brilliant discussion of Alcyon, Astrophel and the Colin of *Colin Clout* as "refractions" of the Colin of *The Shepheardes Calender* is not new in most of its assumptions, but it extends this principle of fragmentation—of dividing to clarify— from the individual poem to Spenser's entire oeuvre.

When he treats them in his fictions Spenser often splits historical figures as well. Spenser's contemporaries usually appear in his poetry as two or more characters, each suggesting an aspect of the original. We have already seen how Ralegh appears alternately as the naive Timias and the polished Shepheard of the Ocean, but the most elaborate instance of this technique is Spenser's extraordinarily original treatment of his queen. The letter to Ralegh describes his initial division:

> In that Faerie Queene I mean glory in my general intention but in my particular I conceive the most excellent and glorious person of our soveraine the Queene, and her kingdome in Faery Land. And yet in some places els, I doe otherwise shadow her. For considering she beareth two persons, the one of a most royall Queene or Empresse, the other of a most vertuous and beautifull Lady, this latter part in some places I doe expresse in Belphoebe, fashioning her name according to your own excellent conceipt of Cynthia (Phoebe and Cynthia being both names of Diana.)[11]

Typically enough, Spenser doesn't stop there: in Book V we have Mercilla in whom the conflict of public and private persons is given a new intensity, and there are as well a series of glancing portraits, figures in the poem which less explicitly present themselves as mirrors. Michael O'Connell points to the most striking of these—the picture of Lucifera in Book I, a queen who embodies all that Elizabeth might at her worst become.[12]

This splitting of historical figures into several versions of themselves has few poetic precedents. There is, of course, something similar in the first part of *The Romance of the Rose* where the presumably real lady that Guillaume de Lorris writes of is parceled out among a number of characters and objects. But she is not a public figure as Elizabeth or Ralegh or even Arthur Gorges were public figures. Spenser's poetic practice probably owes more to the intense awareness of multiple social roles which, as recent criticism has increasingly suggested, was so much a part of Renaissance court life.[13] Such a sense of alternative roles did affect the practice of the visual arts. This was the period, after all, in which Elizabeth sat for a series of allegorical portraits, each of them displaying a different facet of her nature as ruler, and Donne had himself painted in the costumes of lover, courtier, and finally as penitent in his shroud.[14]

Fragmentation as a technique for including historical figures in a poetic fiction has certain obvious advantages. It adapts the historical person to the poem: only thematically relevant aspects of his character are included. It also enables the poet to isolate problematic aspects of the person treated for special investigation. In Book V of *The Faerie Queene* Spenser splits the Lord Grey he knew into two figures—Artegall and his servant, Talus. Talus embodies the violent nature Lord Grey must assume as the enforcer of the queen's rule: this brutal justice is singled out for critical examination.

The fragmentation of historical figures within the fiction can lead to peculiarly complex patterns of reference; it accounts for some of the richness typical of Spenserian allegory. One instance of this complexity of reference occurs in the Ralegh/Spenser relation. The opposition of Colin and the Shepheard of the Ocean in *Colin Clout* clearly starts from the historical meeting of Spenser with his greater friend and patron. But Colin is not Spenser: he is more single-minded, more absolute, more decided than his creator. He can afford the pastoral luxury of absolute decisions. Unlike his creator, he seems willing to give up the court forever, and unlike him he is willing to remain *his* Rosalind's poet and worshiper without demanding sexual fulfillment. The other nature of the historical Spenser—those drives which kept him from returning to London and seek preferment—appears in the courtly figure of the strange shepherd. Thus the Shepheard of the Ocean "refers" to two historical figures, depending on whether one reads the episode as an analysis of the Ralegh/Spenser relation, or as an investigation of Spenser himself. The essential opposition of court poet and pastoral poet in the poem illuminates the historical particulars in several different ways.

PERSPECTIVES ON LUST

The fragmentation of historical characters in the fictional world is thus often associated with perspectivism, the tendency to present multiple views of the same situation. Recent scholarship has increasingly tended to stress the importance of this tendency in Renaissance literature, and it is an important aspect of Spenser's work.[15] Cheney's essay shows how the episode of Timias, Belphoebe, Amoret and Lust presents us with two different— and incompatible—views of the same event, and this confusing double perspective has caused some trouble for commentators. Michael O'Connell comments that "the pressure of the actual upon the fiction causes a strange blurring of the moral focus that is uncharacteristic of Spenser's poem." [16] But one can, I think, take the episode of Timias and Lust as an extreme instance of Spenser's tendency to present several perspectives on an event in order to analyze it more adequately.

A. L. Rowse's biography of Ralegh gives an outline of the historical details behind this episode. [17] In November 1591 Ralegh secretly married one of the queen's ladies-in-waiting, Elizabeth Throckmorton, daughter of Elizabeth's famous ambassador Francis Throckmorton. Ralegh could not ask the queen's permission: she was notoriously jealous of her favorites, and indeed of her ladies in waiting. He could only marry and hope to moderate the royal wrath later when he revealed his act to the queen. However, the circumstances were discovered well before Ralegh was ready to disclose them, and in the most embarrassing way. In March 1592 Elizabeth took leave of the court and secretly bore a baby boy, returning in April to the palace to resume the position of virgin retainer. News leaked out; in May Ralegh (who was attempting to embark on a privateering voyage against the Spanish) was arrested; both he and his wife were placed in the tower. While Ralegh and his wife were subsequently released, Ralegh was barred from court for the next five years (his wife was permanently banished) and he never fully regained the queen's favor.

When he treats this event in his fiction, Spenser splits it into several alternative versions, each of which creates a different perspective on the historical facts. It is the interaction of these distinct perspectives that accounts for the complexity—even the confusion—of the episode. A central instance of this confusion occurs in Timias's battle with Lust which Cheney has already discussed. Amoret has run from Lust's cave where she has been prisoner, and her captor follows her and catches her just as Timias, separated from Belphoebe while hunting, spies them. Timias at once attacks Lust but he is baffled.

> For ever when the Squire his javelin shooke,
> He held the Lady forth before him right,
> And with her body as a buckler, broke
> The puissance of his intended stroke.
> And if it chaunst, (as needs it must in fight)
> Whilest he on him was greedy to be wroke,
> That any little blow on her did light,
> Then would he laugh aloud, and gather great delight.
>
> Which subtill slight did him encumber much,
> And made him oft, when he would strike, forebeare;

> For hardly could he come the carle to touch
> But that he her must hurt, or hazard neare:
> Yet he his hand so carefully did beare,
> That at the last he did himselfe attaine,
> And therein left the pike head of his speare.
> A streame of coleblacke bloud thence gusht amaine,
> That all her silken garments did with bloud bestaine.
> (IV.vii.26–27)

The dominant impression of the stanzas is frustrated stalemate: Timias is "encumbered much" because his effort to help Amoret is likely to hurt her and he is not free to use his full force. The reflexive quality of the fighting that Cheney has noted reemphasizes this sense of bafflement. Timias labors to kill Lust "As he on him was greedy to be wroke" but the doubled male pronoun tends to blur the distinction between the two. As often happens in Spenser's battle scenes, the two antagonists begin to mirror one another. In this line Timias is "greedy" for revenge but the argument to the canto speaks of "greedy lust" and Belphoebe's arrow will soon pierce Lust's "greedy throat"(IV,vii.31). The reflexiveness appears again when Timias succeeds in his effort to wound Lust "That at the last he did himselfe attaine," which makes it sound as if Timias has wounded himself.

Timias has, indeed, a history of such frustrating stalemates. We see him in Book III walking into an ambush in the midst of a ford where his opponents assail him from a high bank. One of the three villainous "forsters" who ambush him throws a dart which "had no powre in his soft flesh to bite:"

> That stroke the hardy Squire did sore displease
> But more that him he could not come to smite;
> For by no means the high banke he could sease,
> But labour'd long in that deepe ford with vaine disease.
> (III.v.19)

The impression of furious and inadequate struggle here — of "vaine disease" is not very different from the encumbrance of the fight with Lust.[18] And the two are near-repetitions. The three forsters are usually identified with the lust of the eyes, the lust of the flesh and the pride of life mentioned in 1 John 2:16. They are, then, internal enemies of the kind familiar from the first two books of *The Faerie Queene*. As Cheney says, Timias is "condemned to the total continence of a Guyon without showing any of Guyon's natural talent in that direction." When he finally does slaughter his opponents, he has himself been so badly wounded that he is near death. The episode suggests that Timias can kill his lusts only at the cost of killing himself, and it needs the new object of desire that Belphoebe represents to restore him to new life. But *that* object of desire is too high for Timias and leaves him again in a baffled sickness, a state near death.

It is not hard to imagine, in such a state, Lust's arising once more and proving a formidable opponent. But to understand more fully Lust's part in this episode we must consider as well his relation to Amoret. For if on the one hand Lust seems identified with Timias's drives, on the other he is associated with Amoret's. The text suggests that Amoret's seizure by Lust is not simply bad luck. As A. C. Hamilton points out, she walks by the dangerous wood "for pleasure or for need" (IV.vii.4), and when Lust seizes her she shrieks "feebly"— so feebly that Britomart doesn't hear her.[19] Spenserian ladies do not normally shriek feebly: when they do it means something. Indeed, "feeble" often has connotations of moral weakness in Spenser.[20] The initial description of Lust also suggests that it is an embodiment of Amoret's own feelings. Commentators have been quick to identify Lust's oversized nose and his elephantine ears with the male genitalia. But there is more to the description:

> His neather lip was not like man nor beast,
> But like a wide deep poke, downe hanging low,
> In which he wont the relickes of his feast,
> And cruell spoyle, which he had spard, to stow.
>
> (IV.vii.6)

The "wide deep poke, down hanging low" has distinctively female associations. Lust is made bisexual because it embodies all sexual desires, male or female; it becomes a demonic parallel to the bisexual Venus of canto x.[21]

When Lust seizes Amoret, then, the allegory suggests that she is not simply the victim of a male predator, but moved by her own passions. She is not, of course, voluntarily unchaste, but she is not proof against the power of Lust as Belphoebe is. Lust's advent is, indeed, presented to us as a sudden, violent, ungovernable onset of passion and Amoret is less blamed than pitied for what happens to her. Lust scoops her up; she shrieks and faints; and he brings her to his dark cave where he keeps her prisoner. The episode recalls Orgoglio's imprisonment of the Redcrosse Knight in Book I: in both cases the human being is overmastered, rendered unconscious and deposited underground, in the dark; in both cases the progression suggests an imprisonment of the rational faculty by the sexual appetite.

We are now in a position to make sense of Timias's battle with Lust.

What Spenser has done brilliantly (and confusingly) is to make a single figure (Lust) embody the passions of both his protagonists. Lust is both male and female because it possesses Amoret and attacks Timias: it is a mutual feeling and thus can mirror man and woman at once. In this situation it is possible to understand the bafflement of the hero: to wound Lust is to reject the lady; not to fight Lust, on the other hand, is to give in and allow oneself to be mastered. But the situation becomes still more complex, for the battle itself becomes an erotic exchange. Whenever Timias's sword lights on Amoret "with any little blow . . . Then would [Lust] laugh aloud, and gather great delight" (IV.vii.26).[22] Timias is in a terrible situation: his best efforts seem doomed to bring about just what he doesn't want. The climax of this encumbered battle comes when Timias wounds Lust so that his blood gushes out staining *Amoret's* silken garments. The suggestion of defloration is recalled later when Timias bends over the lady finding that she has been sorely bruised by Lust, but that "Also of his owne rash hand one wound was to be seene" (IV.vii.35). Spenser captures wonderfully the sense of helpless bafflement when one is fighting against one's own instincts — and losing, for those instincts are subtler than the rational intelligence, perverting it and turning it into an unwitting ally.

This complex allegory of Lust thus develops at once two perspectives on the Ralegh-Throckmorton relation, one dependent on a literal reading of the action (by which Timias and Amoret are simply innocents comically in the wrong place) and the other dependent on the conventions of psychological allegory (by which Timias and Amoret are indeed sexually involved). But both versions of the affair are fundamentally sympathetic to the lovers: at most they are overpowered by mastering emotion, but they are not deeply guilty. Yet Spenser's analysis does not stop here. He concerns himself as well with less elevated views of the relationship, and he presents them through other "fragments" of Elizabeth Throckmorton. Amoret escapes from Lust unsoiled largely because he is already occupied with two ladies who are considerably less chaste and who spell out in some detail different and baser aspects of Elizabeth Throckmorton's relation to Ralegh.

The high-born maiden Aemylia resembles Amoret in several particulars: she has been picked up by Lust in a similar location, "within a grove" which she has come to on her "feeble feet" (IV.vii.17). Yet her seizure, unlike Amoret's, is unambiguously related to her actions. She tells Amoret that she has come to the grove to meet and elope with a "squire of low degree" and her interest in him is primarily sexual. When apologizing for his low birth she insists, "Yet was he meet, unlesse mine eye did faine, / By any Ladies side for Leman to have laine" (IV.vii.15). The coarseness of Aemylia's nature appears in the somewhat clinical assessment of her lover with its significant dependence on the eye. And her story does, in essentials, recall Elizabeth Throckmorton's. Like the queen (who stood in loco parentis to her ladies in waiting), Aemylia's noble "sire" disapproves of the match and, of course, the elopement proves disastrous. There are, to be sure, some differences between the historical incident and the fictional one. Although Ralegh and Elizabeth Throckmorton both came from aristocratic families, the queen's favor placed Ralegh well above his bride on the social scale,[23] and instead of eloping, the couple contracted a secret marriage. But the similarities are sufficient to present Aemylia's story as a second version of the Ralegh disaster, one in which disobedience and physical desire are fully explicit. Amoret has more reason than she knows to exclaim, "Ah sad Aemylia . . . Thy ruefull plight I pitty as mine owne" (IV.vii.19).

Yet Aemylia, too, is spared literal violation, at least by her own account. She informs Amoret that although she has been in Lust's clutches she has remained a virgin:

> Through helpe (quoth she) of this old woman here
> I have so done, as she to me hath showne
> For ever when he burnt in lustfull fire,
> She in my stead supplide his bestiall desire.   (IV.vii.19)

The sexual *act* is still further removed from Amoret: it becomes the sole concern of a character one might dub Old Eve. The Hag is, indeed, interesting precisely because her function is so minimal and so explicit: she is nothing but an image of incorrigible female sexuality. She does the deed that honorable ladies approach only as part of marriage, and bad opinion is centered on her. It is significant that, when Belphoebe has killed Lust, she releases Amoret's companions but responds to them differently. Aemylia issues forth from the cave trembling:

> And after her the Hag, there with her mewed,
> A foule and lothsome creature did appeare;
> A leman fit for such a lover deare.
> That mov'd Belphoebe her no lesse to hate,
> Than for to rue the others heavy cheare.   (IV.vii.34)

The chaste Belphoebe's instinctive dislike of the Hag reemphasizes her function as an embodiment of unchaste sexuality.

Here again Spenser explores a situation by fragmenting it into several alternate situations, affording different perspectives on the same historical character by presenting her in several fictional guises. If a literal reading of the canto reveals a blameless Amoret, an allegorical interpretation presents a woman who, while she is not intemperate, is nonetheless incontinent. Aemylia affords a still less elevated version of the surprised-by-lust theme, in her open disobedience and her explicit physical motivation. Finally, the Hag presents the seamiest version of the affair: she is associated with the act as Elizabeth the queen might have perceived it when she learned that her lady-in-waiting had given birth to the child of her favorite.

We will never know enough of the particular details of Spenser's history and those of his contemporaries to follow all the complex negotiations between his fictions and the reality they interpret. But what we do know stresses the freedom with which Spenser chose to work with his material: what happened is at most a starting point. Spenser had no need to feel himself bound to the actual: to the neoplatonist art with its golden worlds is a step closer to ideal truth than any earthly happening. The golden world of Spenser's fictions plays against particular facts in order to question them. Here in the incident of Timias, Amoret, and Lust, the primary question is one of justice: under what circumstances would Belphoebe's (or the queen's) anger be truly righteous? There is no single answer given; instead, Spenser creates a spectrum of possible situations which enable one to judge the particular historical situation more clearly.

Smith College

NOTES

An early version of this paper was given as a commentary on the preceding essay at the Seventeenth International Congress on Medieval Studies in Kalamazoo, Michigan, May 8, 1982.

1. Paul E. McLane, *Spenser's "Shepheardes Calender": A Study in Elizabethan Allegory* (Notre Dame, Ind.: University of Notre Dame Press, 1961), pp. 13–91; Alexander C. Judson, *The Life of Edmund Spenser,* in *The Works of Edmund Spenser: A Variorum Edition,* ed. Edwin Greenlaw et al. (Baltimore: Johns Hopkins Press, 1932–57), vol. 11, pp. 136–37.
2. Critics like Greenlaw and Renwick did not, however, operate on these reductive assumptions; see esp. Edwin Greenlaw, *Studies in Spenser's Historical Allegory* (Baltimore: Johns Hopkins Press, 1932), pp. 59–103.
3. McLane, *Spenser's "Shepheardes Calender,"* pp. 29–30.
4. Harry Berger, Jr., "The Renaissance Imagination: Second World and Green World," *Centennial Review* 9 (1965), 36–78, esp. 46–52; see also Judith H. Anderson, "'Nor man it is': The Knight of Justice in the *Faerie Queene* V," *PMLA* 85 (1970), 65–77. Recent criticism has stressed the various ways in which Spenser's poem gives fictional shape to historical incident; see Frank Kermode, *Renaissance Essays* (London: Routledge & Kegan Paul),

pp. 33–59; Michael O'Connell, *Mirror and Veil: The Historical Dimension of Spenser's "Faerie Queene"* (Chapel Hill: University of North Carolina Press, 1977); and Thomas H. Cain, *Praise in "The Faerie Queene"* (Lincoln: University of Nebraska Press, 1978).

5. Kathleen Williams, "The Moralized Song: Some Renaissance Themes in Pope," *ELH* 41 (1974), 584.

6. See, for instance, O. B. Hardison, Jr., *The Enduring Monument: A Study of the Idea of Praise in Renaissance Literary Theory and Practice* (Chapel Hill: University of North Carolina Press, 1963), pp. 50–51, 54–57.

7. In canto ix Mercilla is presented as unable to overcome her pity for Duessa, and the fact of the execution is relegated to what William Nelson calls a "sidelong mention" in canto x (*The Poetry of Edmund Spenser* [New York: Columbia University Press, 1963], p. 271). Some critics find that this leaves Mercilla looking less merciful than she might (see O'Connell, *Mirror and Veil*, pp. 150–54) and others find her less resolute than she needs to be (see Cain, *Praise in "The Faerie Queene,"* pp. 136–46). The historical Elizabeth was very—and to her Protestant subjects, inexplicably—unwilling to have her royal cousin put to death.

8. *Colin Clouts Come Home Againe*, 208–11. All quotations from Spenser's works follow *The Poetical Works of Edmund Spenser*, ed. J. C. Smith and Ernest de Selincourt, 3 vols. (Oxford: Clarendon Press, 1909–10).

9. Cain, *Praise in "The Faerie Queene,"* pp. 158–61.

10. Indeed, as Donald Cheney has reminded me, Gorges himself wrote poems to his wife under the name of Daphne. Spenser may, then, simply be using an accepted pastoral name for Francis Howard.

11. *Poetical Works*, vol. 3, p. 486.

12. O'Connell, *Mirror and Veil*, pp. 52–54.

13. See in particular Stephen Greenblatt, *Sir Walter Ralegh: The Renaissance Man and His Role* (New Haven, Conn.: Yale University Press, 1973); and *Renaissance Self-Fashioning from More to Shakespeare* (Chicago: University of Chicago Press, 1980).

14. See Francis A. Yates, *Astraea: The Imperial Theme in the Sixteenth Century* (London: Routledge & Kegan Paul, 1975), pp. 29–87, 215–19; Roy Strong, *The Portraits of Queen Elizabeth* (Oxford: Oxford University Press, 1963), pp. 21–22. Portraits of Donne are reproduced in the Clarendon Press editions of his work (*Songs and Sonnets*, 1965; *Satires*, 1967; and *Epithalamions*, 1978).

15. I am adapting Leo Spitzer's term as he uses it in "Linguistic Perspectivism in Don Quixote," in *Linguistics and Literary History: Essays in Stylistics* (Princeton, N.J.: Princeton University Press, 1967). Recent discussions of this play of differing perspectives in Renaissance literature has emphasized especially the drama and the works of the sixteenth-century humanists. See especially Joel B. Altman, *The Tudor Play of Mind: Rhetorical Inquiry and the Development of Elizabethan Drama* (Berkeley and Los Angeles: University of California Press, 1978), and Duncan Douglas, *Ben Jonson and the Lucianic Tradition* (Cambridge: Cambridge University Press, 1979).

16. O'Connell, *Mirror and Veil*, p. 118; see also Allan Gilbert, "Belphoebe's Misdeeming of Timias," *PMLA* 62 (1947), 622–43; H. M. English, "Spenser's Accommodation of Allegory to History in the Story of Timias and Belphoebe," *JEGP* 59 (1960), 417–29; James P. Bednarz, "Ralegh in Spenser's Historical Allegory" in this volume. For a view of the episode deemphasizing the historical allegory and insisting on Amoret's innocence, see Thomas P. Roche, Jr., *The Kindly Flame* (Princeton University Press, 1964), pp. 136–48.

17. A. L. Rowse, *Sir Walter Ralegh: His Family and Private Life* (New York: Harper and Row, 1962), pp. 158–69.

18. James Bednarz argues convincingly in the following essay that this episode is based on the well-known story of Ralegh holding a ford against the Senechal of Imokelly. In my view, however, the rest of his account tends too much to reduce the meaning of the episode to its historical reference. Spenser's readers might have associated the episode with its historical source while at the same time noticing that it now seemed to shadow forth an internal conflict. Ralegh's heroic defiance of the senechal turns into something more ambiguous and less triumphant.

19. A. C. Hamilton ed., notes to Edmund Spenser, *The Faerie Queene* (London: Longman, 1977), p. 473.

20. See for instance the Orgoglio episode which is somewhat similar: *FQ* I, vii. 5,6,11; I.viii.20,30,40. In the Lust canto we also come across Aemylia's feeble breast (I.vii.14), and her feeble feet (I.vii.17).

21. I know of no literary precedent for this particular version of Lust; the Wodwo or wild man usually cited as Spenser's precedent is emphatically male. See Richard Bernheimer, *Wild Wild Men in the Middle Ages: A Study in Art, Sentiment and Demonology* (Cambridge, Mass.: Harvard University Press, 1952). Harold Skulsky has drawn my attention to a visual parallel, however, in Bruegel's *Allegory of Lust* (1557), one of his series on the Seven Deadly Sins. In the foreground center we see a demon's face with a bulbous nose and an open mouth: the demon's arms are lifted above his head, breaking an egg (supposed at the time to be an aphrodisiac). Yet the figure can be "read" in two ways: Bruegel has drawn the arms so that they can appear as a pair of upthrust legs on either side of a gaping vagina (the "mouth"). The "nose" of the figure suddenly appears a squat penis.

22. See Bednarz's excellent comments on the entanglement of Amoret, Timias, and Lust. Much of my argument here parallels his, though I would stress that Spenser presents this view of the matter as one of the many possible views of the Ralegh/Elizabeth Throckmorton relationship.

23. Sir Walter was not higher born than his wife but he was considerably wealthier. Her very modest marriage portion had been loaned out to the earl of Huntington in 1572 and was never recovered. See Rowse, *Sir Walter Ralegh*, p. 104.

JAMES P. BEDNARZ

Ralegh in Spenser's Historical Allegory

THE ALLEGORY of Timias and Belphoebe in *The Faerie Queene* documents two distinct periods in the ongoing relationship between Sir Walter Ralegh and Queen Elizabeth. The first describes an early era of mixed fortune in which Ralegh's preeminence was being undermined by the earl of Essex, and the second alludes to a later time of disgrace, occasioned by his clandestine marriage to Elizabeth Throckmorton in 1592. The 1590 and 1596 installments of *The Faerie Queene,* considered together, trace a historical pattern that moves from Ralegh's participation in the quelling of the Desmond Rebellion, through which he gained the queen's attention, to their first meeting, his rejection, and later reconciliation with her. The 1590 edition of the poem shows Ralegh engaged in acts of war (III.v.12–26) and love (III.v.27–55). The 1596 sequel continues this allegory, but shifts its interest to the more pressing issue of whether or not Ralegh had broken faith with the queen by violating her trust. In detailing the court history of Elizabeth and Ralegh, Spenser inevitably found himself in a difficult social situation, when the two principal patrons of his poem became engaged in a bitter feud that he recreates—as a "biographical fiction"—in the pages of *The Faerie Queene.*

In the summer of 1589, Spenser had the good fortune to be visited by Ralegh on his Kilcolman estate. Ralegh and Spenser, who may have met in the earl of Leicester's service or on military maneuvers with Lord Grey in Ireland, were landholding neighbors in Munster County. And in November of the same year, Ralegh, acting as Spenser's patron, accompanied him back to London for the purpose of publishing the first three books of *The Faerie Queene* and enjoying an audience with Queen Elizabeth. Spenser evidently saw the acquisition of Ralegh's patronage as one of the great turning points of his career, since Ralegh's prominent position at court assured him a fitting reception. Spenser's joy upon receiving this golden opportunity for advancement must have been considerable—especially if we agree with Edwin Greenlaw's persuasive theory that the poet had brought exile upon himself in 1579 for attacking Lord Burghley and the duke of Alençon in the caustic farce of *Mother Hubberds Tale.*[1] Spenser's outspoken objection to the French match had placed him at the outskirts of empire, in the "waste" of Ireland, that "savadge soyle, far from Parnasso mount."[2] The arrangement of this audience with the queen would be the most important of the "singular favours and sundrie good turnes" for which he vows an "infinite debt" to Ralegh in the dedicatory epistle of *Colin Clouts Come Home Againe.*

But even though Ralegh's patronage came as a propitious event, it drew Spenser into a potentially dangerous position at court. He would arrive in London with a patron whose status was tensely ambiguous. In 1589, at the age of thirty-seven, Ralegh saw his role as the queen's favorite unexpectedly upset by the rising star of the twenty-three-year-old earl of Essex. Before 1587, the year in which the earl of Leicester introduced his red-haired stepson to the queen, Ralegh's meteoric rise to power had been unhampered. From the time of his first appearance before the queen in 1582, Ralegh had been showered with honors.[3] After 1587, however, he would never again enjoy Elizabeth's undivided attention. Spenser must have been aware of the precariousness of his patron's situation at court, which had deteriorated to the point where Essex could disdainfully reproach Ralegh by reminding the queen of Ralegh's humbler days, of "what he has been and what he was."[4] Indeed, the arrogant, erratic Essex even had the audacity to "disdain his competition of love" and ferociously taunted Ralegh by asking Elizabeth, "What comfort can I have to give myself over to a mistress that [is] in awe of such a man?"[5]

We do not know if Spenser was aware that Essex had challenged Ralegh to a duel, prevented only by the intervention of the Privy Council.[6] Nor can we be sure whether he heard gossip that his patron's excursion to Munster was a concession to Lord Essex, who, in Sir Francis Allen's words, "hath chased Mr. Ralegh from the court, and hath confined him in Ireland."[7] We do know, however, that as early as 1589 Spenser had heard poetry by Ralegh complaining of his mistreatment at court, since he writes in *Colin Clout* that he and Ralegh had recited verses to each other, and that Ralegh's

> song was all a lamentable lay,
> Of great unkindnesse, and of usage hard,
> Of *Cynthia* the Ladie of the sea,
> Which from her presence faultlesse him debared.
>
> (164–67)

One of the extraordinary features of Spenser's comment on Ralegh's poetry is the fact that he wrote it in the crossrimed quatrains that his patron often employed. Spenser also picked up another characteristic element in Ralegh's poetry—the "undersong" or refrain. Spenser states that while the queen's besieged favorite recited his verse,

> He cryed out, to make his undersong
> Ah my loves queene, and goddesse of my life,
> Who shall me pittie, when thou doest me wrong?
>
> (169–71)

After suffering his great disgrace of 1592, in "The 11th: and last book of the Ocean to Scinthia," Ralegh repeats the undersong—"Of all which past the sorrow only stayes"—from his complaint "A Farewell to the Court," and notes that the refrain was written in his previous period of mixed fortune:

> Of all which past the sorrow only stayes.
>
> So wrate I once, and my mishapp fortolde,
> My minde still feelinge sorrowfull success
> Yeven as before a storme the marbell colde
> Douth by moyste teares tempestious tymes express.
>
> So fealt my heavy minde my harmes att hande
> Which my vayne thought in vayne sought to recure;
> At midel day my soonn seemde under land
> When any littel cloude did it obscure.[8]

In this explicitly autobiographical passage we hear of two periods of crisis in Ralegh's service to the queen. Plunged into a far greater disgrace, buffeted by the "storme" that sweeps through *The Ocean's Love to Cynthia,* he remembers the oxymoronic season of "sorrowfull success." This was the period before 1592—while the marble still gently wept—which probably occasioned the composition of a short complaint that begins: "Fortune hath taken the away my love / my lives soule and my soules heaven above / fortune hath taken the away my princes." Recent scholarship has uncovered the fact that the queen wrote a reply to this poem which encourages Ralegh to "Revive againe & live without all drede, / the lesse afraid the better thou shalt spede."[9] But what modern scholarship has uncovered Spenser must have known, for in *Colin Clout* he has the Irish shepherd Marin attest to the mollifying effect that Ralegh's complaints had upon the queen:

> Right well he sure did plaine:
> That could great *Cynthiaes* sore displeasure breake:
> And move to take him to her grace againe.
>
> (*CCCHA* 173–75)

Before Spenser arrived in London at the end of 1589, he seems to have been vividly aware of his patron's difficulties at court. He had heard the "lamentable lay" of his fellow courtier-poet, whom he names "the sommers Nightingale" in his dedicatory sonnet to Ralegh in the 1590 edition of *The Faerie Queene,* recalling the mournful strains of his Philomela-like poetry from the summer of their friendship.

Spenser embedded Ralegh's complaint in the Book of Chastity. But he prefaces his depiction of the grieving Timias with an example of Ralegh's martial prowess, in a portion of the poem that has escaped detailed analysis by critics. At the beginning of the Book of Chastity, Arthur, his squire Timias, Guyon, and Britomart are outraged at the sight of "A goodly Ladie" (III.i.15), fiercely pursued by "a griesly Foster . . . Breathing out beastly lust her to defile" (III.i.17). Arthur and Guyon instantly race after the frightened Florimel, while Timias spurs onward to punish her beastly assailant. Timias reappears in the fifth canto, where he continues to follow him, "To bene avenged of the shame, he did / To that faire Damzell" (III.v.13). But the villain soon outdistances him, "through swiftnesse of his speedy beast, / Or knowledge of those woods, where he did dwell" (III.v.14), and enlists the aid of his two brothers. Armed with "sad instruments / Of spoyle and murder," vowing that "never he alive, / Out of that forest should escape their might" (III.v.16), they wait in ambush for Timias, in "a covert glade, / Foreby a narrow foord" (III.v.17). Once he comes into sight, they spring from cover and launch an attack, during which the brothers are swiftly dispatched by Arthur's valiant squire.

This brief martial episode, which precedes Timias's initial encounter with Belphoebe, seems at first to be little more than one of the hundreds of anonymous battles in *The Faerie Queene.* Upon closer examination, however, it turns out to be a glorified account of the part Ralegh played in suppressing the Desmond Rebellion, which ripped through Munster County, Ireland, from 1579 to 1583.[10] The allegory conflates two distinct (but related) historical events: the ambush Ralegh weathered on the road from Youghall to Cork in February 1581 and the service he rendered in the execution of the revolt's instigators: the earl of Desmond and his brothers John and James.

Spenser is quite specific about the place where the "fosters" [foresters] lie in ambush for Timias. He writes that within the forest they inhabit

> there was a covert glade,
> Foreby a narrow foord, to them well knowne,
> Through which it was uneath for wight to wade;
> And now by fortune it was overflowne:
> By that same way they knew that Squire unknowne
> Mote algates passe; for thy themselves they set
> There in await, with thicke woods overgrowne,

And all the while their malice they did whet
With cruell threats, his passage through the ford to let.

(III.v.17)

This incident at the ford transformed Ralegh into an English hero, who
was first recorded as such in the 1586 edition of Holinshed's *Chronicles*. There,
in John Hooker's addition to the *Chronicles of Ireland,* the historian describes the outstanding valor that Ralegh exhibited when, as a captain de-
livering dispatches, he was suddenly attacked by a band of Irish rebels.
Hooker relates:

> This capteine making his returne from Dubline, & the same well
> knowne unto the seneschall of Imokellie, through whose countrie
> he was to passe, laie in ambush for him to have intrapped him be-
> tween Youghall and Corke, lieing at a foord, which the said capteine
> must passe over. . . . The capteine little mistrusting anie such mat-
> ter, had in his companie onelie two horssemen and foure shot on
> horssebacke, which was too small a force in so doubtfull and dan-
> gerous times.[11]

Hooker then proceeds to describe how Ralegh, riding slightly ahead of his
troop, singlehandedly routs the entire gang of rebels led by the seneschal
of Imokelly (Eustace Fitz Edmond) and saves the life of his fellow Devon-
shireman, Henry Moile. In a paragraph that must have particularly pleased
Ralegh, we read:

> The Captaine being come toward the foord, the seneschall had espied
> him alone, his companie being scattered behind, and verie fiercelie
> pursued him, and crossed him as he was to ride over the water, but
> yet he recovered the foord and was passed over. . . . The captaine being
> thus over the water, Henry Moile, riding alone about a bowes shoot
> before the rest of the companie, when he was in the midel of the
> foord, his horsse foundered and cast him downe; and being afraid
> that the seneschals men would have folowed him and have killed him,
> cried out to the captaine to come and save his life; who not respect-
> ing the danger he himselfe was in, came unto him, and recovered
> both him and his horsse.

Ralegh's courage so impresses his adversaries that they soon abandon their
siege and slink back into the woods whence they came:

The capteine neverthelesse staid still, and did abide for the coming
of the residue of his companie . . . sat upon his horsse in the meane
while, having his staffe in one hand, and his pistoll charged in the
other hand. The seneschall, who had so fiercelie folowed him upon
spur, when he saw him to stand and tarrie as it were for his coming,
notwithstanding he was counted a man (as he was indeed) of great
service, and having also a new supplie of twelve horssemen and sundrie shot come unto him; yet neither he nor anie one of them, being
twentie to one, durst to give the onset upon him, but onelie railed
and used hard speeches unto him, untill his men behind him had
recovered and were come unto him, and then without anie further
harme departed.[12]

In his superb history of English colonialism in sixteenth-century Ireland,
The Twilight Lords, Richard Berleth writes that through this act of bravery,
Ralegh became "the talk of the army" early in 1581. "This gallant action
was to shape his future," Berleth notes. Because of it "Elizabeth would
hear of his heroism from Burghley."[13] Less than three years after Holinshed's *Chronicles* made the occurrence general knowledge, Spenser could
count on the fact that his readers would have little trouble in pinpointing
the actual historical event he was alluding to, when he sends Timias headlong into the trap set by the "fosters." The incident at the ford would
immediately come to mind, when they read how

> The gentle Squire came riding that same way,
> Unweeting of their wile and treason bad,
> And through the *ford* to passen did assay;
> But that fierce foster, which late fled away,
> Stoutly forth stepping on the further shore,
> Him boldly bad his passage there to stay,
> Till he had made amends, and full restore
> For all the damage, which he had him doen afore.
>
> (III.v.18)

Spenser highlights Ralegh's courage at the ford, however, by fusing the incident with the execution of the principal leaders of that "treason bad," those
"three / Ungratious children of one graceless sire" (III.v.15): the Desmonds.

Timias's destruction of the "fosters" is narrated with unusually acerbic
wit. After the squire painfully fights his way to the opposite bank, he
spears "the third brother" through "both his sides" (III.v.21). As this "foster" dies, Spenser writes:

He tombling downe, with gnashing teeth did bite
   The bitter earth, and bad to let him in
   Into the balefull house of endlesse night,
   Where wicked ghosts do waile their former sin.

                                   (III.v.22)

The next brother to feel Timias's wrath, the one who attempted to assault Florimel, is struck on the skull "so rudely . . . That to the chin he cleft his head in twaine" (III.v.23). But the full thrust of Spenser's black humor surfaces in the stanza illustrating the last brother's brutal death. The remaining "foster" tries to escape the vengeful Timias, after his two siblings have been butchered:

With that he would have fled into the wood;
  But *Timias* him lightly overhent,
  Right as he entring was into the flood,
  And strooke at him with force so violent,
  That headlesse him into the foord he sent:
  The carkas with the streame was carried downe,
  But th' head fell backeward on the Continent.
  So mischief fel upon the meaners crowne;
They three be dead with shame, the Squire lives with renowne.

                                   (III.v.25)

When Spenser states that the last brother's head fell "backeward on the Continent," causing "mischief" to fall "upon the meaners crowne," he subtly traces the full political thrust of his allegory. Here, Spenser, using remarkable linguistic compression, spices his sardonic commentary with three wry puns on the words: "Continent," "meaner," and "crowne." The capitalized noun "Continent" refers to the land adjoining Spenser's fictional ford, but it also undoubtedly stands for the European mainland, from which Philip II of Spain incited the Irish to rise against British rule. The slain "foster" is the "meaner" or plotter, who unsuccessfully plans Timias's ambush and is also more debased or "meaner" in spirit than his intended victim. He suffers the effects of retributive justice. However, Spenser's allegory looks beyond the Desmonds and, with brilliant wordplay, implicates Philip II in their treachery. Philip II — in Spenser's elaborate system of puns — is the "meaner" or prime instigator behind the Desmond revolt, who is "meaner" in birth and nobility than Elizabeth of England. According to Spenser, the treasonous "mischief" promoted by the king of Spain, which was thwarted by the Desmonds' execution, has redounded upon his tarnished "crowne." This reading is verified by the facts of a struggle in which both Ralegh and Spenser played active roles.

The ill-fated Desmond Rebellion erupted in 1580, after an army of Spanish and Italian mercenaries, financed by Philip II, had landed in Dingle Bay. The landing signaled a general insurrection against English control of Ireland that constituted the greatest threat to British security before the Armada of 1588. The revolution, led by the Desmonds, was viciously crushed by an English state that feared the expansionist ambitions of Spain, ambitions that would lead to an attempted invasion of the British mainland only eight years later. English power was first released in the wholesale massacre of all mercenaries captured at Smerwick. Approximately 500 soldiers were hacked apart in a single day. As Latin secretary to Lord Grey, who engineered the assault, Spenser probably witnessed the massacre.[14] Ralegh was one of three captains directly responsible for the annihilation of this invading force that hoisted their white flag of surrender in vain.[15] The continued exercise of English power led to the vindictive executions of the three rebel leaders who collaborated with Spain—the Desmonds. Thus James was hunted down in 1580, John in 1582, and Gerald, the earl, in 1583, at which point the conflict was terminated. Ralegh was closely connected with the first two of these executions. After James was captured by the sheriff of Cork, he was imprisoned for several months, and then, as Berleth records, "he was hanged, drawn, and quartered under the supervision of Sir Warham St. Leger and Ralegh."[16] Ralegh was also present at the garrison in Cork, when Captains Zouch and Dowdall returned with the body of Sir John, who was shot in the neck and bled to death soon after being apprehended.[17]

Ralegh's thorough familiarity with the Desmonds' fate is evident in his introduction to *A Report of the Fight about the Iles of the Açores,* published in 1591. There he recalls how "one Morice Fitz John, sonne of old John of Desmond, a notable traitor," tried to rally English sailors to the cause of Catholic Spain. When John of Desmond's son promises them good fortune under a Spanish flag, Ralegh ironically adds: "If he had withall vaunted of this successe of his owne house, no doubt the argument woulde have moved much, and wrought great effect; which because he for that present forgot, I thought it good to remember in his behalfe." The "successe" of Morice's father and two uncles was well known to Ralegh, who summarizes the demise of the ancient house of Desmond for the edification of his crew. He had the story by heart and repeats it at length:

For the Earle his cosen being one of the greatest subjects of *Ireland,* having almost whole contries in his possession; so many goodly manners, Castles, and Lordships; the Count Palatine of *Kerry,* five hundred gentlemen of his owne name and familie to follow him, besides others. All which he possessed in peace for three or foure hundred yeares: was in lesse then three yeares after his adhering to the Spaniards and rebellion, beaten from all his holdes, and not so many as ten gentlemen of his name left living, him selfe taken and beheaded by a soldiour of his owne nation, and his land given by a Parlament to her Majestie, and possessed by the English. His other Cosen, *Sir John* of *Desmond* taken by M. *John Zouch,* and his body hanged over the gates of his native citie to bee devoured by Ravens: the third brother of Sir *James* hanged, drawne, and quartered in the same place.[18]

In *The Faerie Queene,* Timias brings the Desmonds to ruin. When the Squire chases the "foster" who menaces Florimel, Spenser may be recalling Gerald Desmond's reputation for lechery, which would then thematically unite the preservation of chastity, the titular virtue of the third book, with the historical allegory of the fifth canto.[19] The depiction of the Desmonds as forest dwellers who wage guerilla warfare against their foes is remarkably accurate. As traitors to the English crown, they die "with shame" in Spenser's narrative, deprived of proper names that would perpetuate their identities. The decapitation of the last brother to feel Timias's power is a vivid emblem of the Desmonds' overthrow that had specific relevance for Elizabeth. When Gerald, the earl, was finally captured, they cut off his head on the spot and forwarded it to the queen. Berleth provocatively observes that, according to legend, "she spent the morning sitting quietly and looking at it, before having it impaled on London Bridge."[20]

Both Ralegh and Spenser had reason to rejoice over the Desmonds' cruel fate. Each acquired possession of an Irish estate that had been confiscated by the Crown from Sir John of Desmond. In all, Ralegh received the bulk of his 42,000-acre estate from territory carved out of the rebel's holdings, while Spenser's Kilcolman castle and its surrounding 3,028 acres of ploughland and forest came from the same confiscation.[21] Spenser must have especially appreciated Ralegh's help in securing an audience with the queen in 1589, because in that year he faced the possibility of losing some or all of the land on which he had just settled. At that time, Lord Roche, Viscount Fermoy, who had joined in the revolt led by the Desmonds but later recanted, was seeking the restoration of his inheritance — title to land in Munster given to English settlers after its seizure by the queen. On October 12, 1589, Lord Roche complained bitterly to the queen and Sir Francis Walsingham that Spenser was depriving him of his rightful property and molesting his servants. In his letter to Walsingham, Roche enclosed a list of specific grievances, which included the allegation that "one Edmund Spenser, clerk of the council in Munster, by color of his office, and by taking their cattle pasturing upon his lordship's own inheritance, and by refusing and beating of his lordship's servants and bailiffs, hath made waste six other ploughlands of his lordship's inheritance to his no small undoing."[22] The prominence of the Desmonds in *The Faerie Queene*'s historical allegory can then be attributed to the fact that Spenser had not yet received complete and undisputed title to the Kilcolman estate and was struggling for control of the land on which he had settled. By reminding the queen of the Desmonds' treachery, he implicitly strengthened his own claim. On October 26, 1590, due in part perhaps to the queen's acceptance of the poem, Spenser was granted full title to the Kilcolman estate. When he returned to Ireland several months later, the lease he had obtained from the Crown, symbolizing his victory, displayed the name of the castle's former tenant—Sir John of Desmond.[23]

But if the destruction of the "fosters" is meant to demonstrate Timias's power, it is also paradoxically intended to show his complete dependence on the queen. At the moment when he has finally achieved mastery over the "fosters," Timias is suddenly leveled by a wound he received in combat. With alarming rapidity, he slips into a "deadly swowne," only to be revived by the virgin huntress Belphoebe, who accidentally discovers his bleeding body. Upon awakening, he utters a short prayer of thanksgiving, in a stanza that expresses immense gratitude for her extraordinary kindness:

> Mercy deare Lord (said he) what grace is this,
>   That thou hast shewed to me sinfull wight,
>   To send thine Angell from her bowre of blis,
>   To comfort me in my distressed plight?
>   Angell, or Goddesse do I call thee right?
>   What service may I do unto thee meete,
>   That hast from darknesse me returned to light,
>   And with thy heavenly salves and med'cines sweete,
> Hast drest my sinfull wounds? I kisse thy blessed feete.
>
> (III.v.35)

Timias's prayer humbly acknowledges Belphoebe to be an instrument of grace extended to "sinfull" humanity. He realizes that her "heavenly salves" have delivered him from death and requests to be of service to her, in recompense for the love she has manifested. Among these "med'cines sweete," Spenser includes "divine *Tobacco*" (III.v.32)—which Ralegh had introduced to the English nation.[24]

It is important to remember that Spenser's name for the fictional character representing Elizabeth in his allegory—"Belphoebe"—was coined in response to Ralegh's poetic name for the queen. In his letter to Ralegh, Spenser notes that she is sometimes portrayed under the appellation *"Belphoebe,"* which he has fashioned *"according to your owne excellent conceipt of Cynthia, (Phoebe and Cynthia being both names of Diana.)"* Years later, in "The 11th booke of the Ocean," Ralegh would repeat Spenser's variation to recall the period in his life when *The Faerie Queene* entertained Elizabeth with an allegory inspired by his own mythological name for the queen. Remembering an earlier and happier period of his career, Ralegh laments that "Bellphebe's course is now observde no more, / That faire resemblance weareth out of date" (271–72). Spenser created the Timias-Belphoebe allegory during the period of Ralegh's "sorrowfull success," and so his narrative demonstrates the queen's double influence on her "gracious servant" (III.Pr. 4). She cures Timias of a thigh wound received in battle that continues to afflict him. Without intending to cause him pain, stirred with "soft passion" (III.v.30), Belphoebe is true to her name, when her Diana-like visage overpowers Timias, even as she attempts to cure him. While gazing at Belphoebe, Timias is again wounded by an "unwary dart" from her eyes that strikes "his hart." This wounding can be construed as an allegorical distillation of the pain that Ralegh endured in his era of mixed fortune—pain that would appear insignificant in the ensuing years of disgrace.

Soon after the publication of the 1590 edition of *The Faerie Queene*, Ralegh suffered a major fall from power. In 1592, the Queen discovered that Ralegh, who was then captain of the guard, responsible for her personal welfare, had conceived a child with Elizabeth Throckmorton, one of her maids-in-waiting. The most accurate information we possess on the chronology of events leading to Ralegh's fall is recorded in the diary kept by Arthur Throckmorton, Elizabeth's brother. Arthur confides that he first heard of his sister's secret marriage to Walter Ralegh on November 19, 1591. On March 29, 1592, he reveals, "My sister was delivered of a boy between 2 and 3 in the afternoon." This notation is followed by the words: "I writ to Sir Walter Ralegh."[25] The child, named Damerei, was sent to nurse at Enfield, and Lady Ralegh quietly resumed her neglected position as personal attendant to the queen after a long absence. But in less than three months news reached the queen and the Raleghs were promptly incarcerated. Sir Edward Stafford caustically wrote to Anthony Bacon in August of that year: "If you have anything to do with Sir Walter Ralegh, or any love to make to Mistress Throckmorton, at the Tower tomorrow you may speak with them."[26] Elizabeth was always angered by the marriage of her favorites. After the earl of Leicester secretly married Lettice Knollys, he was temporarily banished from court, as was the earl of Essex, after he wed Sir Philip Sidney's widow. In Ralegh's case, the queen evidently believed that he had betrayed her trust and had made her demonstration of affection seem ridiculous." [27] He had, after all, used his privileged position as her personal servant to seduce one of her handmaids.

Even before Damerei's birth (and short life—he died months later), rumors of Ralegh's secret marriage had reached the son of the queen's closest counselor. When Robert Cecil, Lord Treasurer Burghley's son, wrote to Ralegh concerning the affair, Ralegh adamantly denied everything, evidently terrified that his union would be discovered. In a letter dated March 10—almost five months after Arthur Throckmorton heard of his sister's marriage and just a few days before the birth of her son—Ralegh denied reports of his personal alliance. He responded to Cecil with a bold lie, claiming that news of his marriage was a slander meant to discredit him at court: "I mean not to cume away, as they say I will, for feare of a marriage, and I know not what. If any such thing weare, I would have imparted it unto yourself before any man living, and therefore, I pray believe it not, and I beseich you to surpress, what you can, any such malicious report. For I protest before God, there is none on the face of the yearth, that I would be fastened to." [28] Ralegh's letter illustrates the cultivation of the art of deceit. Faced with imminent exposure, he even dares to invoke his Creator's name to bluff his way through a scandal that was becoming increasingly more volatile. His strategy, at this point, was simply to refute the charge and to attribute it to his enemies' spite. His first impulse was to "give the lie" (in the terms of his famous poem) to all those who were telling the truth, albeit maliciously. The queen, however, was not impressed with these protestations of innocence and imprisoned him and his wife in the Tower at the end of July.

Ralegh's first, temporary reprieve was hastened by a matter of expediency. On September 7, the huge East Indian carrack, *Madre de Dios,* which his ships had captured off the Azores, was brought into Dartmouth harbor. Since Ralegh was the person most familiar with the intricate financial arrangements behind this act of piracy (from which the Crown received a substantial portion), he was set free. Robert Cecil, in whose charge he was placed, sensed his eagerness to atone for his indiscretion and wrote that he found Ralegh "marvelous greedy to do anything to recover the conceit of his brutish offense." [29] Although the Raleghs were released in the autumn of that year, the stigma lingered on. Indeed, Ralegh was still brooding on his fall from favor in November 1596; he wrote to Cecil, describing new enterprises he had been devising in the queen's service, troubled that "because of [his] disgrace all men feare to adventure with [him]." [30]

The difficulty of interpreting Spenser's treatment of Ralegh's public dishonor stems from the fact that Spenser creates an allegorical narrative that can be construed either as a vindication or as a condemnation of his patron's conduct.[31] The complexity of Spenser's depiction of this crucial event in Ralegh's career can, in part, be attributed to the peculiar situation regarding patronage that Spenser occupied after 1592, when the two major sponsors of his poem were at odds with each other. Equidistant from the moral perspectives of Elizabeth and Ralegh, the historical allegory of the fourth and sixth books of *The Faerie Queene* is a point of convergence for conflicting versions of the same event. Here Spenser's generous moral understanding embraces a comprehensive vision which is, as a result, fundamentally ambiguous. The pivotal moment in Spenser's allegory, in the second installment of *The Faerie Queene*, when he first reflects on the Throckmorton affair, occurs when Belphoebe returns from her execution of Lust only to find Timias comforting Amoret in what she deems to be a highly improper manner.[32] Angered by the attention Timias has lavished on Amoret, Belphoebe first thinks of killing him and his "new lovely mate" and then rebukes the squire, before forsaking him. Returning from her conquest:

> There she him found by that new lovely mate,
> Who lay the whiles in swoune, full sadly set,
> From her faire eyes wiping the deawy wet,
> Which softly stild, and kissing them atweene,
> And handling soft the hurts, which she did get.
> For of that Carle she sorely bruz'd had beene,
> Als of his own rash hand one wound was to be seene.
>
> Which when she saw, with sodaine glauncing eye,
> Her noble heart with sight thereof was fild
> With deepe disdaine, and great indignity,
> That in her wrath she thought them both have thrild,
> With that selfe arrow, which the Carle had kild:
> Yet held her wrathfull hand from vengeance sore,
> But drawing nigh, ere he her well beheld;
> Is this the faith, she said, and said no more,
> But turnd her face, and fled away for evermore.
>
> (IV.vii.35–36)

The poised tendencies of Spenser's thought, evident in this episode, lead analysis in opposing directions. On the one hand, Timias seems innocent of all wrongdoing, victimized by a jealous Belphoebe, who acts unadvisedly and in wrath. Spenser had previously presented Belphoebe's rescue of the wounded Timias as a paradigm of virtuous action. When Belphoebe aids the unconscious Timias, she administers grace that is freely bestowed upon victimized humanity. In the third book, the virgin huntress pursues the chase with a company of followers and comes upon the injured squire. In the fourth book, Timias is part of her retinue and repeats her kindness when he cares for Amoret. These acts of mercy are thus analogous in this regard. But, on the other hand, even though there are basic similarities shared by these two actions, significant differences also exist, which question Timias's integrity in manifesting love for Amoret.

It is the voice of the *poet* and not that of a possibly mistaken Belphoebe which informs us of the sudden emotional bond uniting Timias and "his new lovely mate." The adjective "lovely" is a pun on Amoret's name; the word "new" suggests that Timias has abandoned Belphoebe, his "old" mistress. The term "mate" stresses the special attachment of "that lovely boy" (IV.vii.23) with the "lovely" Amoret, the allegorical figure of desire. Spenser had previously hinted at this union in his quatrain introducing the seventh canto, where he outlines this episode:

> *Amoret rapt by greedie lust*
> *Belphoebe saves from dread,*
> *The Squire her loves, and being blam'd*
> *his dayes in dole doth lead.*

The statement that "*The Squire her loves*" is a marvelous example of Spenser's use of ambiguous pronouns. If the antecedent for "her" is "Belphoebe," then the squire has been unjustly accused of betrayal. But if, instead, it refers to "Amoret," then Belphoebe's charge is again validated by the narrator. Furthermore, Timias's ministration to Amoret's wounds is related in a tone that insinuates a sexual dimension, but with immense subtlety. After he wipes "the deawy wet" from "her faire eyes," he ventures past the bounds of discretion and courtesy by "kissing atween" her eyes and "handling soft" her "hurts." With these phrases an act of salvation is transformed into an act of foreplay. Belphoebe recognizes this erotic motivation instantly and considers killing both lovers with the same weapon with which she dispatched Lust. Through this impulse we are prompted to identify Timias and Amoret—Ralegh and his wife—with the inordinate desire they were unable to resist.[33]

Criticism of Ralegh is also implied in Timias's wounding of Amoret. As the squire comforts his "new lovely mate," Spenser tells us that "of his own rash hand one wound was to be seene." This line recalls an event that immediately precedes Belphoebe's destruction of Lust and her rebuke of Timias. As soon as Amoret drifts away from her protector, Britomart, she is captured by "a wilde and salvage man" (IV.vii.5), from whose dungeon she escapes. The savage, described at the beginning of the canto as "greedie lust," pursues her past Timias, who is now Belphoebe's hunting companion. But Timias, who accosts the villain, is unable to overcome him and, indeed, adds to Amoret's torment; Lust defends himself by using her as a shield, which he repeatedly strikes:

> Thereto the villaine used craft in fight;
>   For ever when the Squire his javelin shooke,
>   He held the Lady forth before him right,
>   And with her body, as a buckler, broke
>   The puissance of his intended stroke.
>   And if it chaunst (as needs it must in fight)
>   Whilest he on him was greedy to be wroke,
>   That any little blow on her did light,
> Then would he laugh aloud, and gather great delight.
>   (IV.vii.26)

Timias's desire to overcome Lust works a contrary effect, adding to Amoret's ravishment and degradation. The pain she suffers is a consequence of his unintended collaboration with unchecked sexual desire. To make certain that this point does not go unnoticed, Spenser mentions Timias's part in Amoret's misfortune on two other occasions outside the context of this incident. First, the poet discusses Timias's culpability, as we have seen, when the squire soothes the injured Amoret in IV.vii.35. And he repeats this observation again, when Prince Arthur comes across Amoret in "sad and sorrowful estate," only to find her still suffering, "Through her late hurts, and through that hapless wound / With which the Squire in her defence her sore astound" (IV.viii.19). Timias does manage to wound Lust, but the poet uses this action to further emphasize Amoret's connection with the vice: "A streame of coleblacke bloud thence gusht amaine / That all her silken garments did with bloud bestaine" (IV.vii.27). Amoret and Lust are pressed together so closely that an assailant cannot attack one without affecting the other. Bathed in Lust's blood, Amoret, like Timias, becomes associated with excessive desire. Only Belphoebe is powerful and pure enough to drive off the villain, who is terrified by the sight of the virgin huntress, "Well knowing her to be his deaths sole instrument" (IV.vii.29). She soon defeats him by shooting an arrow through his "greedy throte" (IV.vii.31), destroying this archetype of consuming passion. After Belphoebe rejects

Timias, he wanders wildly through the forest, like the mad Orlando forsaken by Angelica. But he does not blame the virgin huntress for his plight; instead, he rebukes himself for his disgrace, seeking only "on him selfe to wreake his follies owne despight" (IV.vii.39).[34]

However, a reader sympathetic to Ralegh's plight can readily locate elements in the 1596 edition of the poem that absolve Ralegh of guilt—that prove he is innocent of any transgression—even as Ralegh had protested in his letter to Cecil. One could argue, for instance, that Timias, being Lust's adversary, is thereby aligned with virtue. He attacks Lust for the same reason that he challenges the beastly "foster": to interrupt an attempted rape and punish the assailant. Spenser even manages to generate pity for Timias by making him Lust's victim rather than his ally. This qualification certainly mitigates the severity of the fourth book's allegory. As the tale continues toward its conclusion, the poet becomes much more emphatic in supporting Ralegh and emphasizing the case against the queen. When they meet again, in the next canto, he accuses her of having misjudged him. She at first does not recognize her former companion in his present state of neglect and asks him to explain the reason for his agonizing self-abuse. Timias then replies with a scathing rebuke:

> Ne any but your selfe, O dearest dred,
>   Hath done this wrong, to wreake on worthlesse wight
>   Your high displeasure, through misdeeming bred:
>   That when your pleasure is to deeme aright,
>   Ye may redresse, and me restore to light.

After Timias blames her for misunderstanding his actions, Belphoebe has a sudden change of heart, based on his complaint:

> Which sory words her mightie hart did mate
>   With mild regard, to see his ruefull plight,
>   That her inburning wrath she gan abate,
>   And him receiv'd againe to former favours state.

>   (IV.viii.17)

Timias's innocence is predicated on Belphoebe's guilt. He charges her with having caused his distress and the narrator supplies the reason for her mistake—"inburning wrath." According to this pattern of vindication, a strong passion colored her judgment when she rejected Timias and thought of killing the pair "in her wrath." She is temporarily blinded with rage and only later comes to recognize her error. The historical allegory, viewed from this perspective, proves that "the displeasure of the mighty is / Then [than] death it selfe more dread and desperate" (IV.viii.1). The shifting attitudes of monarchs cause them to abuse their subjects, when this "displeasure" is melded to a failure to "deeme aright."

Commenting on Timias's reproach, Allan Gilbert asserts that the squire's alleged faithlessness is here shown to be an inaccurate perception. "This breach is not real," he argues, "for as Timias explains, Belphoebe's inference is incorrect."[35] But Gilbert simply overlooks the extensive pattern of incrimination that I have previously suggested, against which we are meant to balance Timias's protestations of innocence. He forgets that Timias's "rash hand" has played a part in his catastrophe. Belphoebe's bitter taunt—"Is this the faith?"—and the squire's later retort—that her "misdeeming" has produced "this wrong" she has perpetrated—compel us to consider the Throckmorton affair from the divergent perspectives of Spenser's quarreling patrons. Spenser incorporates *both* perspectives in his narrative, and thus remained faithful to both Ralegh and Elizabeth in his historical allegory.

The incident that brings Belphoebe and Timias together includes yet another reconstruction of a historical event. She is drawn to Timias through the mediation of a turtle dove that steals a jewel from the squire with which to lure her to his side. The jewel is described as "a Ruby of right perfect hew, / Shap'd like a heart, yet bleeding of the wound, / And with a litle golden chaine about it bound" (IV.viii.6). In January 1595, Arthur Throckmorton wrote to Robert Cecil asking to be numbered among the masquers celebrating the wedding of Elizabeth Vere to the earl of Derby. Sir John Davies had composed the "Epithalamion of the Nine Muses" to commemorate the event, and Throckmorton hoped that during this masque he might be allowed to prostrate himself before the queen and then arise to give her "a ring made for a wedding ring set round with diamonds, and with a ruby like a heart placed in a coronet, with the inscription *Elizabetha potest.*"[36] It is likely that Spenser introduces the heart-shaped ruby into his narrative as a historical detail symbolizing Ralegh's hopes for reconciliation with his sovereign. Arthur Throckmorton construed his offering as an attempt to "modify the easy softened mind of her Majesty as both I and mine may find mercy." He certainly included the fate of his sister and his brother-in-law in this wish for benevolent treatment. The reconciliation of Timias and Belphoebe, however, does not distribute blame equally between Ralegh and Elizabeth. Instead, it contradicts the imputation of guilt leveled against Ralegh and criticizes the queen for her rashness.

In the final book of *The Faerie Queene*, the Legend of Courtesy, Ralegh and his wife appear for the last time. Spenser tactfully omits any mention of their misfortune in the Book of Justice, where his advocacy of severe justice culminates with the execution of Mary, Queen of Scots, under the guise of Duessa. Walter still retains his identity as Timias, but his companion is now called "Serena," which was Ralegh's poetic name for his wife.[37] The three Desmond brothers are here replaced by the three masters of the Blatant Beast: Despetto, Decetto, and Defetto, who ambush Timias in "a woody glade" and "gan him to invade" (VI.v.14). The vindication of Ralegh in the sixth book utilizes the method of circular composition in *The Faerie Queene*, through which narrative patterns are made to echo, by analogy, previous events in the poem. A sense of Ralegh's virtue is affirmed by this recreation of the incident at the ford in which he overcame treason and lust. The 1590 and 1596 editions of *The Faerie Queene* are symmetrically balanced; in the fifth canto of the last book of each installment, Timias triumphs over ignominious foes. As masters of the Blatant Beast, Ralegh's new adversaries are manipulators of slander. Despite ("Despetto") defines the attitude of Timias's rivals, while deceit ("Decetto") signifies the method they employ to ensnare him "in treasons subtill traine" (VI.v.14). Their plan to use the Blatant Beast "To worke his utter shame, and thoroughly him confound" (VI.v.14) is a result of their own defective natures — the "Defetto" that represents the state of inadequacy which engenders evil. This link between the traitors of the third book and the slanderers of the sixth parallels the treason of the Desmonds with the malice of Ralegh's unnamed rivals at court.

But Timias is by no means completely absolved of error in the narrative of the sixth book. After he and Serena are bitten by the Blatant Beast and seek to be cured by a "carefull Hermite" (VI.vi.2), we are paradoxically told that the wounds they have received were internally induced. The hermit enjoins the couple to be vigilant in resisting "fraile affection"—the source of their distress:

> First learne your outward sences to refraine
> From things, that stirre up fraile affection;
> Your eies, your eares, your tongue, your talk restraine
> From that they most affect, and in due termes containe.

> For from those outward sences ill affected,
> The seede of all this evill first doth spring,
> Which at the first before it had infected,
> Mote easie be supprest with little thing:
> But being growen strong, it forth doth bring
> Sorrow, and anguish, and impatient paine

> In th' inner parts, and lastly scattering
> Contagious poyson close through every vaine,
> It never rests, till it have wrought his finall bane. (VI. vi. 7–8)

Through the hermit, Spenser acknowledges that the Raleghs' indulgence in "this evill" has brought about their ruin. In the hermit's homily, we are again confronted with the issue of Timias's guilt, as the poem reinforces Belphoebe's suspicion that he has been unfaithful. The hermit's comforting of Timias and Serena provides the third and final example of this motif of compassion in Spenser's historical allegory. Having been cured of the Blatant Beast's venomous bite, the characters of this fiction again lose their identities as analogues to contemporary political figures.

The historical allegory of Timias and Belphoebe is both a chronicle of court events and a vital part of their development. Spenser filled a dual role as both spectator to and actor in the incidents he commemorates. As a vehicle for social aspiration, the 1590 edition of *The Faerie Queene* unfolds an allegory of power wherein Ralegh defeats the queen's Irish opponents and then submits himself, in turn, to her authority. As a historical commentary, it continues the depiction of Ralegh's early career beyond the limit of Holinshed's *Chronicles,* in a bipartisan narrative that dramatizes Ralegh's sudden rise and subsequent misfortune. Unlike Dante in exile or Milton in retirement, Spenser composed his epic during a period of political involvement. Perhaps the most poignant aspect of his "biographical fiction" resides in the courage that he demonstrates in sympathetically responding to Ralegh's fate even during the years of his disgrace. In the fourth and sixth books, Spenser at times concedes that Ralegh was guilty of betraying his sovereign's trust. The case against him was strong and the evidence remains irrefutable. In seducing Elizabeth Throckmorton, Ralegh's unchecked desire had compelled him to violate what was regarded as a sacred confidence. But Spenser also realizes that this "crime" was clearly not commensurate with the "inburning wrath" that it engendered, or the imprisonment and calumny that were its consequences. Ralegh had, after all, remedied his lapse of judgment by marrying his "Serena." Continued vindictiveness toward him could surely be termed a vice. These competing sympathies moved Spenser to create a complex meditation that combines the conflicting interpretations of his embittered patrons.

While outlining his *"whole intention in the course of this worke"* in the letter to Ralegh appended to the 1590 edition of *The Faerie Queene*, Spenser, referring to himself as "a Poet historical," notes that he has chosen to write an Arthurian legend—set far back in the past—because it is *"furthest from the daunger of envy, and suspition of present time."* Having decided to incorporate analogues to the activities of Elizabeth and Ralegh in his poem, he was nevertheless fully aware of the fact that he was again exposing himself to the Blatant Beast's "venemous despite," just as he had in 1579, the year of his self-exile. It was then that he first suffered for his "former writs, all were they clearest / From blamefull blot" (VI.xii.41), which he recalls in the poem's final stanza. In mirroring contemporary court politics, however, Spenser decided to risk the bite of slander to repay a debt of gratitude and to reunite Ralegh and the queen.

C. W. Post College

NOTES

1. See Edwin Greenlaw, "Spenser and the Earl of Leicester," *PMLA* 25 (1910), 535–61; Greenlaw maintains that Spenser embarrassed Leicester, in whose service he was temporarily employed in 1579, by writing *Mother Hubberds Tale,* and was quickly shipped off to the wilds of Ireland.

2. From the dedicatory sonnet in *The Faerie Queene* addressed to Lord Grey, line 12. All quotations are taken from *The Works of Edmund Spenser: A Variorum Edition,* ed. Edwin Greenlaw et al., 11 vols. (Baltimore: Johns Hopkins Press, 1932–57).

3. See Kathrine Koller, "Spenser and Ralegh," *ELH* 1 (1934), 39, for a list of the gifts and grants heaped upon Ralegh before 1587.

4. Quoted in Walter Oakeshott, *The Queen and the Poet* (London: Faber and Faber, 1960), p. 28.

5. Ibid.

6. From an account of the Pomeranian traveler Leopold von Wedel, in W. B. Rye, *England as Seen by Foreigners* (London, 1865; rpt. New York: B. Bloom, 1967), p. 113.

7. Oakeshott, *The Queen and the Poet,* p. 36.

8. Sir Walter Ralegh, "The 11th: and last book of the Ocean to Scinthia," 123–31. All quotations from Ralegh's poetry are taken from *The Poems of Sir Walter Ralegh,* ed. Agnes Latham (Cambridge, Mass: Harvard University Press, 1951), unless otherwise cited.

9. Oakeshott includes late seventeenth-century versions of these verses in *The Queen and the Poet,* pp. 217–19, from MS 3602 of the Phillips collection. Sixteenth-century copies of both poems have subsequently been located: Ralegh's in Archbishop Marsh Library (MS 2.3.5.21. f. 30ʳ); and the queen's in the Petyt collection of the Inner Temple Library (MS Petyt 538, vol. 10).

10. This correspondence is cited by R. W. Church, *Spenser* (London: Macmillan, 1906), pp. 88–90. Church writes that "the *Faerie Queene* might also be called the Epic of the English wars in Ireland under Elizabeth" (p. 89). See also Philo Buck, "On the Political Allegory of *The Faerie Queene,*" *Nebraska University Studies* 11 (1911), 184–85; and Koller, "Spenser and Ralegh," p. 46.

11. John Hooker, *The Supplie of the Irish Chronicles* (London, 1586), p. 173.

12. Ibid.

13. Richard Berleth, *The Twilight Lords* (New York: Knopf, 1978), p. 180.

Ralegh in Spenser's Historical Allegory

14. In August 1580, Spenser was appointed to be Lord Grey's private secretary. He records the Smerwick massacre in his *View of the Present State of Ireland*, ed. W. L. Renwick (London: Partridge, 1934), pp. 139–40.

15. Hooker, *Irish Chronicles*, p. 171; Berleth, *The Twilight Lords*, pp. 167 ff.

16. Berleth, *The Twilight Lords*, p. 147.

17. Ibid., pp. 188–90; Hooker, *Irish Chronicles*, p. 175.

18. Sir Walter Ralegh, *A Report of the Truth of the fight about the Iles of Açores* (London, 1591), C4^r–C4^v.

19. Hooker, *Irish Chronicles*, p. 144, writes in a marginal note of how Gerald "putteth away his wife and married another mans wife." However, Berleth, *The Twilight Lords*, pp. 80–82, tempers this opinion of the earl's imputed vice.

20. Berleth, *The Twilight Lords*, p. 204.

21. See Fredric Carpenter, *A Reference Guide to Edmund Spenser* (New York: Kraus, 1969), p. 32, for grant 5473 to Spenser.

22. Quoted from Alexander Judson, *The Life of Edmund Spenser, Var.* 11.23.

23. It seems likely that Spenser read either part or all of the Timias-Belphoebe episode, when he entertained the queen, with selections from *The Faerie Queene*, "at timely houres" (*CCCHA* 362). One could hardly imagine a more apposite excerpt.

24. Thomas Roche, ed., *The Faerie Queene* (Bungay, Suffolk: Penguin, 1978) comments of III.v.32 that "this is the first reference to tobacco in English literature" (p. 1151).

25. Arthur's diary notations can be found in A. L. Rowse, *Sir Walter Ralegh, His Family and Private Life* (New York: Harper and Row, 1962), p. 160; Ralegh's child is mentioned on pp. 159–60.

26. Ibid., p. 167.

27. Fred Sorenson, "Sir Walter Ralegh's Marriage," *SP* 33 (1936), 182–202.

28. Edward Edwards, *Life of Ralegh* (London: Macmillan, 1868), vol. 2, p. 46.

29. Rowse, *Sir Walter Ralegh*, p. 167.

30. Oakeshott, *The Queen and the Poet*, p. 50.

31. Thomas Roche, *The Kindly Flame* (Princeton, N.J.: Princeton University 1964), pp. 142–49, offers a different reading of this episode, which defines it as an "allegory of honor" wherein Timias is first accepted and then wrongfully rejected by Belphoebe, who temporarily misprizes his virtue. I state that the poem exhibits two opposing strands of argumentation: one that shows Timias being victimized by Belphoebe's error and another, no less significant, that hints at Timias's misconduct, thereby justifying Belphoebe's wrath.

32. This generally accepted allusion can be found in Allan Gilbert, "Belphoebe's Misdeeming of Timias," *PMLA* 62 (1947), 627–28; and E. M. English, "Spenser's Accommodation of Allegory to History in the Story of Timias and Belphoebe," *JEGP* 59 (1960), 418 ff.

33. I agree with William Oram, whose essay in this volume argues that the poet's "fictional distortion" of history "seizes on the problematic." Yet I fear that his final assessment of Amoret as being "essentially blameless" — "only unlucky" — is not successfully reconciled with Oram's previous remark that "the text suggests that her seizure by Lust is not simply bad luck." Since Oram's analysis is attuned to the subtle suggestion at IV.vii.4 that Amoret contributes to her own ravishment, that she is not merely the victim of bad luck, his closing remark unduly simplifies Spenser's complex treatment of Amoret, in distinguishing her from Aemylia. Using Oram's terminology, we might maintain that the character of Amoret has been "fragmented" and "reshaped . . . as a question."

34. Arthur Gorges identifies Ralegh with the mad Orlando in a letter to Cecil, dated 9 August 1592 (Oakeshott, *The Queen and the Poet*, p. 46). During this same period, Ralegh

JAMES P. BEDNARZ

also writes to Cecil, admitting his guilt and lamenting that "once amiss hath bereaved me of all" (ibid., p. 47).

35. Gilbert, "Belphoebe's Misdeeming," p. 634.

36. The foregoing commentary is indebted to J. R. Brink, "The Masque of the Nine Muses: Sir John Davies's Unpublished 'Epithalamion' and the 'Belphoebe-Ruby' Episode in *The Faerie Queene*," *RES* 23 (1972), 445–47.

37. See J. H. Adamson and H. F. Folland, *The Shepherd of the Ocean: An Account of Sir Walter Ralegh and His Times* (Boston: Gambit, 1969), pp. 200–06; Oakeshott, *The Queen and the Poet,* p. 46; and Agnes Latham, ed., *The Poems of Sir Walter Ralegh* (Cambridge, Mass.: Harvard University Press, 1951), pp. 118–19, in her gloss on "Now Serena bee not coy."

THOMAS P. ROCHE, JR.

The Menace of Despair and Arthur's Vision, *Faerie Queene* I.9

*T*HE NINTH canto of Book I of *The Faerie Queene* is generally described as the "despair canto," that is, the canto in which Redcross meets the figure of Despair, one of the great episodes in the poem. Its brilliance has obscured for readers, especially for those of us who write about this strange poem, the fact that Spenser devotes two-thirds of the canto to two other stories, which, if remembered, do not seem to be related to the later adventure in ways that make sense of Spenser's exquisite taste in structuring his cantos.[1] I do not want to make a general theory of canto structure, but I would like to suggest that the collocation of the three stories in this canto might serve as a general model for considering other cantos of the poem as structural units.

The canto begins just after the rescue of Redcross from Orgoglio by Prince Arthur, and in the twenty stanzas devoted to him, Arthur tells Una and Redcross the story of his *enfance*, his upbringing by Timon and Merlin, and his visionary encounter with the fairy queen. This is the only time in the poem that we hear what must be considered the primary plot vision. Did Spenser see a relation between Arthur's vision of the fairy queen and Redcross's encounter with Despair? If so, by what logic did Spenser want to link love and despair together?

Part of the answer lies, I believe, in the middle stanzas of the canto in which an unidentified knight with a rope around his neck rides up to tell Redcross a story about his friend Sir Terwin's encounter with Despair, who is not named until the fifth line of I.9.28, the precise midpoint of the five stanzas devoted to Sir Trevisan's story—a point to which I will return. Redcross rushes off to encounter this Despair, bringing with him both Una and Sir Trevisan, who "Would faine haue fled, ne durst approchen neare, / But the other [Redcross] forst him stay, and comforted in feare" (I.ix.34). Redcross now meets Despair alone, beginning in the next stanza, although the narrative tells us "That darkesome caue *they* enter, where *they* find / That cursed man" (I.ix.35). Spenser never specifies who the *they* are. We might suspect that they include Trevisan and Una, but Spenser in his usual manner never mentions Trevisan again. We must ask the question why Spenser even bothered to introduce this character when he could equally well have had Redcross and Una just arrive at the cave as they happen on the Cave of Error in canto i. Una, who has not been mentioned since the departure of Arthur in stanza 20, resurfaces in the fiction only after Redcross is handed the dagger to kill himself in stanza 52. It is, as my colleague A. Walton Litz suggested to me long ago, as if the dialogue between Redcross and Despair were taking place only in Redcross's mind. Only when he makes the physical action of grabbing the dagger does Una see what is happening. It is a brilliant perception, but only if Auerbachean mimesis is allowed to be lord of misrule over Spenserian creation. Principles other than mimesis are required to deal with Spenser's poetics. Canto ix tells two stories, Arthur's (stanzas 3–15) and Trevisan's (26–30), and then reveals Redcross's encounter with Despair in the fictional present. We must inquire how and why these three episodes function in this canto and to what extent Arthur's vision is threatened by the menace of despair.

I

Spenser's poetics is triumphantly nondramatic: he seldom sets the scene with anything more than the bare boards; he rarely blocks the action; he never clears the stage and very often does not conclude the action. Hence the patchy description of Despair's abode, hence the thereness and nontherenss of Trevisan and Una, hence the dismissal of Redcross at the conclusion: "So vp he rose, and thence amounted streight" (I.ix.54)—without so much as the twitching of a mantle blue or a loving glance toward Una. These are not lapses in Spenser's poetic abilities. The problem is our own inability to describe the ontology of Spenser's fiction with any degree of accuracy. Alpers has suggested that Tasso and Spenser use essentially different narrative techniques, but the difference between *Gerusalemme liberata* 15–16 and the Bower of Bliss is less a matter of narrative-direct versus poet-using-narrative-to-persuade-reader than Alpers would allow.[2] I do not dispute Alper's basic point, but if that is taken fully as the difference between Tasso and Spenser, it deprives both poets of their common moral purpose and their common subordination of their fictions to the Christian beliefs that their fictions are meant to figure forth. Tasso is reduced to writing a narrative about a crusade to rescue Jerusalem; Spenser is reduced to persuading his readers to achieve a Jerusalem, for which his narrative is not necessary. By shifting our attention from narrative fulfillment in Tasso to reader psychology in Spenser, Alpers avoids the main question of Christian doctrine that occupied both authors. It is therefore important to understand that the narrative "inadequacy" of Spenser's poem is simply his different way of handling the same problems of demonstrating Christian truths. Because of this theological dimension of his poem it was absolutely essential for Spenser to let Trevisan tell his story of Terwin's despairing love and to have Una play such a self-effacing part in the final section of the canto.

This canto treats three "couples": Arthur and the fairy queen, Terwin and the unnamed proud lady, and Redcross and Una. It is strange to think of them as "couples," because they are not, in any conventional sense of the word, but Arthur has been enthralled by the fairy queen who has vanished — a Cupid and Psyche in reverse; Terwin and his lady are totally at odds; and then there are Redcross and Una, surely the chastest couple this side of heaven. If one stops to think that Spenser, the great poet of marriage, allows only the marriage of Florimell and Marinell to be celebrated in the poem (V.3), then one has to reconsider the relation of Spenser's poem to the earlier epic-romance. Virgil allows Aeneas his false marriage to Dido but ends his epic before Aeneas marries Lavinia, an "omission" corrected by Mapheus Vegius in the thirteenth book he added to sixteenth-century editions of the poem. Ariosto allows his Bradamante to marry the converted Ruggiero, and Tasso at least suggests that his converted Armida will be wed to his Rinaldo. In celebrating these marriages, these poets are in actuality praising their patrons, who are always the descendants of these couples.[3]

Spenser's poem is within this same tradition, but his lovers — Redcross and Una, Britomart and Arthegall, Calidore and Pastorella, Arthur and Gloriana — do not marry in the poem as written. These unions were all reserved for that final unwritten book in which all the questing knights were to have returned triumphant to Cleopolis, and a general feast was to have ended the poem.[4] One set of dynastic progenitors was enough for Virgil, Ariosto, and Tasso. Spenser doubles the number. In imitation of the earlier poems, Britomart and her knight-equal-to-Arthur begin the line that leads to Elizabeth, but there are also Arthur and Gloriana, the beginning and end of the plot. There is no doubt in my mind that in the early stages of planning and writing *The Faerie Queene* Spenser meant Arthur to represent his patron the Earl of Leicester, who was ambitious to make himself consort to Elizabeth but whose marital intrigues and early death (1588) prevented Spenser's becoming the English Virgil he had intended. To base an epic poem on historical prediction is to invite disaster. The death of Marcellus before the completion of the *Aeneid* was a serious blow for Virgil, but since he had made Marcellus only the putative bud of his epic intentions, that death only increased the *lacrimae rerum* so deeply entrenched in the fabric of that poem. Spenser's epic intentions were spared because he

was writing an allegorical poem in which Arthur figured not only Leicester but also Magnificence, and this Arthur could still search for the fairy
queen without Leicester's support in the significance of the design of the
poem. Arthur could still be Magnificence and the fairy queen Glory, and
that is how we apprehend them in reading the poem today as in 1590.

II

The tripartite structure of the canto ix of Book I presents three different aspects of love, figured by the three "couples." Arthur in search of
Gloriana is Magnificence, the sum of all virtues, seeking its earthly reward,
Glory, and the import of this quest is mainly moral. Trevisan's story of
Terwin and his despairing love is a negative example of human love meant
to balance the positive love vision of Arthur and to show the potential danger inherent in love as a passion. The despair episode moves from human
story to theological meaning—man's apprehension of God's love for him—
with not a word about love as a passion. This is the reason that Una must
be kept unobserved until the climax lest we concentrate on the merely human
aspects of Redcross's breach of faith with Una once more. These three aspects of love—love as visionary quest, love as despair, and despair as the
total absence of love—are played off against one another through an intricate series of poetic details.

The first is a parallel between Arthur and Redcross, for Spenser makes
Arthur point out that parallel in relating his vision of the fairy queen. After
two stanzas (10–11) of conventional description of love's power to catch even
those who scorn its blandishments, Arthur points to Redcross:

> Ensample make of him your haplesse ioy,
>   And of my selfe now mated, as ye see;
>   Whose prouder vaunt that proud auenging boy
> Did soone pluck downe, and curbd my libertie.
>   For on a day *prickt forth* with *iollitie*
>   Of *looser* life, and heat of hardiment,
>   Raunging the forest wide on courser free,
>   The fields, the floods, the heauens with one consent
> Did seeme to laugh on me, and fauour mine intent.

> For-*wearied* with my sports, I did alight
>   From loftie steed, and downe to sleepe me layd;
>   The verdant gras my couch did goodly dight,
>   And pillow was my helmet faire displayd.
>   (I.ix.12–13, emphasis added)

Surely we are to be reminded of that knight "*pricking* on the plaine," that "full *iolly* knight" who in canto vii "*wearie* sate, / To rest him selfe, foreby a fountaine side. . . . Pourd out in *loosenesse* on the grassy ground" (I.vii.2,7).

Both loves have been inspired by the fairy queen who appears to Arthur as fleeting vision and who imposes the rescue of Una's parents on Redcross as the task to test his knightly mettle.

The parallel goes further, in that neither Arthur nor Redcross knows his lineage. Arthur asks Merlin:

> Of what loines and what lignage I did spring:
> Whose aunswere bad me still assured bee,
> That I was sonne and heire vnto a king,
> As time in her iust terme the truth to light should bring.
>
> (I.ix.5)

The "truth to light" is brought in the next stanza in the person of Una:

> Well worthy impe, said then the Lady gent,
>   And pupil fit for such a Tutours hand.
>   But what aduenture, or what high intent
>   Hath brought you hither into Faery land,
>   Aread Prince *Arthur,* crowne of Martiall band?   (I.ix.6)

This is the first time that Arthur is named in the poem proper. He had been named in the arguments to cantos vii, viii, and ix, but it seems decorously appropriate that it should be Una, she who is named "Truth" in the argument to canto ii, who brings his name to light. We do not know by what means Una learned his name, nor whether Arthur knew his name before, but Spenser's ceremony of naming is clearly intended as revelation.

Redcross is led to an analogous revelation in the following canto when Fidelia leads him to Contemplation's hill where he has a vision of the New Jerusalem and finds out his own true name and destination:

> And thou faire ymp, sprong out from English race,
>   How euer now accompted Elfins sonne,
>   Well worthy doest thy seruice for her grace,
>   To aide a virgin desolate foredonne.
>   . . . .
>   For thou emongst those Saints, whom thou doest see,
>   Shalt be a Saint, and thine owne nations frend
>   And Patrone: thou Saint *George* shalt called bee,
>   Saint *George* of mery England, the signe of victoree.
>
> (I.x.60–61)

In their naming and in their destinies, in their setting forth, in their submission to love, in their visions, Arthur and Redcross are meant to be both parallel and contrast, the first a prince (and as I have suggested, in Spenser's original intention, eventually a king), the second a saint. Therefore the usual interpretation of Arthur as a symbol of grace entering into the poem to rescue the titular knight of the book from the nature that is his really does not apply in this episode of Book I. Both prince and saint-to-be are sustained by grace, as all in nature must be. The question in this canto is not nature *and* grace (*pace* Woodhouse) but nature *in* grace as expressed by the gifts exchanged by Arthur and Redcross. Within the earthly kingdom, both prince and saint must interchange their special gifts, according to Paul:

> Now there are diuersities of giftes, but the same Spirit.
> And there are diuersities of administrations, but the same Lord.
> And there are diuersities of operations, but God is the same, which worketh all in all. . . .
> For to one is giuen by the Spirit the worde of wisdom; and to another the worde of knowledge, by the same Spirit:
> And to another is giuen faith, by the same Spirit: and to another, the giftes of healing, by the same Spirit. (I Cor.12.4–9)

Spenser is only following out Paul's adjudication of the gifts of the spirit in describing the gifts exchanged between Arthur and Redcross:

> Prince *Arthur* gaue a boxe of Diamond sure,
>   Embowd with gold and gorgeous ornament,
>   Wherein were closd few drops of liquor pure,
>   Of wondrous worth, and vertue excellent,
>   That any wound could heale incontinent:
>   Which to requite, the *Redcrosse* knight him gaue
>   A booke, wherein his Saueours testament
>   Was writ with golden letters rich and braue;
> A worke of wondrous grace, and able soules to saue.
>
> (I.ix.19)

If any discrimination must be made between these gifts, it should be between the healing power of the sovereign and the reliance of the saint on the word. Other discriminations such as nature and grace, works and faith, or Nohrnberg's suggestion about the golden pot of manna (Heb. 9.4; Exo-

dus 16.32) and God's Word overlook the essential unity of the interchange —
the *Una*-fication of Arthur's rescue of Redcross:[5]

> Als *Vna* earnd her traveill to renew.
>   Then those two knights, fast friendship for to bynd,
>   And loue establish each to other trew,
>   Gaue goodly gifts the signes of gratefull mynd,
> And eke as pledges firme, right hands together ioynd.
>
> (I.ix.18)

The gifts exchanged are really the same thing expressed in different modes,
as the passage from Corinthians suggests. The gifts are an image of unity
in diversity, the manifestation of the spirit at work in this world.

III

Immediately after Arthur and Redcross part, up rides Sir Trevisan with
his story of a companion lost to Despair. Once more we hear of two men
who have been given "gifts," the one a hempen rope, the other a knife
with which he kills himself. The victim, suffering from the unrequited
love of a lady, proud and unrelenting,

> Sir *Terwin* hight, that well himselfe aduaunst
>   In all affaires, and was both bold and free,
>   But not so happie as mote happie bee:
>   He lou'd, as was his lot, a Ladie gent,
>   That him againe lou'd in the least degree:
>   For she was proud, and of too high intent,
> And ioyd to see her louer languish and lament.
>
> From whom returning sad and comfortlesse,
>   As on the way together we did fare,
>   We met that villen.   (I.ix.27–28)

Sir Terwin, the "thrice-winner," who is named for the first and only time
in this third line of the twenty-seventh stanza (3 × 3 × 3) of this fifty-
four stanza canto, is centrally placed between love's vision and despair.[6] His
story is told by Sir Trevisan (the thrice viewer?) who has witnessed his
friend's unavailing love and his subsequent death. In relating the story to
Redcross and Una, Trevisan witnesses it again in the telling of the story
and then sees it enacted once more in Redcross's doughty replacement of
Terwin in the third episode of the canto.

His name notwithstanding, Terwin (a thrice loser) is the despised lover. He does not speak at all in Spenser's poem but that unspeaking lover is that very lover whom we have heard speak for himself in so many sonnet sequences, poems that do not end but merely stop with the poet-lover in a state of despair. The logic is all too clear unless we pay too much attention to the illogical rhetoric of the poet-lover. No matter how brilliantly the poet-lover pleads his case, it is always the same old game: I love you so much that I will die unless you love me and by that statement I mean that you are killing me. The rhetoric of sonnet sequences is brilliant poetic blackmail to which no lady should succumb. Astrophil's blackguardly assailment of Stella is a case in point,[7] but I call to witness the more than fifty sequences in English that leave the poet-lover in the inconclusive limbo of despair. The problem for all these sequences is the use of human love and the self-destructive effects of love as a passion on the poet-lover himself. We see the poet-lover becoming more and more resourceful, and less successful, in controlling the idol he has created. The end of this unrewarding encounter with love in sonnet sequences is almost always despair for the poet-lover. Only Spenser, Barnabe Barnes, and William Habington offer different solutions to the problem of poetic closure of the sonnet sequence. Spenser and Habington chose marriage as the solution to their sonnet problems. Barnes chose the more problematical solution of enchanting the lady and raping her, after she is brought in to him, naked, on the back of a goat.[8]

I am not suggesting for a moment that either Sir Trevisan or Sir Terwin were sonneteers, but I see in their story a mediation between the love vision of Arthur and the plight of Redcross, almost duplicating Terwin's submission to the arguments of Despair. I am led to this conclusion by the first simile Spenser uses to describe Sir Trevisan's approach to Redcross and Una:

> Als flew his steed, as he his bands had brast,
> And with his winged heeles did tread the wind,
> As he had beene a fole of *Pegasus* his kind.   (21)

Pegasus, the winged horse, associated with poetic creation for having struck out the well Hippocrene for the Muses, was sprung from the blood of his mother Medusa, along with his brother Chrysaor.[9] The Pegasus reference is particularly relevant in this context because Medusa, a female monster that turned men to stone when they looked at her, had been used from the time of Dante and Petrarch to represent the poet-lover's view of a female who killed those who looked on her.[10] Once beautiful, she was turned into a monster by Minerva because she had slept with Neptune in one of Minerva's temples. Because of this sexual submission she became a monster, and produced from this union both the winged horse Pegasus and the warrior Chrysaor, born only after Perseus had decapitated Medusa by the subterfuge of viewing her through a mirror shield given him by Minerva. This extraordinary myth works into the fabric of sonnet literature through the following distortion of the myth: female Gorgon becomes monster and enemy to men only after sexual submission; her monstrosity and hostility is subdued only by an equally hostile act performed through a mirror by another man (a male version of the Lady of Shallot). The avenging male becomes then the midwife of Pegasus and Chrysaor, the winged horse of poetry and the armed warrior. The poet-lover, armed for battle against his lady, uses the power of poetry to win her over through mirroring his love in his poetry. This grisly reinterpretation of the Medusa myth is the psychological basis of much of our sonnet literature in which the pedestal on which the sonnet lady is put is only an extension of the male attempt to dominate or to vilify as in the case of Shakespeare's "dark lady" so compliant. The lady cannot win in a sonnet sequence. We hear only the male voice enchanting us to believe in his need, at our peril as readers. The nexus between Arthur's love vision and Redcross's despair is the lot of the poet-lover whose brilliant desires do him in.

Against this interpretation of sonnet literature, I hope, Trevisan's story of Terwin's defeat will make some sense. Trevisan can only tell of the despair of his friend in love but never tells us of what the Elizabethan reader must have thought of this failure of love. They could only have thought that Terwin's death was self-induced, that he had succumbed to despair and that his lady's disdain was only the mediating cause in his own self-defeat.[11]

We never hear what arguments Despair uses to make Sir Terwin succumb, but we are meant, I think, to assume that they are the same used against Redcross, which we do hear. Those arguments, which Kathrine Koller relates to a diabolical misrepresentation of the conventional comfort of the *ars moriendi,* speak unremittingly of a failure of love, of a logic that misconstrues the largesse of God's justice and mercy, of an egotism that borders on the Faustian in its presumption against the love of God.[12] The theological import of Despair's argument afflicts the lovesick as well as saints-to-be; only Arthur's steadfast vision allows him to escape.

Despair's argument is merely the obverse of the pride that prompts Redcross's boast on his first encounter:

> Thou damned wight,
> The author of this fact, we here behold,

> *What iustice* can but iudge against thee right,
> With thine owne bloud to price his bloud, here shed in sight.
>
> (I.ix.37, emphasis added)

Redcross's bravado is based on the scene he sees before him; his reaction is knightly and just, but the relationship of his sense of justice and the price of the blood he wants to exact is merely human vengeance, a point that Despair seizes on immediately:

> What *franticke fit* (quoth he) hath thus distraught
> Thee, *foolish* man, so rash a doome to giue?
> *What iustice* euer other iudgement taught
> But he should die, who merites not to liue?
>
> (I.ix.38, emphasis added)

Despair's attack is a distorted echo of Redcross's boast. The repeated *What iustice* merely picks up Redcross's threat of righteous indignation and turns it against him by universalizing it, and at this point Redcross is lost even before the battle begins. Hamlet, an even more famous would-be avenger, uses Despair's argument as a foil against Polonius: "Use every man after his desert, and who shall scape whipping?" (act 2, scene 2). Unlike Redcross, Hamlet even in his putative madness, or perhaps because of it, taunts Polonius's worldly courtesy: "My lord, I will use them according to their desert." His taunt, however we interpret his intention, disallows man's desert as a significant part in that burden of sin that God has already lifted from him. We cannot know how Polonius responded to the truth of Hamlet's taunt, but Spenser goes to great pains to show how Redcross is engulfed by his desire to avenge a knight he never knew in a disavowal of God's mercy through an argument that presents only half the case. Despair's victims come unsought, and sometimes not even knowing their parlous state.

We need not go through the entire argument; its rhetorical brilliance and its logical flaws have been amply witnessed by many commentators, as has Una's rebuttal of his argument in stanza 53:

> Come, come away, *fraile, feeble, fleshly* wight,
> Ne let vaine words bewitch thy manly hart,
> Ne diuelish thoughts dismay thy constant spright.
> In heauenly mercies hast thou not a part?
> Why shouldst thou then despeire, that chosen art?

Where iustice growes, there grows eke greater grace,
The which doth quench the brond of hellish smart,
And that accurst hand-writing doth deface,
Arise, Sir knight arise, and leaue this cursed place.

(I.ix.53, emphasis added)

Una not only refutes Despair's argument theologically; Spenser makes her
begin by picking up the basic alliteration of Despair's opening speech. Here
the full impact of Redcross's "*f*rantic *f*it, his *f*oolishness" of stanza 38 is
reappraised as the *f*railty, the *f*eebleness, and the merely *f*leshly knowledge
of the earthly knight. The simple poetic device, effective in and of itself,
becomes a structurally important detail of the whole canto. The alliterative
words used by Despair and Una characterize Redcross as much as his actions and carry the argument from initial assault to resolution, from wil-
ful extravagance to sustained purposiveness. Within the encompassing alliteration Redcross is saved, not by a poetic device but by the intellectual
definitions that the poetic device imposes on the whole argument.

IV

The enclosure of Despair's argument and its rebuttal within alliterative
repetitions is only one of the means Spenser uses to enforce his intellectual
argument. He also uses rhyme words as structural signposts, linking the
various parts of the canto together.

Stanza 35 describes Despair in appropriately negative terms, "low sitting on the ground," "griesie lockes . . . Disordred . . . hid his face," "hol-
low eyne," "raw-bone cheekes . . . shronke into his iawes, as he did neuer
dine." Anorexia is the least of his problems, for each of the details is a negative inversion of its life-giving function, and this inversion continues in the
description of his garments and his latest victim:

His garment nought but many ragged clouts,
  With thornes together pind and patched was,
  The which his naked sides he wrapt abouts;
  And him beside there lay vpon the gras
  A drearie corse, whose life away did pas,
  All wallowd in his owne yet luke-warme blood,
  That from his wound yet welled fresh alas;
  In which a rustie knife fast fixed stood,
And made an open passage for the gushing flood.

(I.ix.36)

The unnamed corpse becomes almost a sur-garment, a reluctant extension
of Despair himself, but even in death this corpse has more liveliness than
Despair. It lies "vpon the gras," its "yet luke-warme blood . . . yet welled
fresh" in a "gushing flood." Even death shows more life than Despair. That
brilliant stroke of putting this corpse "vpon the gras," although we know
that we are in a "darkesome caue," recalls two other occurrences of the word
earlier in the canto when Arthur recounts his vision of the fairy queen:

> For-wearied with my sports, I did alight
> From loftie steed, and downe to sleepe me layd;
> The *verdant gras* my couch did goodly dight.
>   . . . .
> When I awoke, and found her place deuoyd,
> And nought but *pressed gras* where she had lyen.
>
> (I.ix.13,15, emphasis added)

Both Arthur and Terwin have been subjected to visions on the grass, one
of hope, one of despair, one of life, one of death.

   The association of grass with life and growth is one of those unsurpris-
ing graces of Spenser's poetry—quiet, solid, and sustaining. He plays the
trick three more times in this canto with the rhyme word *greene* (italicized
below). Arthur relates that at birth he was brought to

> Old *Timon*, who in youthly yeares hath beene
> In warlike feates th'expertest man aliue,
> And is the wisest now on earth I weene;
> His dwelling is low in a valley *greene*,
> Vnder the foot of *Rauran* mossy hore,
> From whence the riuer *Dee* as siluer cleene
> His tombling billowes rolls with gentle rore:
> There all my dayes he traind me vp in vertuous lore.
>
> (I.ix.4)

The lush exuberance of the green that sustained Arthur in his early years
and those "tombling billowes" of the Dee are meant to be a contrast to
the "gushing flood" of Terwin dying on the grass in stanza 36 and to the
description of Despair's cave:

> And all about old stockes and stubs of trees,
> Whereon nor fruit, nor leafe was euer seene,
> Did hang vpon the ragged rocky knees;

> On which had many wretches hanged beene,
> Whose carcases were scattered *on the greene,*
> And throwne about the cliffs.   (I.ix.34)

Even the blighted landscape of Despair's habitation retains a little life as background, as rebuttal of its desolation.

The final *greene* rhyme occurs in the climactic stanza 51 in which Redcross is about to succumb to Despair:

> But when as none of them he saw him take,
> He to him raught a dagger sharpe and keene,
> And gaue it him in hand: his hand did quake,
> And tremble like a leafe of Aspin *greene,*
> And troubled bloud through his pale face was seene
> To come, and goe with tydings from the hart,
> As it a running messenger had beene.
> At last resolu'd to worke his final smart,
> He lifted vp his hand, that back againe did start.   (I.ix.51)

Once more there is the contrast between the greenness and the "troubled bloud" unwilling to make itself into the "gushing flood" that had been Terwin a few stanzas before. As Alpers has pointed out, it is as if the hand felt a "natural revulsion from self-murder."[13] I think that Spenser's insight into the natural condition led him to "highlight" the story of each of the three main male figures in this canto with that *greene* rhyme: Arthur, raised in his "valley greene," Despair's victims, lying "on the greene," and Redcross, in his life or death struggle, trembling "like a leafe of Aspin greene."[14]

V

It is at this point that Una breaks through Redcross's reverie to rescue him with her alliterative rebuttal of Despair, but even here there is a deliberate reference to Trevisan's initial story about Despair, through the rhyme words of two pairs of stanzas:

> *Which when* he knew, and felt our feeble harts
> Embost with bale, and bitter byting griefe,
> Which loue had launched with his deadly darts,
> With wounding words and termes of foule repriefe,
> He pluckt from vs all hope of due reliefe,

That earst vs held in loue of lingring *life;*
  Then hopelesse hartlesse, gan the cunning thiefe
  Perswade vs die, to stint all further *strife:*
To me he lent this rope, to him a rustie *knife.*

With which sad instrument of hastie death,
  That wofull louer, loathing lenger light,
  A wide way made to let forth liuing breath.
  But I more fearefull, or more luckie *wight,*
  Dismayd with that deformed dismall sight,
  Fled-fast away, halfe dead with dying feare:
  Ne yet assur'd of life by you, Sir *knight,*
  Whose like infirmitie like chaunce may beare:
But God you neuer let his charmed speeches heare.

. . . .

Which when as *Vna* saw, through euery vaine
  The crudled cold ran to her well of *life,*
  As in a swowne: but soone reliu'd againe,
  Out of his hand she snatcht the cursed *knife,*
  And threw it to the ground, enraged rife,
  And to him said, Fie, fie, faint harted *knight,*
  What meanest thou by this reprochfull *strife?*
  Is this the battell, which thou vauntst to fight
With that fire-mouthed Dragon, horrible and bright?

Come, come away, fraile, feeble, fleshly *wight,*
  Ne let vaine words bewitch thy manly hart,
  Ne diuelish thoughts dismay thy constant spright.
  In heauenly mercies hast thou not a part?
  Why shouldst thou then despeire, that chosen art?
  Where iustice growes, there grows eke greater grace,
  The which doth quench the brond of hellish smart,
  And that accurst hand-writing doth deface,
Arise, Sir knight arise, and leaue this cursed place.
                    (I.ix.29–30, 52–53, emphasis added)

The rhyme words *life, strife, knife, wight,* and *knight* appear in both pairs of stanzas, and nowhere else in the entire poem in this combination. In an uninflected language like English, rhyme words are always important. In a vast poem like *The Faerie Queene,* in which Spenser allowed himself only three rhymes to a stanza, the coincidence of five rhymes repeated in two pairs of stanzas in one canto is astonishing and suggests that we have paid less than sufficient attention to Spenser's talents and intention as a rhyming poet. His decision to write a rhymed stanzaic poem must have been as conscious and serious as Milton's decision not to write such a poem, but Spenser's achievement has always fallen under the shadow of Milton's magisterial establishment of epic diction in English.

I would like to suggest that the collocation of rhymes in these two pairs of stanzas is meant to attune us to a moral and intellectual judgment that would not be possible without these particular rhymes in this particular sequence. There seems to be a purposeful progression in the placement of the rhymes, descending in the first pair and ascending in the second. That is, Trevisan's story of despairing death seems to be retold in Una's rebuttal of Despair simply in the placement of the rhyme words. In stanza 29 we proceed from Trevisan's description of Terwin's plight, to his assessment of his part in the story, to Redcross's possible involvement. We move from Trevisan's and Terwin's abandonment of hope, "That earst [them] held in loue of *lingring life*," to the abandonment of all will power, as Despair began to persuade them *"to stint all further strife,"* to his gifts of the instruments of death, a "rope, [and] a *rustie knife*" (I.ix.29, emphasis added).

In stanza 30 Terwin separates himself from Trevisan, "loathing longer light," leaving Trevisan in doubt about his own state; he cannot decide whether he is the "more fearefull, or more lucky *wight*." Transferring the burden to Redcross, Trevisan continues his story: "I,"

> Dismayd with that deformed dismall sight,
> Fled-fast away, halfe dead with dying feare;
> Ne yet assur'd of life by you, Sir *knight*.
>
> (I.ix.30, emphasis added)

The *wight-knight* rhymes in both pairs of stanzas play off against each other and offer two different interpretations of Redcross. Trevisan defers to Redcross's superiority; he is "Sir knight" as opposed to Trevisan: the "more fearefull, or more lucky wight." But the deference to Redcross carries with it a warning in the last two lines of the stanza to that very same "Sir knight":

> Whose like infirmitie like chaunce may beare:
> But God you neuer let his charmed speeches heare.
>
> (I.ix.30)

But that is precisely what happens in the next few stanzas because of Redcross's derring-do. Ignoring the advice of Trevisan, Redcross takes on the role of the unlucky knight, Sir Terwin, and goes to his assignation with Despair, relying solely on his title to get him through.

Trevisan's prediction would have proven true if Una had not been with Redcross, but Spenser is not trying to prove Redcross derelict in his doughtiness. Una has been assigned to him by that very fairy queen who has visited Arthur. Forcefully allegory raises its head to keep us from reading this passage as just another story of a knight and a lady. Redcross is totally feckless in encountering Despair, and simply as a knight he succumbs to Despair. But he is Redcross, *and* accompanied by Una, *and* to be named a saint in the next canto, and therefore the simple story of his defeat by Despair cannot be the simple story it might appear.

Una, who emerges after stanzas of fictional neglect in stanza 52, reverses the *wight-knight* rhymes and in doing so reverses Trevisan's exaggerated opinion of Redcross. For Una Redcross is first of all a "faint harted *knight*" but more importantly she specifies the cause: "fraile, feeble, fleshly *wight*." Una rightly sees that all "Sir knights" are nothing more than the "*fraile, feeble, fleshly wight*" she sees before her. Her instinctive reaction, from her "well of life," is to snatch the "cursed knife" from his hand, to reproach him (once more those alliterative *f*'s) for "this reprochful strife," and to bid him, "Come, come away, fraile, feeble, fleshly wight." We move from her instinctive reverence for life, to the disposal of the instrument of death, to chastisement for the agent because of the ignoble nature of the act, and finally to the cause of the action: the frailty, the feebleness, the fleshliness of this or any other wight.

The placement of these rhymes in both pairs of stanzas carries out the psychology of the argument as much as the stanzas themselves. The rhymes seem to exchange their valency as words. The effectiveness of this interplay depends partly on the context in which words take on ironic or subsidiary meanings, which is the ordinary use of words in poetic discourse, but in these repeated rhymes Spenser is badgering language in his gentle but persistent way to make us see that Redcross has taken on the roles of both Terwin and Trevisan. Like Terwin he has been tempted, and like Trevisan he has escaped, not through fear but in being the "more luckie wight" in having Una for a companion. The technique is not that of Henry James with Una as Millie Theale and Kate Croy as Duessa. Spenser does not create characters but fictions. His rhyme words help him to relocate moral and intellectual responsibilities not in terms of character as would happen in a novel but in terms of large moral and intellectual issues that inform the action of his poem. Redcross and Una and Despair are both characters and something else, and that otherness derives from what we should call their allegorical function, if we can in fact separate that function from their depiction in the text. Redcross is but a bumpkin knight in the letter to Ralegh, an errant knight in the text of Book I—and also a saint to be proclaimed. There is no possibility for him to fail in the fiction. He will be Saint George. Una is both a lady needing help, a figure and what her name implies: unity, the church, truth, troth—Una. Despair is a philosophical abstraction. When brought together in a poetic fiction, they assume a similarity that the fiction demands but will finally not allow because of those other burdens of meaning.

So with the closure of the canto; one line is devoted to Redcross: "So vp he rose, and thence amounted streight" (I.ix.54). There is no response to Una's recriminations, no admission of despair, no indication that he has been through an experience. The rest of the final stanza is given over to a redundancy, the despair of Despair, in which Spenser shows the never to be resolved activity of his poem beyond its fictional matrix. In novels passions are begun and concluded because they are *en*cluded within the lives of the characters in the fiction; in allegorical poems the conquest of a vice or a passion can only be a momentary victory because of the unending continuance in this world of the vice or passion, and thus the allegorical narrative can never end with closure. It is here that Spenser's use of moral abstractions is most triumphant and most problematic for modern readers. The triumph of Redcross through Una is apparent, not through a triumphal procession away from Despair, but through a direct focusing on the defeat of Despair, presented in two separate clauses. The first describes his action, and the second the result of the action:

> So vp he rose, and thence amounted streight,
>> Which when the carle beheld, and saw his guest
>> Would safe depart, for all his subtill sleight,
>> He chose an halter from among the rest,
>> And with it hung himselfe, vnbid vnblest.
>> But death he could not worke himselfe thereby;
>> For thousand times he so himselfe had drest,
>> Yet nathelesse it could not doe him die,
> Till he should die his last, that is eternally.   (I.ix.54)

In the first clause one can hardly restrain the impulse to recall the despair of Judas and his self-imposed fate (Matt. 27.3; Acts 1.18). I think the allusion is operative but not definitive—that is, Despair includes Judas but is not bound by him. Despair is the universal, of which Judas is but one notable particular, and for that very reason, as Spenser is at pains to show in that second clause, he cannot kill himself. Despair because of his very nature has power neither over his "guest" nor over himself, even in Spenser's fictive world. Here mimesis will not work. Even though "drest" like his human victims, Despair is of a different order of reality from Redcross. The narrative technique is part and parcel of the allegorical mode in which dark conceits weave a darker and denser tapestry than mimesis will allow. Despair presents the same enigma as the Old Man in Chaucer's *Pardoner's Tale,* that old man who wants to die but cannot, and cannot because he is not an old man but the Old Man in all of us, as Paul tells us in Romans 6 and Ephesians 4. Fiction cannot destroy him because in a very real sense fiction (at least in the Middle Ages and Renaissance) derives its being from the life of this universal as it inheres in our fallen natures. Spenser is telling us that only Love can kill Despair. We have just seen that happen tropologically in Una's saving Redcross, and we are promised an ultimate death for him in that awesomely simple last line, in which the whole burden of Christian eschatology hangs on that one word, "eternally." The ultimate defeat of the enemy is assured, but Spenser's stanza equally assures us of the ever present lurking menace of Despair.

VI

By the end of this canto our apprehension of what human love means has been gradually widened to accommodate theological overtones of the ultimate source of that love, mainly through the confrontation with Despair. Our own most "natural" responses, like Una's, rush in to fill the vacuum created by Despair's total eradication of God's love for mankind. Arthur's love vision and Terwin's despairing love must be viewed in a different context after Redcross's and our own experience of Despair's argument. Spenser has moved us beyond the simple romance response of rooting for Arthur and of heaving a little sigh for Terwin. Spenser will not let us dispose of Love so simply because for him the problem was "as dark as day." Love in a Christian context such as Spenser's has so many ramifications, amplifications, contradictions that definitions of love are as dark as day, and how could it be otherwise when the most beloved of the apostles assures us (1 John 4.8) that God is love? Thus we are left with an ultimate simplicity that must be continually adjudicated with our daily uses of the word, the emotion, the passion, the reality of our participation with that reality that is love. Thus when Augustine magisterially gave the two names of *caritas* and *cupiditas* to love in this welter of meanings, he was not constricting our understanding but pointing us to the infinite variety of experience that could be subsumed within his two terms. Much vituperation has been expended on the uses of Augustine's terms in literary criticism, and like love itself these terms have been misused, but they are firmly based on an antecedent formula: Thou shalt love the Lord God with thy whole heart, and thy whole soul, and thy neighbor as thyself. The plighting of God and neighbor and what these terms may mean plighted, is the work of a lifetime, and in the Christian context a paradox as "dark as day." Spenser's preoccupation with this paradox is amply witnessed by the *Amoretti and Epithalamion,* and the *Fowre Hymnes,* but in this particular canto we can see Spenser using another strand of scriptural love imagery in one more repeated rhyme word, *ground* (italicized below). It is used four times in this canto. The first is Una's gracious inquiry about Arthur's first declaration of his "fresh bleeding wound":

> Ah curteous knight (quoth she) what secret wound
> Could euer find, to grieue the gentlest hart on *ground*?

The second is Arthur's disconsolate assessment of the love quest on which he is embarked:

> Nothing is sure, that growes on earthly *ground.*

And at the end of Arthur's story even Una can take on some of Arthur's unease about his predicament:

> True Loues are often sown, but seldom grow on *ground.*
>
> (I.ix.7,16)

Una's comments are as hilariously ominous as auntie's first meeting with the prospective fiancé of a favored niece. (I introduce this anachronism only to qualify the solemnity of the statements as if Una were Ingrid Bergman playing Joan of Arc.) The interchange is serious talk, but we should not miss the submerged courtly humor of our "sage and serious" Spenser. Even church wardens have been known to indulge in gentle wit without forgetting the seriousness of their calling. The resonance of that word *ground* is like ballast holding back the soaring aspirations of Arthur and the commitment of Una to his enterprise, and it is reinforced when we first meet Despair,

> That cursed man, low sitting on the *ground.*
>
> (I.ix.35)

In the first three occurrences of this rhyme the word *ground* is vague, almost a euphemism for earth, the transitory, all that is associated with the flesh, beyond which we must rise if anything truly human can transpire. It is as if the word *ground* were a charade they were playing with human existence. But with the fourth repetition of the rhyme word, "That cursed man, low sitting on the *ground*," we must recognize a sinister possibility in that ground that supports the *greene* and the *grasse.* It is also a dark ground that can support Despair, not that Spenser is espousing a Manichaean dualism. For Spenser God's creation is constantly good except when misapprehended or misused by fallen men. Despair does not grow out of the ground, like love; he merely covers it, occupies it, misappropriates it. Una's and Arthur's uncertainties about the ground and the love that grows from it are merely darkened by Despair's sharing that rhyme word with them. The rhyme assures us that Arthur's love is being played at higher stakes than he knows.

Paul in the eleventh chapter of Hebrews provides a text that may elucidate Spenser's linking of love and despair: "Now faith is the *grounde* of things which are hoped for, and the evidence of things which are not sene" (Heb. 11.1). Paul continues with a long litany of the faithful, begin ning with the offering of Abel, on through the great acts of faith in the Old Testament:

All these dyed in faith, and receiued not the promises but sawe them a farre of, and beleued them, and receued them thankefully, and confessed that they were strangers and pilgremes on the earth.

For they that say suche things, declare plainely that they seke a countrey.

And if they had bene mindeful of that countrey, from whence they came out, they had leasure to haue returned.

But now they desire a better, that is an heauenlie; wherefore God is not ashamed of them to be called their God: for he hathe prepared for them a citie. (Heb. 13–16)

Both Arthur and Redcross are seeking cities. Arthur was eventually to make his way to Cleopolis where he would have found his vision enthroned. Redcross, who has set out from Cleopolis on his quest with Una, finds in the very next canto an even greater city, his vision of the New Jerusalem (I.x. 57–61), which gives him a new city, a new name, and a vision to sustain him through the task ahead, when he is returned to ground.

O holy Sire (quoth he) how shall I quight
The many fauours I with thee haue found,
That hast my name and nation red aright,

And taught the way that does to heauen bound?
This said, adowne he looked to the *ground*,
To haue returnd, but dazed were his eyne,
Through passing brightnesse, which did quite confound
His feeble sence, and too exceeding shyne.
So darke are earthly things compard to things diuine.

(I.x.67, emphasis added)

Errant human action always has a destination, if it can but find its way. Despair intervenes when human love is not returned (Terwin) or when divine love is not apprehended (Redcross). Only Una and Arthur escape the menace of despair, because their love is faith both in the loved one and in love itself. The three stories in this canto are unified because all three deal with different aspects of human love and their relationship to faith, the "*ground* of things which are hoped for, and the evidence of things which are not seen."

Princeton University

NOTES

1. See Paul J. Alpers, Jr., *The Poetry of "The Faerie Queene"* (Princeton, N.J.: Princeton University Press, 1967), pp. 349–61, who also treats the relation of Arthur's vision to Despair.

2. Paul J. Alpers, Jr., "Narrative and Rhetoric in *The Faerie Queene,*" in *Elizabethan Poetry: Modern Essays in Criticism,* ed. Paul J. Alpers, Jr. (Oxford: Oxford University Press, 1967), pp. 380–400.

3. See Peter V. Marinelli, "The Dynastic Romance: A Study in the Evolution of the Romantic Epics of Boiardo, Ariosto, and Spenser" (Ph.D. diss., Princeton University, 1964); and Andrew Fichter, *Poets Historical: Dynastic Epic in the Renaissance* (New Haven, Conn.: Yale University Press, 1982).

4. See Thomas Roche, *The Kindly Flame: A Study of the Third and Fourth Books of Spenser's "Faerie Queene"* (Princeton, N.J.: Princeton University Press, 1964), pp. 47–50.

5. James Nohrnberg, *The Analogy of "The Faerie Queene"* (Princeton, N.J.: Princeton University Press, 1976), p. 277, suggests this to be a reference to Eph. 1.20; however, a more likely reference would be Rev. 5.1, 7. All Bible references are to the Geneva version, 1560.

6. The etymology of these two names has never been satisfactorily explained, but see C. A. Hebert's query in *Spenser Newsletter* 5, no. 3 (1974), 18; and Russell J. Meyer's reply, ibid., 6, no. 1 (1975), 18–19.

7. See Thomas P. Roche, Jr., "Sidney's *Astrophil and Stella:* A Radical Reading" in *Spenser Studies* 3 (1982), 139–91, and *Petrarch and the English Sonnet Sequences,* forthcoming.

8. Spenser, *Amoretti and Epithalamion* (1595); Barnabe Barnes, *Parthenophil and Parthe-*

nophe (1593); William Habington, *Castara* (1634), and the not so triumphantly or domestically happy ending of Robert Tofte, *Laura* (1597).

9. Ovid, *Met.* 4.775–803.

10. Kenelm Foster, O.P., "Beatrice or Medusa," in *Italian Studies Presented to E. R. Vincent,* ed. C. P. Brand et al. (Cambridge: Heffer's, 1962), pp. 41–56; and John Freccero, "Medusa: The Letter and the Spirit," *Journal of Italian Studies* 2 (1972), 1–18.

11. That Spenser emphasizes the as-it-were unbridling of this as-it-were descendant of Pegasus suggests the hempen rope around Trevisan's neck, and his warrior brother Chrysaor, whose name Spenser uses as the name of Arthegall's sword (V.1.8), may even suggest the knife given to Sir Terwin. Whether Spenser intended this complicated allusion to be part of his poetic innuendo I cannot be sure, but Terwin's problem is despised love, which brings him to despair and that problem he shares with the legions of sonneteers in the sixteenth century.

12. Kathrine Koller, "Art, Rhetoric, and Holy Dying in *The Faerie Queene* with Special Reference to the Despair Canto," *SP* 61 (1964), 128–39; and Vernon Torczon, "Spenser's Orgoglio and Despaire," *TSLL* 3 (1961), 123–28.

13. Alpers, *Poetry of "The Faerie Queene,"* p. 357.

14. The significance of rhyme words as guides to structure within cantos has been argued by Maren-Sofie Røstvig, "Canto Structure in Tasso and Spenser," *Spenser Studies* 1 (1980), 177–200. I cannot find such a neat geometrical precision in the rhymes of this canto, but the fact that the three *greene* rhymes occur in stanzas devoted to Arthur, Despair, and Redcross seems to recapitulate the tripartite structure of the canto. I suggest that this rhyme, centrally located in each stanza, is significant symbolically. The word *greene* appears 49 times in the poem, in 25 instances as a rhyme word: 5 in Book I, 3 each in Books II–IV, and 4 each in VI and VII. The fact that three of the five *greene* rhymes in Book I occur in this canto supports my contention that they are placed purposely.

HUGH MacLACHLAN

The Death of Guyon and
the *Elizabethan Book of Homilies*

The last temptation is the greatest treason:
To do the right deed for the wrong reason.
— T.S. Eliot, *Murder in the Cathedral*

AFTER THREE days and nights continually on his feet in Mammon's Cave,
Guyon's "vitall powres," Spenser tells us, "gan wexe both weake and wan, /
For want of food, and sleepe" (II.vii.65).[1] The knight's predicament can
be appreciated, since he has resolutely refused the god's offer of both "fruit
of gold" to eat and a "siluer stoole" on which "To rest [his] wearie person." And it is no surprise that when he reaches the surface,

> all so soone as his enfeebled spright
> Gan sucke this vitall aire into his brest,
> As ouercome with too exceeding might,
> The life did flit away out of her nest,
> And all his senses were with deadly fit opprest.
>
> (II.vii.66)

In other words, Guyon faints.

Guyon's collapse, and its relationship both to his experience in the Cave
of Mammon and to his role in the entire book, have provoked much schol-
arly debate.[2] Essentially, however, the interpretive problems are these: is
Guyon's faint the result of merely physical exhaustion, or should we read
it symbolically as reflecting a moral or spiritual state; is it a state implying
Spenser's condemnation of the knight's decision to enter the cave in the first
place or, if not that, at least of his actions while in it; or is it rather the
poet's affirmation of a successful trial which has taxed the knight's strength,
physical or otherwise, to the limit but which he has triumphantly passed?
Clearly, any interpretation of the faint leads to a hypothesis concerning the
nature and function of Guyon in the entire book, his status as protagonist

or hero, his assumptions concerning the universe in which he operates, and his role either as a perfected exemplar or as a mind undergoing some process of education, moral or spiritual. And even more radically, the interpretation must assume some understanding of Spenserian allegorical technique. Guyon, we are told, collapses "For want of food, and sleepe," and those readers who believe that Guyon's decision to enter the cave and his trials there are exemplary, perhaps even Christlike, usually insist on a literal acceptance of Spenser's explanation here—the knight is physically exhausted. Other readers, however, who assume that the literal level of the allegory should point to another level—in this case moral or theological—insist that we are not dealing with a physical situation at all. This second group usually finds in Guyon's faint a revelation of some weakness in his conscious or unconscious being.

Perhaps we can solve the problem of the nature of Guyon's "faint" and in so doing clear the way for a more acceptable reading of the knight's role in the poem—not, as other readers have done, by looking back to his experience in the cave itself but forward to what is said about him in canto viii while he lies there unconscious.

No critic has attempted to explain a very curious fact: Guyon is not merely said to be unconscious throughout most of canto viii; he is repeatedly described, by characters who in fact know better, as though he were *dead*.[3] Spenser tells us that, as the Palmer approaches the knight, "*Guyon* lay in traunce" (II.viii.3) and that he discovers him "slumbring fast / In senselesse dreame" (II.viii.4). Although horrified at what he thinks are the mortal remains of the knight, the Palmer is assured by the angel that, "Whiles deadly fit thy pupill doth dismay . . . dread of death and dolour doe away" (II.viii.7), for Guyon will soon revive. Apparently not quite convinced, the moment the messenger departs the Palmer feels for the knight's pulse, "Where finding life not yet dislodged quight, / He much reioyst" (II.viii. 9). Thus there can be no question of the Palmer's knowledge of Guyon's living state. What then are we to make of his remark to Pyrochles and Cymochles when they too arrive on the scene and assume that Guyon is dead? Pyrochles instructs the Palmer to "Abandone soone . . . the caitiue spoile / Of that same outcast carkasse" (II.viii.12), and declares, "Loe where he now inglorious doth lye, / To proue he liued ill, that did thus foully dye." But the Palmer does not correct the mistake:

> Certes, Sir knight, ye bene too much to blame,
> Thus for to blot the honour of the dead,
> And with foule cowardize his carkasse shame,
> Whose liuing hands immortalizd his name.

> Vile is the vengeance on the ashes cold,
> And enuie base, to barke at sleeping fame.   (II.viii.13)

Granted that he may be hinting in the last line that Guyon is merely unconscious, the Palmer's condemnation of Pyrochles is, nevertheless, based
on the premise that the knight is dead. Moreover, he never again suggests
to the brothers that Guyon is not dead. Cymochles, in his observations
on Guyon, either misses the Palmer's hint or else assumes that Guyon is
suffering from an eternal sleep:

> The worth of all men by their end esteeme,
> And then due praise, or due reproch them yield;
> Bad therefore I him deeme, that thus lies dead on field.
>
> > (II.viii.14)

Pyrochles certainly misses the Palmer's drift, for his own frustration is only
that he himself was not given the opportunity to kill Guyon, with whom
he had an old score to settle:

> Good or bad . . .
> > What doe I recke, sith that he dyde entire?
> > Or what doth his bad death now satisfy
> > The greedy hunger of reuenging ire,
> > Sith wrathfull hand wrought not her owne desire?
> > Yet since no way is left to wreake my spight,
> > I will him reaue of armes, the victors hire,
> > And of that shield, more worthy of good knight;
> > For why should a dead dog be deckt in armour bright?
> >
> > > (II.viii.15)

The Palmer again replies as though acknowledging that Guyon is dead:

> To spoile the dead of weed
> Is sacrilege, and doth all sinnes exceed;
> But leaue these relicks of his liuing might,
> To decke his herce, and trap his tomb-blacke steed.
>
> > (II.viii.16)

When Arthur arrives, Spenser himself informs us that the Prince sees at
the Palmer's feet "an armed corse . . . In whose dead face he red great mag-

nanimity" (II.viii.23). But when Arthur asks for an explanation of Guyon's death, the Palmer quite openly reveals what he has known all along, assuring the Prince that the knight is not dead, "but cloudes of deadly night / A while his heauie eylids couer'd haue, / And all his senses drowned in deepe senselesse waue" (II.viii.24).

Arthur's disgust at the brothers' intention "to doen outrage to a sleeping ghost" (II.viii.26) by despoiling Guyon, indicates that he apparently now too understands the knight's condition. Yet, like the Palmer, he seems to imply in his argument with the brothers that Guyon is still alive but at the same time bases his request for their mercy on the premise that he is dead:

> Ye warlike payre, whose valorous great might
> It seemes, iust wrongs to vengeance doe prouoke,
> To wreake your wrath on *this dead seeming knight,*
> Mote ought allay the storme of your despight,
> And settle patience in so furious heat?
> Not to debate the chalenge of your right,
> *But for this carkasse pardon I entreat,*
> *Whom fortune hath alreadie laid in lowest seat.*
>
> (II.viii.27, emphasis added)

As he had in his response to the Palmer, Cymochles assumes that Arthur means him to believe that Guyon is dead:

> who shall let me now,
> On this vile bodie from to wreake my wrong,
> And make his carkasse as the outcast dong?
> Why should not that dead carrion satisfie
> The guilt, which if he liued had thus long,
> His life for due reuenge should deare abie?
> The trespasse still doth liue, albe the person die.
>
> (II.viii.28)

And in his reply, Arthur continues in the same vein:

> Indeed (then said the Prince) the euill donne
> Dyes not, when breath the bodie first doth leaue,
> . . . .
> But gentle knight,
> That doth against the dead his hand vpheaue,

His honour staines with rancour and despight,
And great disparagment makes to his former might.

(II.viii.29)

Are Arthur and the Palmer liars? Or are they, to put perhaps a better face on it, merely virtuous equivocators? If we treat this episode only as a romantic narrative, we might argue that the Palmer has found himself in a delicate situation after the departure of the angel and before the arrival of Arthur. He is certainly not in a position to protect the knight himself and may have decided that to reveal to Cymochles and Pyrochles that Guyon is, in fact, still alive would only shorten that life considerably. But surely, even if we credit the Palmer with such a ploy, Arthur himself has no reason to equivocate. As he will shortly demonstrate, he is quite capable of protecting the prostrate Guyon from the two brothers. What then is the purpose of this continued equivocation?

There is, I think, no way to explain satisfactorily this curious episode except to understand Guyon's faint, not as a physical collapse, but as a metaphor for his spiritual state after (and before) his stay in the Cave of Mammon. Moreover, I think that it would have been almost impossible for Spenser's original audience to have read it in any other way. Several times a year,[4] during compulsory church attendance, they would have heard the following admonition:

Whatsoeuer worke is done without fayth, it is sinne. *Faith giueth life to the soule, and they be as much dead to God that lacke fayth, as they be to the world, whose bodies lacke soules. Without fayth all that is done of vs, is but dead before God,* although the worke seeme neuer so gay and glorious before man. Euen as the picture grauen or painted, is but *a dead representation of the thing it selfe, and is without life, or any maner of moouing: so be the workes of all vnfaythfull persons before God.* They doe appeare to bee liuely workes, and indeed *they bee but dead,* not auayling to the euerlasting life. They be but shadowes and shewes of liuely and good things, and not good and liuely things indeed. For *true fayth, doth giue life to the workes,* and out of such fayth come good works, that be very good workes indeed, and without fayth, no worke is good before God, as sayth S. Augustine. We must set no good works before fayth, nor think that before fayth a man may doe any good works: for such workes, although they seeme vnto men to be prayse worthy, yet indeed they be but vaine, and not allowed before God. . . . For good deedes bee not measured by the facts themselues, and so discerned from vices, but by the ends and intents for the which they were done. If a Heathen man clothe the naked, feed the hungrie, and doe such other like workes: yet because he doeth them not in fayth, for the honour and loue of God, *they be but dead, vaine, and fruitlesse workes to him;* . . . where [faith] is not, there is but fained vertue, although it be in the best workes. . . . *And for a similitude . . . they which glister and shine in good workes without fayth in God, bee like dead men, which haue goodly and precious tombes, and yet it auayleth them nothing.* . . . A man must needes bee nourished by good workes, but first hee must haue faith. Hee that doeth good deedes, yet without faith *hee hath no life.*[5]

The affinities between this passage and Guyon's circumstances suggest that, without his Palmer, Guyon may be one of those who glister and shine in good works but who are "like dead men." In spirit (and therefore in deed) "hee hath no life."

In Book II, as we will see, Guyon, Spenser's protagonist and ultimately his hero, begins his quest in the awkward position of being a Roman Catholic in a staunchly Protestant poem. If, however, we are to understand how Guyon has managed to get himself into this embarrassing predicament, and why "A Sermon of Good Workes Annexed vnto Faith" from the *Elizabethan Book of Homilies* provides us with a proper understanding of the nature of Guyon's faint, we have first to understand his character and his motivations by putting Book II into both a moral and a theological perspective.

Several critics have, to a limited extent, recognized the indebtedness of Guyon's characterization to that of Aristotle's description of the magnanimous man in *The Nicomachean Ethics.*[6] There the virtuous man "is thought to be proud [magnanimous] who thinks himself worthy of great things, being worthy of them."[7] The greatest reward he can deserve he believes to be honor, for it is "surely the greatest of external goods." The greatest thing he fears is shame. In this desire for honor, he is not to be blamed, since "he is coming by his own or even less than his own; for there can be no honour that is worthy of perfect virtue," a virtue which he possesses. He gains honor, however, not only by doing great moral deeds but also by inheriting or acquiring, and then using for honorable purposes, other internal and external goods including nobility, wealth, and power. Although he values these gifts as an aid to honor in harmony with his moral goodness, nevertheless, living as he does in a universe controlled by chance, he is moderate in his attitude toward these things, "neither over-joyed by good fortune nor over-pained by evil." Because he is ultimately indifferent to these things, although they can bring him honor when he has them, he is regarded as disdainful. Moreover, this same remoteness informs his relations with others, for he desires to do good but is shamed to receive good himself, since this makes him inferior. Thus, in an exchange of good deeds, he will always reciprocate, if possible, with a greater deed in order to put the other person in his debt. He will affect modesty among those below him and bear no grudges for wrongs done to him (for that would be to be controlled by a lower impulse), though he does expect the proper reward of honor for his acts. Finally, he is quite conscious of the good deeds he has done, but refuses to acknowledge and remember good done to or for him, and as a consequence will not ask favors.

Aristotle's sketch of the *megalopsychos* explains much of Guyon's attitude and behavior in the first eight cantos of Book II. As Berger and others have recognized, Guyon assumes that he lives in a world governed by fortune,[8] a world in which he sees himself surrounded by the less fortunate on whom he moralizes with the slightly censorious tone of a member of the moral elite. If, after meeting Redcrosse, he finds it difficult to act *holier*-than-thou, still he manages to make everyone else he meets aware of his rank as more-*temperate*-than-thou. Unlike Redcrosse in Book I, who tends to be ignorant of the meaning of what he experiences, Guyon has not only a self-righteous confidence in his own capacities but also a certainty of what it is that others are lacking which he possesses — rational temperance and, with that, the magnanimous man's sense of his own honorable worth. Looking at the dead Amavia, for example, he lectures his own Palmer on her problem (II.i.57–58),[9] having already offered the dying woman a smattering of self-assured aphorisms ("He oft finds present helpe, who does his griefe impart," II.i.46). The fact that she imparts her grief on his advice but promptly dies having done so does not shake Guyon's self-confidence in his philosophic stance. It is Guyon, moreover, who offers the reader a meditation on Ruddymane's predicament (II.ii.2), and it is Guyon who lectures Pyrochles on shame and honor after the latter refuses to acknowledge Guyon's martial supremacy (II.v.15–16). His self-assurance and self-reliance (in the face of experiences which he does not understand)[10] are in danger of seeming pedantic.[11] Archimago, well aware of Guyon's Aristotelian (and Roman Catholic) character, knows exactly what to say in order to provoke him into a righteous rage against Duessa's supposed ravisher, the Redcrosse Knight:

> Faire sonne of *Mars,* that seeke with warlike spoile,
> And great atchieu'ments great your selfe to make,
> Vouchsafe to stay your steed for humble misers sake.
>
> (II.i.8)

And when Guyon questions Duessa, his concern is not with her presumed physical bruises and emotional pain but with finding out: "who hath ye wrought this shamefull plight?" (II.i.18) The only "emotional" reaction he can understand is one which he would suffer himself were he a woman, living as he does in a culture in which honor and shame are much more understandable than sin and the necessity of grace.[12]

Mammon's temptations are focused most clearly on Guyon's magnanimity, the god systematically offering him "Riches, renowme, and principality, / Honour, estate, and all this worldes good" (II.vii.8). And while Guyon step-by-step refuses, it is not because these things do not attract him but because: "Me list not (said the Elfin knight) receaue / Thing offred, till I know it well be got" (II.vii.19). In other words, he is prepared to explore Mammon's Cave to make sure that the god is not trafficking in stolen goods, "Or that bloud guiltinesse or guile them blot." His abrasiveness with his host is only because Mammon treats his offerings as ends in themselves, while for Guyon, insulted by being assumed equally crass, they are only valuable as means to a greater end—his own personal glory. As an Aristotelian, he can take power and wealth or leave them ("All that I need I haue; what needeth mee / To couet more, then I haue cause to vse?" II.vii.39), for these worldly goods are valuable only insofar as he can use them to further his honor. And we can understand why he is not prepared to accept any indebtedness to Mammon in exchange for his gifts (II.vii.9), leaving him, as it would, obligated and hence inferior to the god.

Mammon's trump card, the offer of his daughter Philotime (desire for honor), is clearly not a paternal afterthought but what Mammon (at least now) knows is the potential weakness in Guyon's moral armour—the overriding desire for glory as an end in itself, perhaps even at the expense of moral perfection (II.vii.47). Wed to her, Guyon would be "aduance[d] for workes and merits iust" (II.vii.49), a temptation not only to his Aristotelian ethical position but also to what may be seen as his latent Roman Catholic tendencies. This explains why, for once, Guyon's tone changes in response to Mammon's offer: it touches very close to home, the god finally having properly sorted out Guyons's priorities. But to succumb to the world of malicious ambition presided over by Philotime would demand that Guyon reject his serene belief in virtue as the central ingredient of the magnanimous life, for this "desire for honor" is a corruption of his own, returning him as it would to the world of fortune and backbiting in order to achieve that honor.

Those who climb Philotime's golden chain do so in order "to *raise themselues* to high degree" (II.vii.47, emphasis added), like Guyon seeking to be advanced for his own meritorious works. It is hard not to see throughout the first eight cantos of Book II not only an attack on the self-reliance of Aristotle's magnanimous man but also the most obvious attack on the popular (though faulty) Protestant notion of Roman Catholic doctrine concerning the efficacy of good works in assuring salvation. The ideal of Aristotle's magnanimous man had been easily assimilated as a Christian ideal in the Middle Ages primarily because, like Christ and his followers, the magnanimous man was in the world but not of it. With his desire for glory spiritualized, his metaphysics reoriented from fortune to providence, and—most importantly—his belief in his own independent capacity to do great deeds of virtue tempered by an acknowledgment that divine grace must aid him by inspiring and supernaturalizing even the best of those deeds—with these accommodations he became a Christian ideal. What is most difficult, however, for Aristotle's hero to accept is a reorientation concerning human nature itself, for while he does accept viciousness in human *beings,* he does not accept viciousness in human *nature.* Good and evil are the product of moral habits; there is no recognition in Aristotelian thought of anything like original sin. And one of the reasons that the magnanimous man is slow to acknowledge this second theory of human nature is that it takes responsibility for his good deeds at least partially out of his own hands, and with it its reward, personal honor. In other words, like Redcrosse, this pagan ideal has to learn humility.

It is not by chance that in response to the Palmer's "work-oriented" congratulations to Redcrosse ("Ioy may you haue, and euerlasting fame, / Of late most hard atchieu'ment by you doune," II.i.32), the knight, now a good Protestant, corrects him by replying:

> His [God's] be the praise, that this atchieu'ment wrought,
> Who made my hand the organ of his might;
> More then goodwill to me attribute nought:
> For all I did, I did but as I ought. (II.i.33)

And it is not by chance that Guyon makes no comment, flattering or otherwise, on this careful statement of a moral and spiritual philosophy antagonistic to his own belief in the value of individual merit.

But for the Aristotelian magnanimous man in a *Roman Catholic* universe, a qualification can be made to Redcrosse's theology, for human freedom is guaranteed and man cooperates in his salvation, aided by grace, though ultimately saved because of his own choice to be spiritually advanced "for workes and merites iust." The necessity of coming to acknowledge an infection in human nature, not simply in the immoral habits of an individual human being, was made palatable to the virtuous pagan as well. As Aquinas, who in his *Summa theologiae* was most responsible for the assimilation of Aristotelian ethics into Christian theology, argued: "In man there is a quality of greatness possessed by God's gift, and a characteristic defect which comes from the weakness of his nature. Magnanimity therefore makes a man esteem himself worthy of great things through contemplating the gifts which he has from God. . . . But humility makes a man belittle himself by contemplating his own particular weakness."[13]

Inherent in the Christianization of this pagan ideal is a reorientation of perspective (from moral to theological) which gives rise to a necessary reorganization of terminology. The first system, a moral system, is composed of virtues and vices—habits of mind. In the second system, however, those moral conditions must be spiritualized, so that they can be seen in terms of grace and sin.[14] Fortunately, in Roman Catholicism there is a direct correlation between the two systems: an act of moral virtue is also an act of grace; an act of viciousness is also an act of sin. A moral act spiritualized is either a gracious or a sinful act. In other words, the magnanimous man is not completely disoriented when he finds himself baptized, for his new Roman Catholic spiritual system augments his moral system, giving it a new beginning and a new end.

With the Reformation, unfortunately, this harmony was destroyed, for Protestant theology asserted that good deeds (moral acts) are no longer meritorious in themselves, and freedom to choose between salvation and damnation is radically curtailed. While the magnanimous man is still free to choose to develop moral habits and to do great deeds in all the virtues, the greatest deeds of moral goodness still do not save the reprobate from hell. And even less severe Protestants than the Calvinists agreed that this essential division between good deeds and salvation is valid. While it may be true that out of a true and lively faith will automatically come acts of moral goodness as a natural consequence of that faith, justification and salvation are by faith alone, not by works, as the Protestants accused the Roman Catholic "semi-Pelagians" of believing.[15]

As "A Sermon of Good Workes Annexed vnto Faith" asserts, the truly moral man must base his deeds on faith, without which his salvation is denied:

Hee that by nature would withstand vice, either by naturall will, or reason, hee doeth in vaine garnish the time of this life and attaineth not the verie true vertues: for without the worshipping of the true God, that which seemeth to bee vertue, is vice. . . . You shall finde manie which haue not the true faith, and bee not of the flocke of Christ, and yet (as it appeareth) they flourish in good workes of mercy:

you shall finde them full of pitie, compassion, and giuen to iustice, and yet for all that they haue no fruit of their workes, because the chiefe worke lacketh. . . . A man must needes bee nourished by good workes, but first hee must haue faith. Hee that doeth good deedes, yet without faith hee hath no life.[16]

The obvious objection here is that Guyon *does* have faith. He may be momentarily duped by Archimago and Duessa, but the sight of the cross on Redcrosse's shield is enough to "abace / His threatned speare" (II.i.26) and for him to cry

> Mercie Sir knight, and mercie Lord,
> For mine offence and heedlesse hardiment,
> That had almost committed crime abhord,
> And with reprochfull shame mine honour shent,
> Whiles cursed steele against that badge I bent,
> The sacred badge of my Redeemers death,
> Which on your shield is set for ornament.   (II.i.27)

The homilies again provide the necessary answer to this important objection. In fact, faith has not one but two parts: it must be both a *true* and a *lively* faith. In "A Sermon of the Saluation of Mankinde, by only Christ our Sauiour," such faith is defined:

Euen the diuels know and beleeue that Christ was borne of a virgin, that he fasted forty dayes and forty nights without meat and drinke, that he wrought all kinde of myracles, declaring himselfe verie God: *They beleeue also, that Christ for our sakes suffered most painefull death, to redeeme from euerlasting death,* and that hee rose againe from death the third day: They beleeue that hee ascended into heauen, and that he sitteth on the right hand of the Father, and at the last end of this world shall come againe, and iudge both the quicke and the dead. These articles of our faith the Diuells beleeue, and so they beleeue all things that be written in the new and old Testament to be true: and yet for all this faith, they bee but Diuells, remaining still in their damnable estate, lacking the verie true Christian faith. *For the right and true Christian faith is, not onely to beleeue that holy Scripture, and all the foresayd articles of our faith are true, but also to haue a sure trust and confidence in Gods mercifull promises, to be saued from euerlasting damnation by Christ:* whereof doth follow a louing heart to obey his commandements. And this true Christian faith, neither any diuell hath, nor yet any man, which in the outward profession of his mouth, and in his outward receyuing of the Sacraments, in comming to the Church, and in all other outward appearances, seemeth to be a Christian man, and yet in his liuing and deedes sheweth the contrary.[17]

As Sidney would put it, not *gnosis* but *praxis* must be the fruit of our faith.

The next sermon, "A Short Declaration of the True, Liuely, and Christian Faith," argues that we reveal a dead faith not only by doing evil or by remaining idle, but also by doing good deeds not firmly grounded in a complete faith—the three divisions of characters to be found in the Book of Temperance:[18]

Such a manner of fayth haue the wicked and naughty Christian people, which confesse God (as S. Paul sayth) in their mouth, but denie him in their deeds, being abominable, and without the right fayth, and to all good workes reproouable. And this faith is a perswasion and beleefe in mans heart, whereby hee knoweth that there is a God, and agreeth vnto all trueth of Gods most holy word, conteyned in the holy Scripture. So that it consisteth onely in beleeuing in the word of God, that it is true. And this is not properly called faith. But as hee that readeth Caesars Commentaries, beleeuing the same to bee true, hath thereby a knowledge of Caesars life, and notable acts, because hee beleeueth the history of Caesar: yet it is not properly sayd that hee beleeueth in Caesar, of whom he looketh for no helpe nor benefit. . . . [Thus] it is not properly sayd that hee beleeueth in God, or hath such a fayth and trust in God, whereby hee may surely looke for grace, mercy, and euerlasting life at Gods hand, but rather for indignation and punishment, according to the merits of his wicked life.

The word used repeatedly in these sermons to describe the lively faith is "confidence." The true believers "had a speciall confidence and trust, that he was and would bee their God, their comforter, ayder, helper, maintainer, and defender."[19] And the lack of this confidence may be the one flaw in Guyon's otherwise admirable character: he professes what he does not believe, because of his Aristotelian (and, for poorly informed Protestants, Roman Catholic) belief in himself, his *self*-confidence, a heretical residue, essentially pagan, in his personality that causes him ultimately to view the world ethically but not spiritually, and to view himself as beyond the common human predicament (except inasmuch as the heavens are "carelesse" of all mankind, leaving him to pick up the burden).[20] The gods are not con-

cerned with mankind as far as Guyon is concerned; he does not understand
the stain of original sin on Ruddymane's hands, as the Palmer points out;
and he lectures everyone he can find, including the Palmer, on the frailty
of others, a frailty he can only understand in moral, not spiritual, terms:

> Old syre
> Behold the image of mortalitie,
> And feeble nature cloth'd with fleshly tyre,
> When raging passion with fierce tyrannie
> Robs reason of her due regalitie,
> And makes it seruant to her basest part. (II.i.57)

The implication is that, for Guyon, if reason here had controlled the passions, man would live at his proper level.

Guyon's state of moral perfection is evidenced from the beginning of
the book. In this way he never changes. But spiritually he is dead—until
he revives in canto viii and, realizing for the first time his insufficiency,
he swallows his magnanimity and acknowledges the Prince as his "comforter, ayder, helper, maintainer, and defender," "the Patrone of his life"
(II.viii.55). (The *OED*, I.2–3, defines the word *patron* for the sixteenth
century as a protector, defender, advocate, pleader, supporter, upholder,
or champion.)

Hence the superficiality of the debate between those readers who claim
that Guyon, the exemplar of moral virtue, does not change and those
who argue that he does change within a spiritual bildüngsroman. Both
are right. And both are wrong. As I have tried to show elsewhere,[21] in
canto viii Guyon's ethical world is spiritualized and his metaphysics are reoriented from those of fortune to those of providence. Moreover, his proto-
Catholicism is explicitly denied, and he is forced to revalue the merit of
his deeds in this new world-system. Learning that Arthur has saved his
life, on awakening, Guyon, in good Aristotelian (and Roman Catholic)
fashion, asks:

> My Lord, my liege, by whose most gratious ayd,
> I liue this day, and see my foes subdewd,
> What may suffise, to be for meede repayd
> Of so great graces, as ye haue me shewd,
> But to be euer bound. (II.viii.55)

In other words, what does one do in return for salvation? Or, in Guyon's
case, how may he return the favor (and escape indebtedness)? Arthur's reply,

"Faire Sir, what need / Good turnes be counted, as a seruile bond, / To bind their doers, to receiue their meede?" (II.viii.56), makes sure that Guyon, now just beginning to live both a true *and* a lively faith, is an entrenched Protestant. Good deeds, the Prince implies, should not be considered as meriting reward. By implication, only faith should.

And yet some readers may still argue that Guyon, in spite of the above, has a lively faith from the beginning of Book II. The solution involves an understanding of Guyon's relationship with the Palmer and his reason for entering the Cave of Mammon. Guyon, unlike Redcrosse at the beginning of Book I, is in full control of his horse (his passions) at the beginning of his book and led, as he should be, by his Palmer. The Palmer himself is called "his reason" (II.ii.11), and is commonly accepted by critics as such. But we must draw a distinction between two forms of reason recognized by writers on ethics and theology in the sixteenth century. Although the terminology varies considerably, essentially human reason was said to have two parts. The first, man's *natural* reason, is discursive or logical, existing in time and in the part of the mind which the will inhabits. It is the peculiarly human form of experiencing reality. Man has also, however, *right* reason by which he intuits, immediately and thus outside of time, moral and spiritual truth, a form of reason which he shares with the angels and which was unfortunately darkened by original sin—hence Una's veil, removed only momentarily to Redcrosse when he returns successfully to the garden and put on again when he "falls" back into the world to serve Gloriana.

The question then is whether the Palmer represents Guyon's natural reason or his right reason—right reason synonymous with faith. The suggestion by Spenser that Guyon will have a "like race to runne" (II.i.32) to Redcrosse's already completed race leads us to expect that the Palmer and Una may serve similar roles. Moreover, those readers who would have the Palmer stand simply for the knight's "reason" must explain how Guyon can argue quite cogently with Mammon while the Palmer is somewhere on the other side of the Idle Lake. Redcrosse can function mentally without Una because he still has his dwarf (his natural reason) to advise him on rather blatant spiritual and moral affairs (such as the danger of the Seven Deadly Sins in the House of Pride.) But if Guyon can still debate without the Palmer, it must be because his absent guide is his *right* reason, and without him he is still capable of the process of discursive natural reasoning. As Maurice Evans has pointed out, the Palmer's staff is made of the same wood as Mercury's caduceus (II.xii.41) by which Mercury led man to divine truth.[22] Moreover, the Palmer is early identified as the knight's "faithfull guide" (II.ii.1), as well he should be, since a palmer was by definition a pilgrim who had gone to the Holy Land. And it is the Palmer who in-

forms Guyon of his ignorance of the reason for the indelible stain on Ruddymane's hands (II.ii.5)—a spiritual stain. Without his Palmer, when challenged by Cymochles, Guyon "with strong reason maistred passion fraile"
(II.vi.40), a feat impossible if the Palmer represents both aspects of his rational faculty. Most convincing, however, is Spenser's simile which introduces the Cave of Mammon episode:

> As Pilot well expert in perilous waue,
>   That to a stedfast starre his course hath bent,
>   When foggy mistes, or cloudy tempests haue
>   The *faithfull* light of that faire lampe yblent,
>   And couer'd heauen with hideous dreriment,
>   Vpon his card and compas firmes his eye,
>   The maisters of his long experiment,
>   And to them does the steddy helme apply,
> Bidding his winged vessell fairely forward fly:
>
> So *Guyon* hauing lost his trusty guide,
>   Late left beyond that *Ydle lake,* proceedes
>   Yet on his way, of none accompanide;
>   And euermore himselfe with comfort feedes,
>   Of his owne vertues, and prayse-worthy deedes.
>   (II.vii.1–2, emphasis added, l.4)

It is in this state that Guyon, relying only on his natural reason, and with
that self-confidence and self-satisfaction which faith, his Palmer, would
have held in check and educated had he been present, begins his experience with Mammon.

Why does Guyon enter the cave, and is he right to do so? The answer,
as qualifications in the homilies might have led us to expect, is that he
is both right and wrong. Having defined both the dead and the living
faith, the homily "Of the True, Liuely, and Christian Faith" points out
the necessity of identifying which of the two we have:

All holy Scripture agreeably beareth witnesse, that a true liuely faith
in Christ, doeth bring foorth good workes: and therefore euery man
must examine and trye himselfe diligently, to know whether hee haue
the same true liuely faith in his heart vnfeignedly, or not, which hee
shall know by the fruits thereof. Many that professed the faith of
Christ, were in this errour, that they thought they knew God, and
beleeued in him, when in their life they declared the contrary. . . . A

man may soone deceiue himselfe, and thinke in his owne phantasie
that he by faith knoweth God, loueth him, feareth him, and belongeth to him, when in very deede he doeth nothing lesse. For the triall
of all these things is a very godly and Christian life.[23]

Thus Guyon, perfect morally, is *right* to enter the Cave of Mammon, since
it is both proper and necessary to make trial of his faith, "to know what
belongeth to it, and how it doth worke in him. It is not the world that
wee can trust to, the world and all that is therein, is but vanitie. It is God
that must bee our defence, and protection."[24] Spenser does not explicitly
indicate that Guyon consciously accepts the god's offer of a guided tour
of the netherworld in order to make trial of his faith. Spenserian allegory
does not usually work that naively. But it does seem clear, at the least,
that Guyon is aware that the tour has the nature of a trial. Mammon himself tries all that he does in order "to doe him deadly fall" (II.vii.64). And
Guyon refuses each of the god's offers because "he was warie wise in all
his way, / And well perceiued his deceiptfull sleight." Spenser himself explicitly acknowledges the testing nature of the episodes of Book II when,
at the beginning of Book III he remarks that Guyon, instead of returning
with Acrasia to Gloriana's court, continues to journey through fairyland
"To make more triall of his hardiment" (III.i.2). In his confrontation with
the god of worldlings, however, Guyon misunderstands the nature of the
test, so that, although he is capable of refusing to put his trust in the
world, he mistakenly puts his trust in his own magnanimity—his own
human strength. In other words, morally he passes the test, but spiritually
he fails it. And this is why he faints, for his works are not the product
of faith.

What most critics miss when they evaluate Guyon's success in the cave
is that to reject Mammon is not automatically to choose God. Christ may
object that man cannot serve both God and Mammon, but there are other
possible things to serve, including personal dignity and independent moral
perfection. Berger is, in an important way, right in arguing that Guyon
is motivated by *curiositas* in entering the cave, but he is right for the wrong
reason. Guyon should be curious about the state of his faith, not simply
about the power of his own natural virtue to endure this temptation. Berger's quotation from Augustine's *Confessions* is relevant, but not as Berger
applies it. Men falsely tempt themselves with "a certain vain and curious
desire, veiled under the title of knowledge and learning, not of delighting
in the flesh, but of making experiments through the flesh. . . . But by this
may more evidently be discerned, wherein pleasure and wherein curiosity
is the object of the senses; for pleasure seeketh objects beautiful, melodi-
ous, fragrant, savoury, soft; but curiosity for trial's sake, the contrary as

well, not for the sake of suffering annoyance, but out of the lust of making trial and knowing them." [25] Were Guyon to have entered the cave with his Palmer, he would not have fainted.

The lesson of "A Sermon of Good Workes Annexed vnto Faith" seems a pointed comment on Guyon's self-complacency as he wanders along without his Palmer, with no interest in finding him, cataloging his virtuous good deeds: "Let no man therefore . . . reckon vpon his good workes before his fayth: Where as fayth was not, good workes were not. The intent . . . maketh the good workes, but fayth must guide and order the intent of man." [26] When the Palmer, in his very first words to Guyon in the book, exhorts him to let "God guide thee, *Guyon,* well to end thy warke, / And to the wished hauen bring thy weary barke" (II.i.32), he is referring in part at least to his own function, since a lively faith is a gift of God. Moreover, seen within the framework of the present argument, he is almost certainly making a theological statement about the necessity of grace and faith as the foundation of the virtuous life, if it is to lead to salvation. The metaphor of the ship and port, used here for the second time in Book II,[27] is echoed at the beginning of canto vii, where Guyon assumes that he can steer himself without God or his Palmer as guide into the port of salvation, using only natural reason. But as "A Sermon of Good Workes" admonishes: "Hee that *by nature* would withstand vice, *either by naturall will, or reason,* hee doeth in vaine garnish the time of this life and attaineth not the verie true vertues: for without the worshipping of the true God, that which seemeth to bee vertue, is vice. . . . And for a similitude . . . they which glister and shine in good workes without fayth in God, be like dead men." [28]

It has been Spenser who has called the Palmer Guyon's faithful guide and in other places implied it within the allegory. But when Guyon awakes from his symbolic faint, his first words indicate not only his recognition of the Palmer's role but also, now, of his need for that role:

> Deare sir, whom wandring to and fro
> I long have lackt, I ioy thy face to vew;
> Firme is thy faith, whom daunger neuer fro me drew.
>
> (II.viii.53)

From now on the steering of his ship of spiritual state is in the hands of the Palmer. As they leave for Acrasia's Bower, "Said then the Boteman, Palmer stere aright, / And keepe an euen course" (II.xii.3). This time when they meet Phaedria, the Palmer is in control (II.xii.18). As at the beginning of canto vii, the ship enters "foggy mistes, or cloudy tempests" (II. vii.1), but this time it is the Palmer who steers them through "a grosse

fog" which envelopes the boat, making "this great Vniuerse . . . one confused mas" (II.xii.34). Likewise, where Guyon had earlier moralized on the
human condition, now it is the Palmer who condemns the Rocke of Vile
Reproach (II.xii.9). Instead of having, as he always had, a ready answer
for all situations, now Guyon asks the Palmer for the meaning of the beasts
in Acrasia's Bower (II.xii.84) and, after receiving an explanation, asks the
Palmer if it is all right to change them back to human form (II.xii.85). Since
natural reason should be in harmony with right reason and can come to
truth with the aid of the latter, it is proper that Guyon's last words are yet
another moralization on the latest exemplum, Grill, to cross Guyon's path:

> Said *Guyon,* See the mind of beastly man,
>   That hath so soone forgot the excellence
>   Of his creation, when he life began,
>   That now he chooseth, with vile difference,
>   To be a beast, and lacke intelligence.   (II.xii.87)

But this time it is the Palmer who gets the last word—the last word in
the Book of Temperance:

> To whom the Palmer thus, The donghill kind
>   Delights in filth and foule incontinence:
>   Let *Grill* be *Grill;* and haue his hoggish mind,
>   But let vs hence depart, whilest wether serues and wind.
>   (II.xii.87)

Acrasia's Bower is not the final port, though, as Shakespeare said of the
Dark Lady of the Sonnets, she has provided "the bay where all men ride";
and indeed the only reason for stopping there is to put in bondage the con-
cupiscence which, article 9 of the Thirty-nine Articles reminds us, remains
in the regenerate. But with her capture—ensnared in a net which "The
skilfull Palmer formally did frame" (II.xii.81)—Guyon's boat may ultimately
be like Una's (and therefore Redcrosse's): a "weather-beaten ship arriu'd on
happie shore" (II.i.2). Until that time, however, "he him selfe betooke another way, / To make more triall of his hardiment" (III.i.2). However, the
nature of the trial he now plans to pursue is that of faith, and the "hardiment" he possesses he now knows is not his alone, since he will, accompanied by his Palmer, "seeke aduentures, as he with Prince *Arthur* went"
(III.i.2)—the "Patrone of his life."

Wilfrid Laurier University

NOTES

1. *The Works of Edmund Spenser: A Variorum Edition,* ed. Edwin Greenlaw et al., 11 vols. (Baltimore: Johns Hopkins Press, 1932-57). All Spenser quotations are from this edition.

2. See A. S. P. Woodhouse, "Nature and Grace in *The Faerie Queene*," *ELH* 16 (1949), 194–228; Ernest Sirluck, "Milton Revises *The Faerie Queene*," *MP* 48 (1950), 90–96; Robert Hoopes, "'God Guide Thee, Guyon': Nature and Grace Reconciled in *The Faerie Queene,* Book II," *RES* 5 (1954), 14–24; Harry Berger, Jr., *The Allegorical Temper: Vision and Reality in Book II of Spenser's "Faerie Queene"* (New Haven, Conn.: Yale University Press, 1957), chs. 1–2; A. C. Hamilton, "A Theological Reading of *The Faerie Queene,* Book II," *ELH* 25 (1958), 155–62, and "'Like Race to Runne': The Parallel Structure of *The Faerie Queene,* Books I and II," *PMLA* 73 (1958), 327–34; Theodor M. Gang, "Nature and Grace in *The Faerie Queene:* The Problem Reviewed," *ELH* 26 (1959), 1–22; Frank Kermode, "The Cave of Mammon," in *Elizabethan Poetry,* ed. John Russell Brown and Bernard Harris (London: Edward Arnold, 1960), 151–74; Maurice Evans, "The Fall of Guyon," *ELH* 28 (1961), 215–24, and *Spenser's Anatomy of Heroism: A Commentary on "The Faerie Queene"* (Cambridge: Cambridge University Press, 1970), ch. 6; Carl Robinson Sonn, "Sir Guyon in the Cave of Mammon," *SEL* 1 (1961), 17–30; Lewis H. Miller, Jr., "Phaedria, Mammon, and Sir Guyon's Education by Error," *JEGP* 63 (1964), 33–44, and "A Secular Reading of *The Faerie Queene,* Book II," *ELH* 33 (1966), 154–69; Paul J. Alpers, *The Poetry of "The Faerie Queene"* (Princeton, N.J.: Princeton University Press, 1967), 235–75; Patrick Cullen, "Guyon *Microchristus:* The Cave of Mammon Re-examined," *ELH* 37 (1970), 153–74, and *Infernal Triad: The Flesh, the World, and the Devil in Spenser and Milton* (Princeton, N.J.: Princeton University Press, 1974), 68–96; A. Kent Hieatt, "Three fearful symmetries and the meaning of *Faerie Queene* II," in *A Theatre for Spenserians,* ed. Judith M. Kennedy and James A. Reither (Toronto: University of Toronto Press, 1973), 19–52; Humphrey Tonkin, "Discussing Spenser's Cave of Mammon," *SEL* 13 (1973), 1–13; Geoffrey A. Moore, "The Cave of Mammon: Ethics and Metaphysics in Secular and Christian Perspective," *ELH* 42 (1975), 157–70; Peter D. Stambler, "The Development of Guyon's Christian Temperance," *ELR* 7 (1977), 51–89; Roger G. Swearingen, "Guyon's Faint," *SP* 74 (1977), 165–85; Madelon S. Gohlke, "Embattled Allegory: Book II of *The Faerie Queene*," *ELR* 8 (1978), 123–40; Hugh MacLachlan, "The 'carelesse heauens': A Study of Revenge and Atonement in *The Faerie Queene*," in *Spenser Studies* 1, ed. Patrick Cullen and Thomas P. Roche, Jr. (Pittsburgh, Pa.: University of Pittsburgh Press, 1980), pp. 135–61. The footnotes to Patrick Cullen's chapter, "Guyon *Microchristus*," in his *Infernal Triad* usefully summarize many of the positions held by the critics listed above.

3. In their edition, Robert Kellogg and Oliver Steele do not annotate Guyon's "death" but seem aware of this metaphoric motif in canto viii. They suggest that the faint represents

the ideal of death to the world expounded by Socrates in the *Phaedrus.* The so-called "philosopher's death" is probably best known from Plato's use of it in the myth of the cave in the *Republic.* On the fictional level, Guyon has been forced through his intense, but self-inflicted, duel with Mammon to neglect his body and the satisfaction of nature's legitimate demands. On the moral level, this neglect leads to the extreme condition of the philosopher's death, an ideal of the contemplative man in the dualistic tradition of Greek and Christian thought but an unsatisfactory condition for the renaissance man of action whose responsibilities keep him in this world and whose ethics make ample allowance for the control rather than the total subjection and death of the lower faculties of human nature.

Books I and II of "The Faerie Queene," "The Mutability Cantos," and Selections from the Minor Poetry, ed. Robert Kellogg and Oliver Steele (New York: Odyssey Press, 1965), p. 67. I will attempt to show that Guyon's "death" is not positive, even in the qualified way that Kellogg and Steele suggest. Rather than being a mistaken (contemplative) triumph over the world, it is a spiritual failure within the world, the result of Guyon's mistaken self-confidence in the sufficiency of his own natural (i.e., worldly) powers successfully to reject the world.

4. The preface to the *Homilies* demanded that the sermons be read, in rotation, "euery Sunday and Holyday in the yeere, at the ministring of the holy Communion, or if there be no Communion ministred that day, yet after the Gospel and Creede . . . except there be a Sermon, according as it is enioyned in the Booke of her Highnesse Iniunctions, and then for that cause onely, and for none other, the reading of the sayd *Homilie* to bee deferred vnto the next Sunday, or Holyday following. And when the foresayd Booke of *Homilies* is read ouer, her Maiesties pleasure is, that the same be repeated and read againe, in such like sort as was before prescribed [sig. a2ᵛ–a3ʳ])." In *Certain Sermons or Homilies Appointed to be Read in Churches in the Time of Queen Elizabeth I* (1623), intro. Mary Ellen Rickey and Thomas B. Stroup (Gainesville, Fla.: Scholars' Facsimiles and Reprints, 1968).

5. "A Sermon of Good Workes Annexed vnto Faith," in ibid., pp. 30–32.

6. See G. W. Kitchen, ed., *Faery Queene, Book II* (1910), quoted in *Var.* 2.253; and Berger, *The Allegorical Temper,* pp. 15–17.

7. Aristotle, *Ethica Nicomachea,* in *The Works of Aristotle,* ed. W. D. Ross, (Oxford: Oxford University Press, 1915), vol. 9, pp. 991–95. All quotations from *The Nicomachean Ethics* come from this edition.

8. See Berger, *The Allegorical Temper,* pp. 3–38, 44–61; and MacLachlan, "The 'carelesse heauens.' "

9. Stanza 58 is often assumed to be spoken by the Palmer, but there are better reasons for ascribing it to Guyon. First, although the Palmer can make moral comments when appropriate (see his observation on Phedon's state, II.iv.34–35), it is much more common for Guyon to do so. Moreover, the explanation given for Amavia's suicide is essentially pagan as is the decision not to pass judgment on it, a philosophy in keeping with Guyon's metaphysics at this moment.

10. Unable to wash Ruddymane's hands clean of their indelible stain, Guyon offers several explanations; we know them to be wrong, however, when the Palmer finally remarks: "of your ignorance great maruell make, / Whiles cause not well conceiued ye mistake" (II. ii.5).

11. It is curious that Guyon should have his horse stolen during his quest, leaving him to walk, fully armored, for the rest of the book (which may explain why he travels by boat as often as he does). C. S. Lewis in *The Allegory of Love* (Oxford: Oxford University Press, 1936) remarks somewhat cryptically, that Guyon loses his horse because temperance is a "pedestrian" virtue (p. 338). Another, punning, possibility may arise from Guyon's "pedantry." The word "pedantical" derives from the Italian *pedante,* from *pedare,* "to foot it." Although the *OED* indicates that the earliest known example of this meaning for "pedantical" dates from 1622, Sidney seems to be punning on its etymology at the beginning of his *Apology for Poetry:*

The Death of Guyon

When the right vertuous *Edward Wotton* and I were at the Emperors Court together, wee gaue our selues to learne horsemanship of *Iohn Pietro Pugliano*, . . .[who] sayd, Souldiours were the noblest estate of mankinde, and horsemen the noblest of Souldiours. Hee sayde they were the Maisters of warre, and ornaments of peace; speedy goers, and strong abiders; triumphers both in Camps and Courts. Nay, to so vnbeleeued a poynt hee proceeded, as that no earthly thing bred such wonder to a Prince as to be a good horseman. Skill of gouernment was but a Pedanteria in comparison.

In *Elizabethan Critical Essays,* ed. G. Gregory Smith (Oxford: Oxford University Press, 1904), vol. 1, p. 150. The "pedant" of the sixteenth century was not necessarily contemptible; he was a man of knowledge and a teacher. Pedants inspire contempt not just because of an ostentatious display of learning but partly because they often give intellectual assent to a body of knowledge without living according to that knowledge, a division between *gnosis* and *praxis*—to use Sidney's terms—that lies at the heart of Guyon's lack of faith.

12. Here is a distinction between what anthropologists and psychologists identify as "shame-cultures" and "guilt-cultures." See Ruth Benedict, *The Chrysanthemum and the Sword: Patterns of Japanese Culture* (Cambridge, Mass.: Houghton Mifflin, 1946); Helen B. Lewis, *Shame and Guilt in Neurosis* (New York: International Universities Press, 1971); Helen Merrell Lynd, *On Shame and the Search for Identity* (New York: Harcourt Brace, 1958); *Honour and Shame: The Values of Mediterranean Society,* ed. J. G. Peristiany (Chicago: University of Chicago Press, 1966); Gerhart Piers and Milton B. Singer, *Shame and Guilt: A Psychoanalytic and a Cultural Study* (New York: W. W. Norton, 1971). These theories are central to our understanding of the Renaissance and the Reformation, when the courtly and chivalric ideal of personal honor and fear of its concomitant, shame, augmented by the prevailing humanist philosophy that "a man can do all things, if he will," was confronted with a reactionary Protestant assertion of human depravity, original sin, and *its* concomitant, guilt. See Lee W. Patterson, "Christian and Pagan in *The Testament of Cresseid,*" *PQ* 52 (1973), 696–714.

13. Aquinas, *Summa Theologiae,* 2.2.129.3, *res.* 4. The apparently contradictory attitudes of the mistress of the *Amoretti* which bothered J. W. Lever (*The Elizabethan Love Sonnet,* ch. 5) so much that he had to separate the sonnets into two collections is actually the poet's portrayal of this christianized magnanimity. The lover's final understanding of the justice of his mistress's attitudes toward herself and him indicated in sonnets 58 and 59 comes significantly at the end of their first year of courtship.

14. Unfortunately, we do not have a term that is the spiritual equivalent of an act of moral virtue, as "sin" is the spiritual equivalent of "vice."

15. Pelagius had heretically denied original sin. The sixteenth-century Anabaptists were often identified as Pelagians because of their similar doctrine; but Roman Catholics were also so accused because Protestants believed that they had dangerously undermined the role played by original sin in the spiritual life. Calvin frequently identifies Roman Catholicism with Pelagianism: "The Schools have gone continually from bad to worse until, in headlong ruin, they have plunged into a sort of Pelagianism" (*Institutes of the Christian Religion,* ed. John T. McNeill and trans. Ford Lewis Battles, [Philadelphia: Westminster Press, 1960], vol. 1, pp. 745–46). See also Harry J. McSorley's *Luther: Right or Wrong? An Ecumenical-Theological Study of Luther's Major Work, "The Bondage of the Will"* (New York: Newman Press, 1969).

16. "A Sermon of Good Works," in *Certain Sermons* (1623), pp. 31–32.

17. "A Sermon of the Saluation of Mankinde," in ibid., pp. 19–20.

18. "Of the True, Liuely, and Christian Faith," in ibid., pp. 21–22; in "A Sermon of the Saluation of Mankinde," in ibid., p. 19, we are told:

> Our office is, not to passe the time of this present life vnfruitfully, and idlely, after that wee are baptised or iustified, not caring how few good workes wee doe, to the glorie of God, and profit of our neighbours: Much lesse is it our office, after that wee bee once made Christs members, to liue contrarie to the same, making our selues members of the diuell, walking after his inticements, and after the suggestions of the world and the flesh, whereby wee know that wee doe serue the world and the diuell, and not God. For that faith which bringeth foorth (without repentance) either euill workes, or no good workes, is not a right, pure, and liuely faith, but a dead, diuelish, counterfaite and feigned faith.

These categories can be applied to the characters of Book II. Under evil deeds (the worst that man can do): Mammon, Pyrochles, Furor, Phedon, Amavia, and Maleger. Under idleness (the least that man can do): Acrasia, Cymochles, Mordant, and Phaedria (with her Idle Lake). The next sermon on "A True, Liuely, and Christian Faith" introduces the third possibility of doing good, but a good not based on faith. Into this category of evil, I am suggesting, can be placed Guyon (until the end of canto viii).

19. "Of the True, Liuely, and Christian Faith," in ibid., p. 25.

20. Only once does he seem to see himself as a member of the common run of humankind. Offered Mammon's daughter in marriage, Guyon rejects the proposal, saying that "I, that am fraile flesh and earthly wight / [Am] Vnworthy match for such immortal mate" (II.vii.50). This acceptance of his own frailty, so out of keeping for Guyon, is also typical of Aristotle's magnanimous man in certain circumstances. He is usually "free of speech because he is contemptuous" of those who speak other than what they believe, but he will also speak "in irony to the vulgar" because he looks down upon them. Guyon has good reason for rejecting Mammon's contemptible offer here, and his impatient replies to the god while he is in the cave indicate his recognition of the inferiority of the offers put forward by his host.

21. See note 7.

22. Maurice Evans, "The Fall of Guyon," in *Critical Essays on Spenser from ELH* (Baltimore: Johns Hopkins Press, 1970), p. 179.

23. "Of the True, Liuely, and Christian Faith," in *Certain Sermons*, pp. 26–27.

24. Ibid., p. 28.

25. Augustine, *Confessions*, X.xxxv.54–55, partially quoted by Berger, *The Allegorical Temper*, p. 26.

26. "A Sermon of Good Works," in *Certain Sermons*, pp. 30–31.

27. The metaphor is first used, significantly, to acknowledge Una's successful return to the state of grace, her prelapsarian homeland, "Where she enioyes sure peace for euermore, / As weather-beaten ship arriu'd on happie shore" (II.i.2).

28. "A Sermon of Good Works," in *Certain Sermons*, pp. 31–32.

RUSSELL J. MEYER

"Fixt in heauens hight": Spenser, Astronomy, and the Date of the *Cantos of Mutabilitie*

*T*HE COMPOSITION date of Spenser's *Cantos of Mutabilitie* has been the subject of considerable debate since their publication ten years after the poet's death. Matthew Lownes, who first published the *Cantos,* is tentative in saying that they "appear to be parcell of some following Booke of the Faerie Qveene, Vnder the *Legend of Constancie.*" While the numbering of the *Cantos* as vi, vii, and viii leave little doubt that they are indeed "parcell" of *The Faerie Queene,* the poet's intention for them is not at all clear. If, as Alice Fox-Blitch suggests, they are a draft for part of Book III,[1] then the date of composition must be quite early, certainly before 1590. If, on the other hand, as James Nohrnberg believes, the *Cantos* are a conscious conclusion to the poem,[2] then they are relatively late — after 1594 at least — for in *Amoretti* 80 Spenser announces that he is halfway through *The Faerie Queene.*

Dates as early as 1580 and as late as 1598 have been suggested. Evelyn May Albright, preferring the earlier, cites Gabriel Harvey's *Letter Book* and his remarks which "seem to be directed at the Mutability Cantos."[3] Arguing for the later date, F. J. Furnivall sees canto viii as appropriately "the last lines that Spenser wrote, on, or in view of, his sad death-bed."[4] Hugh Maclean observes that the *Cantos* cannot be assigned a specific date, but that "their substance and tone encourage the view that they were composed during the relatively troubled last years of the poet's life."[5] Alexander Judson, noting the allusion to Mulla and Bregog (VII.vi.40), "That Shepeard *Colin* dearely did condole / And made her luckless loves well known to be," concludes that the *Cantos* were written "in or after 1595, when *Colin Clouts Come Home Again* was published."[6]

In their attempts to date the *Cantos,* scholars have turned to stylistic analysis, consideration of thematic elements, and such external evidence as the Spenser-Harvey correspondence. To the best of my knowledge, however, no attempt has been made which considers the possibility that in the *Cantos* Spenser alludes to an actual astronomical event.

Early in canto vi, Spenser describes an event which is clearly a lunar eclipse. Mutabilitie, having come from earth to the sphere of the moon, challenges Cynthia for her throne:

> But shee that had to her that soueraigne seat
>> By highest *Ioue* assign'd, therein to beare
>> Nights burning lamp, regarded not her threat,
>> Ne yielded ought for fauour or for feare;
>> But with sterne countenaunce and disdainful cheare,
>> Bending her horned browes, did put her back:
>> And boldly blaming her for coming there,
>> Bade her attonce from heauens coast to pack,
> Or at her perill bide the wrathfull Thunders wrack.
>
> Yet nathemore the *Giantesse* forbare:
>> But boldly preacing-on, raught forth her hand
>> To pluck her downe perforce from off her chaire;
>> And there-with lifting vp her golden wand,
>> Threatened to strike her if she did with-stand.
>> Where-at the starres, which round about her blazed,
>> And eke the Moones bright wagon, still did stand,
>> All beeing with so bold attempt amazed,
> And on her vncouth habit and sterne looke still gazed.
>
> Meane-while, the lower World, which nothing knew
>> Of all that chaunced here, was darkened quite;
>> And eke the heauens, and all the heauenly crew
>> Of happy wights, now vnpurvaide of light,
>> Were much afraid, and wondred at that sight;
>> Fearing least *Chaos* broken had his chaine,
>> And brought againe on them eternall night:
>> But chiefely Mercury, that next doth raigne,
> Ran forth in haste, vnto the king of Gods to plaine.
>
> (VII.vi.12–14)[7]

Whether the eclipse described in these stanzas actually occurred is of course open to question, but there is reason to suspect that Spenser indeed refers to an actual eclipse. In Spenser's lifetime some twenty-seven total lunar eclipses were visible in Europe, thirteen of them between 1573 and 1599, the period most likely to include the composition of the *Cantos*.[8] Of these thirteen, ten were visible in the British Isles. Furthermore, the widespread interest in astronomy and astronomical observation characteristic of the late sixteenth century, a result of the astounding discoveries of that period, is likely to have touched Spenser as well. And, as A. Kent Hieatt has demonstrated, the poet was capable of quite accurate observations of natural phenomena.[9]

But was Spenser sufficiently interested in astronomy to draw his attention to such an event as an eclipse and, more importantly, to incorporate his observations in a poem? The evidence is necessarily circumstantial, but certainly suggestive.

As part of the quadrivium, of course, astronomy was studied in the universities of Spenser's day. In fact, it had been specifically prescribed in the revised statutes for Cambridge University in effect while Spenser was a student there.[10] To be sure, the study of astronomy was unlikely to deal with the most recent discoveries of contemporary astronomers. Copernicus's work, completed some thirty years earlier, was probably not covered in any detail, and his hypothesis of a heliocentric universe had by Spenser's time received only the most cursory notice, if any, in the schools. Spenser no doubt studied astronomy in Ptolemy's *Almagest,* and if an astronomy professor were to have mentioned Copernicus at all, his primary hypothesis would almost surely have been dismissed as foolish.[11]

Copernicus published his *De revolutionibus* in 1543, nearly a decade before Spenser's birth, but the impact of his work was not fully realized until considerably later. It is tempting to believe that the publication of the heliocentric hypothesis created an immediate sensation among the European intellectual community. But it did not; in fact, not until much later in the century did many astronomers take the theory seriously. The view generally held by sixteenth-century astronomers was that the heliocentric hypothesis was an interesting curiosity, but that Copernicus's real contribution to astronomy was his mathematics, calculations which made more accurate predictions of celestial phenomena than were possible with the old Alfonsine tables, based upon the Ptolemaic theory.[12]

Copernicus's heliocentric hypothesis may not have been taught in the schools, but there is considerable evidence to suggest that both his theory and other astronomical events were widely discussed in less formal surroundings. Science in general and astronomy in particular were of great interest to Renaissance thinkers, especially in England. Although university students may not have received very thorough instruction in the sciences from their professors, books on these subjects were virtually at their fingertips. There were, in fact, more vernacular books on scientific subjects published in England than anywhere on the Continent.[13]

Furthermore, while Spenser was still an undergraduate at Cambridge there occurred an astronomical event which spurred both professional and popular interest in astronomy and its recent discoveries: in November 1572 a new star appeared in the heavens, as if to present a celestial challenge to the Aristotelian theory of the immutability of the stellar sphere. Most prominent among the astronomers who observed this event was Tycho Brahe. Robert DeKosky gives this account of Tycho's observations:

> On 11 November 1572, Tycho had noted the appearance of a new star in Cassiopeia which was brighter than the rest of the stars in that constellation. He very carefully measured the angular separation of the new star from the others in Cassiopeia and, in subsequent similar determinations, found that it did not change position relative to the others. Brahe concluded that the new star was therefore in the region of the fixed stars, for if it were in the upper reaches of the terrestrial region or even in the region of the planets, it should have manifested some alteration in its position against the stellar background. Moreover, as Tycho continued to observe this body over the course of months, both its brightness and color varied perceptively: as bright as Venus and white at first, the star progressively dimmed and went from yellow to red in February, 1573, to the color of lead by April, after which the color remained unchanged but the star grew more faint; he could scarcely discern the body after February 1574. Throughout Europe people noticed the new celestial phenomenon, and not a few followed its changes in appearance and measured its position. All told, more than 50 observers composed tracts on the nova. As a result of widespread interest in this heavenly body, confidence eroded seriously in the traditional Aristotelian proposition that the celestial region was constitutionally immutable.[14]

This "new star" called into question the theory of the immutability of the stars, but events in following years added what was to become the final blow to the Aristotelian hypothesis. Between 1572 and 1596, Tycho observed six comets and was able to prove conclusively that they, too, were mutable objects beyond the sphere of the moon, located in the supposedly immutable area.[15]

Given Spenser's probable circle of acquaintances, particularly through his relationship with Walter Ralegh, it would seem to be virtually impossible for him to have remained ignorant of the astronomical advances of the late sixteenth century, even if he chose to disbelieve the contentions of the new astronomy. Among the observers of the momentous "new star" of 1572 were two English astronomers, both of whom came to have close relationships with Ralegh. Thomas Digges and John Dee reached the same conclusion as Tycho: that the new celestial object was indeed a star and thus seriously called into question Aristotle's hypothesis. Dee's interpretation of the event is especially interesting, for he advanced the thesis, published in his *Alae sen scalae mathematica* (1573), that the observable fading quality of the star was caused by its moving directly away from the earth, a direct challenge to the Aristotelian thesis that the universe consisted of a series of solid, although transparent, crystal spheres.[16] Spenser could have become acquainted with both Digges and Dee through Ralegh. Shortly after his graduation from Oxford in 1579, Digges was employed by Ralegh as his mathematical tutor, and Dee served Ralegh as technical advisor on matters of navigation (in addition, apparently, to being a tutor in chemistry to Sir Philip Sidney).[17]

Also among Ralegh's circle was a still more influential astronomer, Thomas Harriot. A member of Ralegh's Virginia expedition and his close friend throughout most of his life, Harriot was described by one of his contemporaries as "the master of all essential and true knowledge."[18] He enthusiastically supported the heliocentric hypothesis, and even corresponded about it with Johannes Kepler, whose work early in the next century would offer the final proof. It seems most unlikely, given Spenser's association with Ralegh, that the poet was not introduced to what Johnson calls "the group of enthusiastic students of astronomy centering about Sir Walter Raleigh and his friend and mathematical adviser, Thomas Harriot."[19] There is, in fact, some reason to speculate that Spenser and Harriot might have been acquainted in Ireland, for, as Henry Stevens indicates, "Hariot is known to have spent some time in Ireland on Raleigh's estates there" in the late 1580's or early 1590's.[20] And it seems even more unlikely that Spenser would not have at least been introduced to their ideas by Ralegh himself.

Of even more importance, however, is Spenser's friendship with Gabriel Harvey. In 1583, Harvey's brother Richard published an *Astronomical Discourse Upon the Conjunction of Saturne and Jupiter,* attempting to prove that this event foreshadowed the end of the world.[21] More to the point, while certainly not an astronomer, Gabriel was clearly quite interested in the subject. He owned books by many of the prominent astronomers, navigators, and mathematicians and apparently knew many of them, including Digges, quite well.[22] It is of course Harvey who informs us that his friend Spenser was deficient in astronomical learning. In Harvey's observation there seems, however, to be something of the tone of the allegation of Shakespeare's "small Latin and less Greek." Spenser may well have been "inexperienced in astronomical canons, tables, and instruments," but he was not "completely ignorant" of the spheres and the astrolabe,[23] nor was he, it seems, totally unfamiliar with such astronomical luminaries as Digges, Harriot, and Dee. By Harvey's standards Spenser must have seemed woefully ignorant, but he must also have been fairly typical of his age—that is, possessed of considerable practical astronomical knowledge when compared to most of his twentieth-century readers.

Although none of this information can be taken as absolute proof that Spenser was intensely interested in the new astronomy, it does contain much circumstantial evidence to support the thesis that he surely had a reasonable degree of interest in astronomical matters. His poetry presents even more evidence.

Astrological allusions abound in Spenser's works, of course, and thus imply a familiarity with astronomy as well, but we need not be concerned with these references here, for there are also those which are more clearly astronomical. In the *Hymne of Heavenly Love,* for example, Spenser refers to "that mightie bound, which doth embrace / The rolling Spheres, and parts their houres by space" (25–26)—that is, the spheres in which the planets and stars were said, in the Aristotelian hypothesis, to be fixed, and the "hours" or system of measurement by which celestial positions were described. These lines clearly refer to the traditional cosmology and, as S. K. Heninger points out,[24] the early stanzas of the *Hymne of Heavenly Beauty* are a nearly perfect gloss on the traditional continuum of the levels of creation, including "that mightie shining christall wall." For proof of the perfection of the world, Spenser says we need

> Looke . . . no further, but affixe thine eye
> On that bright shynie round still moving Masse,
> The house of blessed Gods, which men call *Skye,*
> All sowd with glistring stars more thicke then grasse,
> Whereof each other doth in brightness passe.   (52–54)

Spenser's cosmology here is obviously traditional, based on literary knowledge. Elsewhere, the poet's references imply a more direct interest in astronomy, although they are often based upon the work of ancient writers. In *Amoretti,* 60, for example, he tells us:

> They that in course of heauenly spheares are skild,
> To every planet point his sundry yeare:
> In which her circles voyage is fulfild,
> As Mars in three score yeares doth run his spheare.

If, as Dodge speculates in his notes on this poem,[25] Spenser is referring to the "period of restitution," then the poet is mistaken in his estimate of that "year." The "period of restitution" is the time between planetary conjunctions with the sun at the same point on the ecliptic. For Mars that period is seventy-nine years, a fact known by Ptolemy. As Dodge points out, "had Spenser, then, written '*four* score,' he would have been exact enough for his purpose; but at Kilcolman he was not likely to have access to astronomical tables."

Spenser's error here may indeed reflect, as Johnson suggests, that he never possessed more than the "minimal level of astronomical lore that was the common possession of all his educated contemporaries."[26] But it may also have been a simple lapse of memory. Johnson's disparaging assessment of Spenser's relative ignorance of astronomy is based in large part on a passage early in *The Faerie Queene:*

> Now when *Aldeboran* was mounted hie
> Aboue the shynie *Cassiopeias* chaire,
> And all in deadly sleepe did drowned lie,
> One knocked at the dore, and in would fare.   (I.iii.16)

Johnson bases his estimation of Spenser's ignorance in describing this event (the arrival of Kirkrapine at the house of Abessa and Corceca) on the notion that it occurs at midnight. But, he says, such a relative position of Aldeboran and Cassiopeia can occur only in the winter, "whereas the entire setting of the poem is summertime." He explains his calculation in more detail in a footnote: "Aldeboran is high above Cassiopeia when the right ascension of the meridian is between 5 and 6 hours. If this occurred between midnight and 2:00 a.m., the allowable limits for the right ascension of the sun would fall between 17 and 20 hours, making the time of year December or January."[27] Two difficulties arise with Johnson's criticism. First, as Alastair Fowler points out, there is no reason to be so sure that "the entire setting of the poem is summertime." There are, after all, clear references to spring,[28] and much of the poem takes place at seasons which are, simply, indeterminant. Second, we have no particular reason to believe the event to occur "between midnight and 2:00 a.m." All we know is that "All night [Una] thinks too long, and often lookes for light." (I.iii.15). If, in fact, we suppose the hour to be, say, 4:00 A.M. rather than midnight, then a date in September would be appropriate, or even as early as August.

The poet's remarks in the Proem to Book V would suggest at least an awareness of, if not an actual interest in, astronomical problems, at least insofar as they confirm his belief in a degenerating world. Here he complains that

the world is runne quite out of square,
From the first point of his appointed sourse,
And being once amisse, growes daily wourse and wourse.

(V.Pr.1)

His particular lament is supported by the evidence of the zodiac,

for the heauens reuolution
Is wandred farre from where it first was pight.   (V.Pr.4)

The "golden fleecy Ram," Aries, has moved to the location of Taurus, Taurus to Gemini, Gemini to Cancer, and Cancer to Leo. Spenser is remarking upon a phenomenon known well in his day: the precession of the equinoxes, whereby the constellations of the zodiac appear to shift westward on the ecliptic from year to year at a rate of approximately one degree every seventy-three and one-half years. By Spenser's day they had moved considerably from the positions of several centuries earlier.[29]

Spenser voices similar complaints in the *Mutabilitie Cantos,* but more importantly he exhibits knowledge of contemporary problems in astronomical theory:

Next, *Mercury* who though he lesse appeare
To change his hew, and always seeme as one;
Yet, he his course doth altar every yeare,
And is of late far out of order gone:
So Venus eeke, that goodly Paragone,
Though faire all night, yet is she darke all day;
And *Phoebus* self, who lightsome is alone,
Yet is he oft eclipsed by the way,
And fills the darkened world with terror and dismay.

Now *Mars* that valiant man is changed most:
For, he some times so far runs out of square
That he his way doth seem quite to have lost,
And cleane without his usuall sphere to fare;
That even these Star-gazers stonisht are
At sight thereof, and damne their lying bookes;
So likewise, grim Sir *Saturne* oft doth spare
His sterne aspect, and calm his crabbed lookes;
So many turning cranks these have, so many crookes.

(VII.vii.51–52)

The apparent irregularity of the planetary orbits had, of course, caused severe difficulties for astronomers and astrologers throughout the ages, but by Spenser's day the problem had become particularly acute, for the standard ephemeris (table of planetary locations), the Alfonsine tables, based upon Ptolemaic principles, was almost hopelessly out of date. The projected positions were in some instances off by as much as a full month.[30] The old system (whether as a result of centuries of accumulated errors of observation or a basic error in the model was debated) simply did not account for the observable positions of the planets. The new system, the Prutenic tables, based on Copernicus's calculations, while an improvement, was still far from totally accurate. Tycho Brahe complained vigorously when a projected conjunction of Saturn and Jupiter turned out to be off by two days in these tables. It is little wonder that contemporary astronomers would "damne their lying books." The problem of accurate prediction, it turned out, was not to be solved until early in the next century, when Johannes Kepler turned his attention to "the problem of Mars" and realized that planetary orbits are elliptical rather than circular.

If, then, Spenser was genuinely aware of astronomy, and if he did indeed refer to an actual eclipse, could that event help to date the *Cantos?* To find the answer to these questions, we must turn our attention to the eclipses of the late sixteenth century and the correspondences in the poem. There was an eclipse in 1573, but this one is too early for our consideration: surely Spenser did not write the *Cantos* so early. The next eclipse visible in Britain occurred in 1577, followed by another in that same year, then one each in 1580, 1581, and 1584, two in 1588, and one each in 1591, 1595, and 1598. After that, there was not another total lunar eclipse visible anywhere in Europe until a month after Spenser's death. Any one of these eclipses would seem to be a possible candidate for the event depicted in the *Mutabilitie Cantos,* and without further evidence our search would have to end, an interesting observation, but nothing more.

But there is additional evidence, for the eclipse is not the only celestial event Spenser alludes to in this passage. Of most importance, of course, is the role of Jupiter. The gods, that is the planets, we are told,

> All ran together with a great out-cry,
> To *Ioues* faire Palace, fixt in heauens hight.
>
> (VII.vi.15)

If indeed Spenser is describing a real eclipse in the *Cantos,* then one would expect that the eclipse with which the description corresponds would include the presence of Jupiter in the visible sky. Such a coincidence of an eclipse and Jupiter occurs for only three of the ten visible eclipses between 1577 and 1598: 7 November 1584, 3 March 1588, and 14 April 1595. Furthermore, that "all ran together" would seem to imply a conjunction of the planets near Jupiter. With the aid of an astronomical emphemeris, we can calculate the location of the planets on the nights in question and determine whether, in fact, they were in or near conjunction coincident to the lunar eclipses. That is, we can determine whether the phenomenon Spenser describes in the *Cantos* actually occurred.

In 1584, Jupiter and Mars were both visible, but nowhere near conjunction, Jupiter being at 28 degrees and Mars at 139. In 1588, only Jupiter was visible at the time of the eclipse. But on 14 April 1595, Jupiter, Mars and Venus were all visible, with Jupiter and Venus nearly in conjunction (at 352 and 349 degrees, respectively) and Mars only 28 degrees to the west at 324 degrees.[31] The proximity of these three planets, then, surely suggests that they have "run together."

More important, however, is the particular location where they meet. In the Ptolemaic system, each planet is said to have two special "houses," two zodiacal signs of particular influence, a solar house and a lunar house. The lunar house of Jupiter is the zodiacal sign of Pisces, of which Jupiter is also said to be guardian deity.[32] While, as we have seen, Spenser recognized the precession of the equinoxes, the sign of Pisces was still by tradition placed at from 330 to 360 degrees on the ecliptic. At 352 degrees, then, Jupiter is indeed "in his faire Palace," with Venus close beside, and Mars only 6 degrees to the west of that house. Neither Mercury nor Saturn was visible at the time of the eclipse, but the poet tells us that Jupiter sent Mercury to the circle of the moon to find the cause of the sudden darkness; his absence, then, is easily accounted for. And Saturn, despite Fowler's claims to the contrary,[33] does not play a significant role in the *Cantos;* furthermore, the absence of this outermost of the visible planets readily explains Spenser's reference to "high Jove," a reference that would not, of course, fit with the normal Ptolemaic depiction of the planets, in which Saturn occupies the highest sphere, but one that fits perfectly well with the observable phenomena of the night of 14 April 1595.

If, however, Spenser does indeed refer to this particular event, then how do we account for his reference to "Vesper, whom we the evening-starre intend"? Vesper, or Hesperus, is said to run by the side of the moon as "her page," and

> with his torche, still twinkling like twylight,
> Her lightened all the way where she should wend.
>
> (VII.vi.9)

Although Vesper is traditionally said to be Venus, that planet was clearly in the wrong position on the date in question; Mercury, often an evening star as well, is to the east of the sun and thus would not appear at all. But just 15 degrees west of the moon and directly on the ecliptic is Spica, the brightest star in the constellation Virgo, which could well be the "Vesper" to which Spenser refers, for it would indeed run "by her side" throughout the night.

Perhaps most important of all, however, is the length of the eclipse of 14 April 1595. According to J. Fr. Schroeter's calculations, the eclipse began its partial phase at 2:07 A.M., Greenwich mean civil time, and ended the partial phase at 5:49. The total, or umbral phase, however, did not begin until 3:08 A.M. and was over at 4:48 A.M.[34] The umbral shadow—that is, the darkest shadow of the earth—eclipsed the moon for just 100 minutes. I take the beginning of the eclipse in the *Cantos* to be that point at which Cynthia, the moon, is said to be "bending her horned browes" (VII.vi.12), for this is precisely the shape the moon appears to take at the onset of an umbral eclipse—that is, the "horned browes" would be pointed in the direction of the "approaching" shadow of the earth. The end of the eclipse, presumably, comes at that point at which Mutabilitie releases Cynthia:

> Eftsoones she thus resolv'd: that whil'st the gods—
> After returne of Hermes' embassie—
> Were troubled, and amongst themselues at ods,
> Before they could new counsels re-allie,
> To set upon them in that extasie,
> And take what fortune time and place would lend.
> So forth she rose, and through the purest sky
> To Ioue's high palace straight cast to ascend
> To prosecute her plot. Good on-set boads good end.
>
> (VII.vi.23)

The eclipse ends, in other words, in the sixth line of stanza 23, for in line 7, "forth she rose," having set Cynthia free. The fictional eclipse of the *Cantos*, then, in direct accord with the actual eclipse of 14 April 1595, lasts a total of 100 lines (VII.vi.12–23), one line for each minute of the umbral phase.

Assuming that Spenser did refer to this particular eclipse leads us to some interesting speculations about the *Cantos* themselves. Most importantly, of course, it implies that the *Cantos* were written after mid-April 1595, a date by which we can be certain that Spenser had completed the first six books of *The Faerie Queene*. It would also seem to be fairly certain the *Cantos* were probably not composed much after this date, for surely

Spenser would not have called to mind such details much after the event itself. But what would have drawn his attention at this time to this eclipse? We know little of his frame of mind in April 1595, of course. By 1595, we know from *Prothalamion,* he had again been disappointed at court, but there is nothing in his life records which would recommend April 1596 as the time of the composition of the *Cantos.* Nothing that is, except the date itself, for in the year 1595, 14 April fell on a Monday—the day of the moon—and Easter of that year was just six days later, on 20 April; therefore this was the Monday before Easter, Mutabilitie come at just the time when we are reminded of immutability through the gift of Christ.

But where does all this lead? Does it lend us any significant new interpretation of the poem? Probably not, although it does indeed confirm Sherman Hawkins's speculations regarding the order of the procession of the months in canto vii. Spenser, as Hawkins points out, has used the traditional "year of grace" in his order of months, beginning with March, rather than the more familiar (to us) year beginning in January. The "year of grace," as Hawkins notes, offered Spenser several advantages:

> Most obviously it matched the sequence of his months with that of the seasons. It also allowed him to suggest religious implications which would be obscured in the cycle from January to January. . . . Finally, beginning with March allowed Spenser to harmonize nature and grace as he had already done in the figure of Nature herself. This calendar synchronizes the life of Christ with the progress of the seasons, the cycle of grace with the cycle of nature, "renewing the state of the decayed world" in both a spiritual and a physical sense. The same Providence is at work in the cycle of natural time and in the progress of redemptive history.[35]

But there is an additional point to be made. The "year of grace" is also closely aligned with the astronomical year, for the sun reaches the beginning, as it were, of the ecliptic, zero degrees, at the moment of the vernal equinox, the point at which the ecliptic crosses the celestial equator. And that point occurs in March. March, then, is the beginning of the year for the church, but it is the beginning of the year for the universe as well.

Finally, the fragment called canto viii is perhaps worth quoting in full, for this new information may give us a better insight into what Spenser intended for the ending of this segment of his work. His plea, it would seem, is not directed toward his own illness; he is not, I would venture, aware of his impending death. Rather, he is aware of the season:

When I bethinke me on that speech whyleare,
  Of *Mutability,* and well it way:
  Me seemes, that though she all unworthy were
  Of the Heav'ns Rule; yet very sooth to say,
  In all things else she beares the greatest sway.
  Which makes me loath this state of life so tickle,
  And loue of things so vaine to cast away;
  Whose flowring pride, so fading and so fickle,
Short *Time* shall soon cut down with his consuming sickle.

Then gin I thinke on that which Nature sayd,
  Of that same time when no more *Change* shall be,
  But stedfast rest of all things firmely stayd
  Upon the pillours of Eternity,
  That is contrayr to *Mutabilitie:*
  For, all that moueth, doth *Change* delight:
  But thence-forth all shall rest eternally
  With Him that is the god of Sabbaoth hight:
O! that great Sabbaoth God, grant me that Sabaoths sight.

Despite all the arguments of the new science, the disturbing discoveries of the last decade of the sixteenth century—indeed of nearly all of Spenser's adult life—there remained for him that one anchor of which the very season of the eclipse, Easter, was a constant reminder. Science may disprove the immutability of the natural world, nature itself may revolt against order, but man may still retain that one saving grace, his faith.

We can, of course, never be sure of Spenser's specific intentions for the *Cantos of Mutabilitie.* But, having a more precise dating of the event they describe, we can now be fairly certain that they represent the last of his extant attempts to complete *The Faerie Queene.* The *Cantos* are neither an early draft of portions of Book III nor Spenser's deathbed lament over the state of the mutable universe; rather, they represent his continuing, although foreshortened, effort to continue *The Faerie Queene.* Presumably he intended them as the central portion of Book VII, a book which, for whatever reason, he never completed. Nonetheless, as we have them, the *Cantos* both suggest the major theme of Book VII and provide an appropriate closure for Books I–VI. Having begun *The Faerie Queene* with the quest of the Knight of Holiness and various tests of the Redcrosse Knight's faith, Spenser closes it with the ultimate statement of his own faith, a faith which overcomes even the challenge of new knowledge which calls into question both classical and scriptural authority. That the poem should end with such affirmation in the face of this challenge is indeed fitting.

University of Missouri, Columbia

NOTES

1. Alice Fox-Blitch, "The Mutability Cantos: 'In Meet Order Ranged,'" *ELN* 7 (1970), 179–86.

2. James Nohrnberg, *The Analogy of "The Faerie Queene"* (Princeton, N.J.: Princeton University Press, 1976).

3. Evelyn May Albright, "Spenser's Reason for Rejecting the 'Cantos of Mutability,'" in *The Works of Edmund Spenser: A Variorum Edition,* ed. Edwin Greenlaw, et al., (Baltimore: Johns Hopkins Press, 1932–57), vol. 6, p. 439. Summaries of many of the earlier considerations of the dating of the *Cantos* may be found in appendix 2, *Var.* 6.433–51. A more succinct summary is contained in Fox-Blitch, "The Mutability Cantos," pp. 180–82.

4. F. J. Furnivall, "Spenser's Last Lines," in *Var.* 6.315.

5. Hugh Maclean, *Edmund Spenser's Poetry* (New York: Norton, 1968), p. 400.

6. Alexander Judson, *The Life of Edmund Spenser Var.* 11.204. Interestingly, however, even the composition date of *Colin Clout* is open to question: see *Var.* 7.450–51.

7. All quotations from *The Faerie Queene* are taken from the variorum edition.

8. J. Fr. Schroeter, *Spezieller Kanon der Zentralen Sonnen- und Mondfinsternisse, Welche Innerhalb des Zeitraums von 600 bis 1800 N. Chr. in Europa Sichtbar Waren* (Kristiania: Jacob Dybwad, 1923), pp. 280–85. Schroeter's tables for the years 1551–1599 do not allow for determination of whether a given eclipse is visible at any specific location; that determination, however, can be made from the data furnished in Theodore von Oppolzer's *Canon of Eclipses,* trans. Owen Gingerich (New York: Dover, 1962). See esp. tables, pp. 367–68 and the formula, p. xxxiv.

9. A. Kent Hieatt, *Short Time's Endless Monument: The Symbolism of Numbers in Edmund Spenser's "Epithalamion"* (New York: Columbia University Press, 1960).

10. *Var.* 11.27–28.

11. In *The University of Cambridge from the Royal Injunctions of 1535 to the Accession of Charles the First* (Cambridge, 1884), James Bass Mullinger observes that "in the age of Galileo and Kepler . . . the student at Cambridge and Oxford was still deriving his notions of the celestial system from the Σύνγαξις of Ptolemy" (p. 402). Robert K. DeKosky mentions Owen Gingerich's survey of late sixteenth-century astronomy texts which "reveals that, though Copernicus' name appeared often enough, authors rarely discussed the theory of a mobile earth; when they did, their texts almost always dismissed that proposition as physically preposterous" (*Knowledge and Cosmos: Development and Decline of the Medieval Perspective* [Washington D.C.: University Press of America, 1979], p. 178). Judson notes that the astronomy lectures at Cambridge were still concerned with the "crystal spheres and static earth of Ptolemy" (*Var.* 11.27).

12. DeKosky, *Knowledge and Cosmos,* p. 179.

13. A. J. Meadows, *The High Firmament: A Survey of Astronomy in English Literature* (Leicester: Leicester University Press, 1969), p. 79; see also Francis R. Johnson, *Astronomical Thought in Renaissance England: A Study of English Scientific Writings from 1500 to 1645* (Baltimore: Johns Hopkins Press, 1937), esp. "Introductory Survey," pp. 1–15.

The Date of the *Cantos of Mutabilitie*

14. DeKosky, *Knowledge and Cosmos*, p. 181.

15. Thomas S. Kuhn, *The Copernican Revolution: Planetary Astronomy in the Development of Western Thought* (Cambridge, Mass.: Harvard University Press, 1957), pp. 207–08; see also Angus Armitage, *John Kepler* (London: Faber and Faber, 1966), who notes that by 1577 Tycho was able to prove that the comets were in the stellar regions (p. 54).

16. Colin A. Roman, *Their Majesties' Astronomers: A Survey of Astronomy in Britain Between the Two Elizabeths* (London: Bodley Head, 1967), pp. 27–30.

17. Johnson, *Astronomical Thought*, p. 137.

18. Meadows, *The High Firmament*, pp. 80–81.

19. Johnson, *Astronomical Thought*, p. 211.

20. Henry Stevens, *Thomas Hariot* (1900, rpt. New York: Burt Franklin, 1972), p. 82. Muriel Rukeyser, *The Traces of Thomas Hariot* (New York: Random House, 1970) carries the speculation further, asserting that Harriot "was given as his home the little island with the Abbey of Molanna on it," some fifty miles from Kilcolman and just a few miles from Ralegh's estate (pp. 9, 91). In any event, there seems to be circumstantial evidence for the Spenser-Harriot connection.

21. Meadows, *The High Firmament*, p. 89. Astronomy and astrology were, of course, closely allied in Spenser's day, and many of the great astronomers of the sixteenth century were also astrologers—Dee, Brahe, and Kepler among them.

22. See, for example, Harvey's familiar references to Digges in his marginalia to Twine's translation of Dionysius Periegetes' *Surueye of the World*, in *Gabriel Harvey's Marginalia*, ed. G. C. Moore Smith (Stratford: Shakespeare Head Press, 1913), pp. 159–64.

23. Quoted by Johnson, *Astronomical Thought*, p. 193: "Pudet ipsum Spenserum, etsi Sphaerae, astrolabijque non planè ignarum; suae in astronomicis Canonibus, tabulis, instrumentisque imperitiae. Praesertim, ex quo vidit Blagraui nostri Margaritam Mathematicam. Qui né Pontano quidem, aut Palingenio, aut Buchanano, aut etiam Bartasio cedit, exquisita vtriusque Globi, astrolabij, baculique familiaris scientia. Vt alter iam Diggesius, vel Hariotus, vel eliam Deius videatur. Aureum calcar non rudium aemulorum."

24. S. K. Heninger, *The Cosmographical Glass: Renaissance Diagrams of the Universe* (San Marino, Calif.: Huntington Library, 1977), p. 86–87.

25. R. E. Neil Dodge, *The Complete Poetical Works of Spenser* (Boston: Houghton Mifflin, 1908), p. 811*n*.

26. Johnson, *Astronomical Thought*, p. 194.

27. Ibid., pp. 194–95.

28. Alastair Fowler, *Spenser and the Numbers of Time* (New York: Barnes and Noble, 1964), p. 71, n.2.

29. However, while the actual zodiacal constellations had "moved," both their relative positions and the *signs* of the zodiac had remained the same. That is, while, say, the constellation Pisces had actually moved, the sign of Pisces was still considered for astrological purposes to be where it had been thousands of years earlier.

30. DeKosky, *Knowledge and Cosmos*, p. 179.

31. Bryant Tuckerman, *Planetary, Lunar, and Solar Positions, B.C. 601 to A.D. 1649* (Philadelphia: American Philosophical Society, 1964).

32. Fowler, *Spenser and the Numbers of Time*, p. 65.

33. Ibid.; see esp. pp. 227–33.

34. Schroeter, *Spezieller Kanon*, p. 284.

35. Sherman Hawkins, "Mutabilitie and the Cycle of the Months," in *The Prince of Poets: Essays on Edmund Spenser*, ed. John R. Elliott, Jr. (New York: New York University Press, 1968), pp. 305–06.

ELIZABETH BIEMAN

"Sometimes I . . . mask in myrth lyke to a Comedy": Spenser's *Amoretti*

*T*AKING BOTH its title and its impetus from *Amoretti* Sonnet 54, this essay dons the motley with Spenser's lover to offer some rather subversive readings of the early sonnets in the sequence. Yet its intention is as honorable and serious as the lover's own: to demonstrate the interdependence, and the ultimate comic coherence, of the various modes of love in human experience. In diverging in argument and tone from many established commentaries, it shows that there is more similarity between the representations of love in the sonnets and those in *The Faerie Queene* than has usually been noted.

It may be well to start with a few sober statements that should draw little dispute from any Spenserian. The *Amoretti,* as a sequence, is unique in its occasion and its ending. Unlike all sequences before it, it offers a developing and open-ended mimesis of the events of an actual courtship, that of the poet himself and his lady, which (we slip here from literature into history) led to the marriage of Edmund Spenser, gentleman, to Elizabeth Boyle on June 11, 1594. Also unlike those previous sequences that bewail or repudiate unsatisfied or unsatisfactory passions as they sublimate them into expressions of more spiritual forms of love, Spenser's sequence ends, as published, in the celebratory *Epithalamion,* reconciling the contrary motions of eros in marriage. The poet draws attention to his innovative appropriation of the latter genre to autobiographical purpose as he fills both the heretofore opposed roles of fescennine celebrant and devoutly joyous bridegroom, objectifying in art his subjective experience. The *Epithalamion* itself he has fashioned for his bride as a "goodly ornament," to close the circlet of eighty-nine sonnets and four anacreontic lyrics. In mimesis of conjugal joy and anticipation of the spousals in the Eternal City, the marriage poem stabilizes the oscillations of passion and devotion, and fulfills the successive moments of courtship in the redeeming, and redeemed, time of the wedding day.[1]

What I wish to suggest now is that these truths have had the unfortunate effect of deafening us to witty intricacies in the language of the *Amoretti*. The voice heard by the lady Spenser was courting was probably much more playful and intimate than the sage and serious voice most commentators describe. I shall argue that on grounds of Tudor rhetorical theory, as well as on those of the wordplay often noted in *The Faerie Queene*, we shall be very sensible to trust our lighter responses when—especially when— they run counter to established expectation.

Carol Kaske provides a start in the right direction. In paying attention to the strong motif of bee-stung desire in the Anacreontics, and assessing, in that light, the conflicts in *Amoretti* between desire and propriety or virtue, and between pride and submission in both partners, she finds that "tension is always there in Spenser . . . in the grand design."[2] With this I agree, as true of the level of open discourse. But when Kaske says that prior to the betrothal sonnet 67 the lover's "references to [his lady's] desire are veiled . . . because until she experiences it there is no use in telling her about it," I must differ.[3] I shall argue that much of the verbal energy in the early sonnets is directed to the decorously veiled end of provoking desire in the lady, to "telling her about it," as the open declarations of worshipful devotion and suffering male desire are laid before her.

Another critic reveals the tendency to read the *Amoretti* more delicately than need be. In *Celestial Pantomime,* Justus George Lawler shows himself to be witty and free of all false delicacy in his criticisms of Donne, yet he takes Donald Cheney to task for a mildly salacious, and eminently sensible, imputation of irony to the final lines of *Amoretti* 15.

The lines in question follow a conventional blazon of the lady's rich physical beauty: "But that which fairest is, but few behold, / her mind adornd with vertues manifold."[4] Cheney sees here an anticlimactic irony, "since the finale to this . . . standard list . . . would presumably have been a reference to the lady's 'amarous sweet spoiles'"—that is, to the external genital organs. This Lawler finds similar to Douglas Bush's observation of irony in the lines in *Epithalamion* which echo Psalm 24: "Open the temple gates unto my love," and he rejects both as illustrating a modern tendency to misread what an earlier generation would have found "transparently straightforward." Both passages must be taken seriously, he argues somewhat tautologically, because when Spenser is speaking in his own voice he is "in bondage to Petrarchan conventions," and thus incapacitated for the innovative and comic playfulness we find in much of *The Faerie Queene*.[5]

Not so. We must learn to approach Spenser's autobiographical love poetry with the detachment we take to the epic—to see the *Amoretti* as the fictionalized mimesis of the stages of an actual courtship, as available to us as any fiction. In so doing we may paradoxically come to see it as an agency of persuasion in that courtship.

John Webster finds a Ramist distinction applicable to the poetic methods of Sidney and Spenser, a distinction conducive to—if not the deconstruction of their works—a reconstruction of our perception of their methods.[6] Petrus Ramus distinguished between two methods of organizing discourse: the "natural" and the "prudential." The "natural" organizes, presents in extended fashion, and completes, a clear and direct statement or argument in circumstances that offer an attentive or friendly audience; the "prudential" proceeds by a variety of strategies of indirection when the rhetorician cannot count on the ready assent of those he seeks to persuade. Under the first method, anticipations are created to be fulfilled; under the second, they may be created expressly to be undermined so that the audience, kept off-balance, may be led to unexpected insights and reactions. Webster demonstrates how a mixture of the two methods in *The Faerie Queene*, by rendering any secure apprehension of the narrative difficult, forces compensating attention upon the allegory.

I find that the dominant "natural" method has, as its author may indeed have expected, outweighed for a public audience the naughty suggestiveness "prudentially" hidden in the wordplay of the *Amoretti*. We should be encouraged, therefore, to take note of our anticipations as raised by Spenser's language, even when the progress of the discourse cancels them out.[7]

Concerning Spenser's wordplay, which has drawn considerable attention, I need point only briefly to some of the critics who have addressed the subject. Speaking of *The Faerie Queene*, Martha Craig quotes Sir Kenelm Digby in support of her advice to seek the Spenserian cunning behind the apparent "gentleness and ease;"[8] and A. C. Hamilton counters the image of a severely Miltonic Spenser by maintaining that "in his art of language Spenser is closer to the fabulous artificer Joyce than he is to the allegorist Dante."[9] William Nelson agrees with Louis Martz that Spenser is parodying the conventions in *Amoretti* and believes that "surely the reader is [also] invited . . . to mock, though not merely."[10]

Many details in the early sonnets can function to alert the reader to Spenser's wordplay. Some trigger indecorous anticipations that are denied later, but not obliterated from consciousness. Others establish patterns of expectation that are fulfilled later in the sequence. The oscillations of tone, so typical of the whole, are striking in the first five sonnets.[11]

Amoretti 1, addressing the activity of sonnet writing, declares that the poet's sole aim is "her to please" who holds his life in the "dead doing might" of her "lilly hands." The middle lines, without deviating from conventional sonnet decorum, are different from the others in their tone of pain, as the poet refers to the "happy lines" upon which the lady will look as "sorrowes of [his] dying spright / written with teares in harts close bleeding book." At the start of the next line the poem reapproaches its near serenity with a third instance of "happy," which suggests, in its symmetry, that the second quatrain has been predominantly happy too. The brief allusion to the poet's yearning "hart" is the seed point for the discursive matter of the next sonnet.

The "vnquiet thought" addressed at the outset of sonnet 2 is clearly the lust located in the poet's "loue pined hart." He exhorts it to "Breake forth at length out of the inner part, / in which [it] lurkest lyke to vipers brood," to seek "succour" from "smart" and sustenance in "food." Resisting the temptation to find an aural pun in line 7 at this early stage in the mimed courtship, I merely point to the odd suggestion in line 4 that the phallic pressure is "woxen" greater than [his] wombe." Since the lover's voice is clearly male, this detail must be referred either to his metaphoric "womb," the matrix for his poems, or less directly to the lady's anatomy. If the latter sense prevails, the word "wombe" provides a prod to awaken her sexual consciousness. We may understand this sonnet as a self-fulfilling utterance, lust expressing itself in the poem, as the poem seeks to "please" the lady, and move her to a less literary pleasure.

The sestet pivots on "but" to urge the viperous thought to obeisance at the "feet" of the "fayrest Proud"—to entreat pardon for itself, and "grace" for the speaker. Although the action projected has implications of Petrarchan worship, "grace"—perhaps with "humblesse"—carries the only theological or spiritual tinge in the diction of this very earthy sonnet. It seems then more natural to see the primary implication here as courtly, and see the entreaty for "grace" as one that barely disguises a plea for the lady's sexual favor.[12] Reading it thus yields a syntactically implied subject for the imperatives of the couplet, a subject otherwise lacking. When we realize that the "vnquiet thought" is addressed throughout the fourteen lines of sonnet 2, and is prudently (and "prudentially"?) separated in lines 12 and 14 from the first person pronouns referring to the speaker, then the command to "cherish" in line 13 casts a highly suggestive light back upon the parallel phrase in line 13 of the first sonnet: "seeke her to please alone." The last line of sonnet 2 suggests that the vital force of the lover is so completely channeled into physical desire that a terminal deflation of his "vegetable love" (to borrow from Marvell) will end his life.

Even the discourse of the second sonnet has proved so disquieting that sonnet 3 must enforce the decorum of Petrarchan worship very clearly in the first line and maintain it during the octave. If the poet's method is understood to be what in Ramist logic is called "natural," and the sonnet

is read straightforwardly, the sestet will sustain a totally exalted interpretation. But if we have been conditioned to expect the unexpected in sonnet
3 by the quite open references to lust in sonnet 2—even more forceful references than in sonnet 84, where the lover's potentially "filthy lustful fire"
is suppressed and banished during the first three lines—then we may find
the sestet of sonnet 3 decorous only on the discursive level. Potentialities
of another sort will arise in the "toung" "stopped" by "thought's astonishment," and the "pen . . . rauisht with fancies wonderment." Let us slide
discreetly past the "toung" to focus on the "pen." All seems quite proper
here for the moment: the poet is writing a sonnet after all. But if we stop
on "rauisht," a word-seed with at least as much potentiality of sexual rap-
ture as of spiritual, and on "fancies," a word operative only on the lowest
level of the psyche in classical systems, we get quite another impression.
As the discourse proclaims the *topos* of authorial incapacity, the linguistic
detail proclaims the potency of sexual fantasy. In the couplet, the "natural"
reading gives a parallel to Sidney's "Look in thy heart and write"; but the
undercurrents suggest a psychic realm below that of the higher "wit" in
which issue of "tongue" and "pen" is not "stopped."

Sonnet 4 invites the lady as "faire flowre, in whom fresh youth doth
raine" (with a hint of proleptic wordplay?) to deck herself, as the earth
is doing at the approach of the young year, and to prepare herself "new
loue to entertaine." The exhortation preserves decorum by locating itself
temporally before the time of "new delight," but seeks to awaken the lady
by projecting such words as "lusty" and "wanton," upon the masculine
spring of the new year, and "fresh loue."

In sonnet 5, the lover's open discourse defends his lady against those
who are "finding fault with her too portly pride," retreating thus from
his earlier protestations of suffering desire and his immediately preceding
invitation to love. "Such pride is praise, such portlinesse is honor" he avows,
in apparent support of her "self-pleasing" bearing. It would be easy to rest
in a totally positive reading, were it not for that "self-pleasing pride." Even
in a Petrarchan context the phrase falls strangely on ears conditioned to
find pride and solipsism in Renaissance schemes more satanic than divine.
Should that closing phrase prompt a requestioning of the text, we can arrive at a very different reading.

A syntactical ambiguity in the first line of sonnet 5 follows, across the
sonnet break, the male's exhortation to the female to prepare "new loue
to entertaine." We may be prompted then to understand the phrase "my
dear harts desire" as the desire of the "my dear heart," the lady, especially
when we see the tumescent potentialities in the words "portly" and "pride."
At such an early stage in courtship, signs of passion in the lady would have

been bound to provoke some fault-finding tattle—more, surely, than would virginal resistance. Carrying on, the lover in this reading boldly proclaims his admiration of the demeanor that the unworthy world envies—and the word "envied" thus requires less adjustment for modern ears than it does in the more conventional reading. It then follows that the "lofty lookes" are those of the detractors. So far, such a counter-reading will work. But the syntax of lines 7 and 8 requires a return to the decorum of the "natural" discourse. If we try to make the "thretning rash eies which gaze on her so wide" the subject of an anticipated main verb, we are thwarted upon reaching a clause that is unmistakably subordinate, and are forced to return to the first line. Now, "desire" must function as part of a three-word eponym for the lady; "pride" and "lofty lookes" must assume their normal function as attributes of a Petrarchan mistress, and "thretning" shifts to modify her self-defense against the "rash" eyes of others. The octave reasserts itself as totally conventional.

If, however, we cannot abandon all of our aborted speculation about the octave we may find the lover's praise in the sestet evoking more than one kind of response: the lady's eyes bear "boldned innocence," but not too bold, we may be prompted to muse, remembering Book III of *The Faerie Queene*, published two years earlier; her countenance "like a goodly banner / spreds"—and the banner over him may be love, in this echo of Canticles. The final couplet can function positively in reference to each of the three levels of the Platonic soul: on the vegetative level, the origins of physical life are suggested in "spark"; on the animal, or heroic level, the self-assertion is defended as necessary to any good worldly endeavor; and on the rational or spiritual level we may find that this praise, appropriate to a Belphoebe figure or a lady on a pedestal, is just as appropriate, and more unitive, in application to a lady like Britomart—one who embodies legitimate sexuality, militance, and a brilliant chastity. Since the lover's intentions are moving towards marriage, it is not unreasonable to prefer on reflective reading an image suited to Britomart rather than to Belphoebe.[13]

I wish now to return to a single word, "hart," which is prominent in several of these sonnets. I shall discuss it in contexts provided by other words and images which impinge upon it, both in this grouping and elsewhere in the sequence. The tradition associating "hart" with the poetry of love, human and divine, is based on Psalm 42: "Like as the hart desireth the water-brooks: so longeth my soul after thee, O God" as rendered in the Book of Common Prayer. The usage is confirmed by many images in Canticles. The psalm leads to medieval occurrences of the "white hart" of spiritual longing; but the convertibility of spiritual into sexual longing, and the reverse, is attested to by the literatures of love and mysticism, and sanctioned by the very physical eroticism in the language of Canticles.[14]

When "hart" occurs in sonnet 1, line 8, a metonymy transfers the participle "bleeding" to "book." The transferral isolates "hart" from the blood that would have linked it to the "stricken deer," a commonplace of complaint literature, and perhaps thus would have prevented our seeing the alternative implication. The "sacred brooke" of the succeeding line is not related to the "hart" syntactically, but the constellation prepares, however obliquely, for the realization of the "harts desire" in the self-surrender of the thirsty "deare" by the brook in sonnet 67.

In sonnet 2 another dimension of the iconography associated with "hart" comes into play, evoked by the "vipers brood" that is linked in simile to the "vnquiet thought . . . bred" in the poet's "loue pined hart." The hart of legend is mortal enemy to snakes: he tramples them under foot as Christ tramples Satan. Yet here, paradoxically, the viperous thought of sonnet 2 arises in the "hart" itself, to be split from the hart's person (the speaking "me" and "I" of lines 12 and 14) and ordered to fall at the feet of the virtuous lady in suit for pardon and grace. If the suit be not granted, the "viper" and the suitor will die together as the lady assumes the virtuous role proper to the hart. The more spiritual icon, the hart as soul panting for the sacred brook, must then be obliterated with its alter-icon, the sexually aroused viper, unless the lady in granting suit permits a potentially fruitful coexistence.

The "hart" of sonnet 3 appears in the couplet. In the discursive sense it is clearly a "heart," the site of an outwardly inexpressible worship: the hart of the psalm adds an appropriate aura of mystical eros. If we allow the suggestion of a meaning too bold to be broached in the poem's open discourse, we shall be reminded that there is yet another tradition in English literature associated with deer both male and female, that of strong sexual proclivities.[15]

The word "hart" is absent from sonnet 4, which issues, in decorous conventional trappings, a direct and frank sexual invitation. It is not here but in the sonnets of obeisance and worship that the poet finds need for his subversively "prudential" word games.

This brings to sonnet 5 evidence in support of the tentative reading of a "prudential" reference to the lady in the "deare hart." To a purist who might remind us that a "hind" is the female deer, I respond that in the betrothal sonnet the "deare" is clearly a hind, with desire as well as good will in her heart, at long last.

I wish now to transfer critical attention to the female deer of iconography. The pure white hind, which in ballads could signify an otherworldly mistress, carries in Petrarch and Dryden a fully apocalyptic meaning. But Spenser's "gentle deare" of sonnet 67 is a much more earthly beast, however much we may see the juxtaposition to the Easter sonnet linking her to Christ, and inviting a spiritual dimension in interpretation. Her thirst has become strong enough to lead her back into the danger she has fled, and she surrenders herself willingly. But when her lover takes her "in hand" she is "yet halfe trembling." The ties she submits to are evoking modesty, and more primitive fears like those of the Amoret whose name the sequence bears.

The poet's pursuit has been long; the "assays" he refers to as "vaine" are in this betrothal sonnet now bearing fruit, but the difficulties have been fully anticipated as early as sonnet 6, which immediately follows those to which we have been attending:

> So hard it is to kindle new desire
>   in gentle brest that shall endure for euer:
> deepe is the wound, that dint the parts entire
>   with chast affects, that naught but death can seuer.
> Then thinke not long in taking litle paine,
>   to knit the knot, that euer shall remaine.
>
> (Sonnet 6, lines 9–14)

Whether we see the image of the hunt implied in a wordplay on "chased" does not matter. The "deepe wound" that must be administered and suffered before the eternal knot of marriage can be knit is a sexual wound. Now that marriage has been declared as the suitor's honorable intention (sexual dalliance is nothing, if not transitory), the couplet may be equivocally worded. It can with some "prudential" decorum serve to counter the lady's virginal fears, even as it equivocally administers the self-admonition to perseverance in the "long pursuit."[16]

The female is always hard to win. An oblique and possibly fortuitous light on these interpretations of the poet's "prudential" rhetoric is offered from an entry on the "stag" in a twelfth-century bestiary: "The females may be impregnated beforehand" but "they do not conceive until the time of the star Arcturus."[17] In Plato's *Laws,* Arcturus presides over "the season of vintage" before which no man may licitly "taste the common sort of fruit, whether grapes or figs . . . whether on his own ground or that of another." The fines for a transgression must be paid "in honor of Dionysus."[18]

Within the calendrical and chronological symbolism of the *Amoretti and Epithalamion* Spenser does not use the name of Arcturus (which does appear in Job 38.32, in a context that asserts an ordering power that is not human). Its absence may indicate little (or nothing) of Spenser's putative intentions and method; but for the auditor or reader, the absence of a restrictive seasonal indicator proves imaginatively productive. "The season of the vintage" may be tested with affirmative results against more than one moment of *kairos* in the *Amoretti and Epithalamion*.

When Spenser's female "deare" finally conceives the love that ties her to her mate, the typology of the vintage accords well with the betrothal sonnet's Good Friday location in the sequence. An equally satisfying, if fortuitous, linkage may be made to the *Epithalamion*. There, the season of vintage is celebrated in Catullan commands that manage to suggest the apocalyptic feast as well as a tribute to Dionysus before descending to a pregnant image:

> Make feast therefore now all this liue long day
> This day for euer to me holy is,
> Poure out the wine without restraint or stay,
> Poure not by cups, but by the belly full.   (*Ep* 248–61)

If the lady of *Amoretti*, like an Amoret, has been shrinking from the nuptial act as a terrifying ritual analogue to the disembowelment suffered by the captured deer, the bride who first began to conceive love of word-seeds planted much earlier need now feel no such restraint. Love is mature and sanctified at this time of vintage. Its expression may, in turn, bring on the "timely fruit" of progeny (*Ep* 404) if Juno so ordains in answer to prayer.

I bring this game to a close, having suggested some guidelines and a minimum of regulation. Let me suggest that all may play. I offer a few seed words for consideration: from sonnet 6, again, in reference to the lady: "deepe is the wound, that dints the parts entire / with chast affects." And from sonnet 85, in reference to the poet: "Deepe in the closet of my parts entyre / her worth is written with a golden quill." And from verses later in Psalm 42 where the hart longs for the brook, an epilogue:

> One depe calleth another depe by the noise of thy water spoutes: all
> thy waues and thy floods are gone ouer me. The Lord wil grante
> his louing kindenes in the daie, and in the night shal I sing of him,
> euen a praier vnto the God of my life.   (Ps. 42.7,8)[19]

University of Western Ontario

Notes

1. See Louis Martz, "The *Amoretti*: 'Most Goodly Temperature,' " in *The Prince of Poets*, ed. John R. Elliott, Jr. (New York: New York University Press, 1968), pp. 120–38; Waldo F. McNeir, "An Apology for Spenser's *Amoretti*," in *Essential Articles for the Study of Edmund Spenser*, ed. A. C. Hamilton (Hamden, Conn.: Archon, 1972), pp. 525–33; G. K. Hunter, "*Amoretti* and the English Sonnet," in *A Theatre for Spenserians*, ed. Judith M. Kennedy and James A. Reither (Toronto: University of Toronto Press, 1973), pp. 124–44; A. K. Hieatt, *Short Time's Endless Monument* (New York: Columbia University Press, 1960); Thomas M. Greene, "Spenser and the Epithalamic Convention," in *The Prince of Poets*, ed. Elliott, pp. 152–69.

2. Carol Kaske, in "Spenser's *Amoretti and Epithalamion* of 1595: Structure, Genre, and Numerology," *ELR* 8 (1978) 271–95, argues that the conflict is too often missed by critics and readers, but she explores the conflict primarily as it occurs between sonnet and sonnet.

3. Ibid., p. 284.

4. All quotations from Spenser follow *Spenser's Minor Poems*, ed. Ernest de Selincourt (Oxford: Clarendon Press, 1960).

5. Justus G. Lawler, in *Celestial Pantomime* (New Haven, Conn.: Yale University Press, 1979), pp. 111–15, counters Cheney's observations on the sonnet in *Spenser's Images of Nature* (New Haven, Conn.: Yale University Press, 1966), pp. 111–16. He cites Bush's identification of this allusion in *Epithalamion* as an "unintentional" and potentially bawdy evidence of a modern tendency to find irony where none exists. "It would be ironic," Lawler says, "if in reply to [another] line of the psalm, 'Who is the king of glory?' one were to reply, 'Donne's "prince" who in prison lies.' " He will allow such bawdry to Donne, although not to his near-contemporary Spenser, whose "earlier generation" presumably took things straight. See Douglas Bush, "Ironic and Ambiguous Allusion in *Paradise Lost*," *JEGP* 60 (1961), 631–40; in a gentler decade Bush has not made explicit the potentiality of sexual entrance as the mystical analogue to celestial marriage that is implied in Christian sacramental tradition (recognized by Lawler, but not as applicable to Spenser's personal poetry); but Bush's closely appended citations of Revelation in connection with the nuptials of Red Cross and Una provide a context suggesting that he would not have found Spenser's love ethos as remote from Donne's as Lawler does.

6. John Webster, " 'The Methode of a Poet': An Inquiry into Tudor Conceptions of Poetic Sequence," *ELR* 11 (1981), 22–43.

7. I am conscious, here, of the advice of Hans Georg Gadamer, *Philosophical Hermeneutics*, ed. and trans. David E. Linge (Berkeley and Los Angeles: University of California Press, 1977), esp. pp. 210–11: "The *mens auctoris* does not limit the horizon of understanding in which the interpreter has to move . . . if, instead of merely repeating, he wants really to understand. . . . Insofar as interpretation has to do with linguistic forms" it is not a secondary act but one participating in an unfolding linguistic tradition. My own conviction that reading is an action which develops and transmits meaning has roots in the Neoplatonic tradition: see James A. Coulter, *The Literary Microcosm* (Leiden: E. J. Brill, 1976), pp. 19–31. It was adumbrated in Elizabeth Bieman, "The Ongoing Testament in Browning's 'Saul,' " *UTQ* 43 (1974), 151–68; and explored directly in "Reconstructing *The Victorian House*: Philip Child's Hermeneutic," *Canadian Poetry* 9 (Fall/Winter 1981), 16–33.

8. Martha Craig, "The Secret Wit of Spenser's Language," in *Essential Articles*, ed. Hamilton, p. 333.

9. A. C. Hamilton, "Spenser, 'well of English undefyl'd,' " in *A Theatre for Spenserians*, ed. Kennedy and Reither, p. 105.

10. William Nelson, "Spenser *ludens*," in ibid., p. 87.

11. Five is a number associated with fallen sensuality, with marriage, and with the power of God manifest in creation; see "Numbers" in J. C. Cooper, *An Illustrated Encyclopedia of Traditional Symbols* (London: Thames and Hudson, 1978); and Alastair Fowler, *Spenser and the Numbers of Time* (London: Routledge and Kegan Paul, 1964), p. 35. Five is also the number of the wounds of Christ, an allusion important to the weight I place upon the juxtaposition of betrothal and Easter sonnets.

12. A comparison with the final stanza of "An Hymne of Beavtie" is invited: there the hyperbolic courtly appeal, "faire *Venus* dearling, my deare dread / Fresh flowre of grace," is both an appeal for sexual favour and an anticipation of the language of the heavenly hymns.

13. Robert Kellogg, in "Thought's Astonishment and the Dark Conceits of Spenser's *Amoretti*," in Elliott, ed., *The Prince of Poets*, p. 150, finds the triune complexity in Spenser's "personal experience as religious worshipper, lover, and poet," less the basis for the fiction of Colin in the *Amoretti* than "his more general imaginative assertion of the doctrine that in the highest civilization the three persons are ideally one." The fictional mistress is no less complex.

14. For hart and other deer symbolism, see Beryl Rowland, *Animals with Human Faces* (Knoxville: University of Tennessee Press, 1973), pp. 94–101; Cooper, *Encyclopedia*, p. 80; and T. H. White, *The Bestiary* (New York: Capricorn, 1960), pp. 37–40.

15. Eric Partridge, in *Shakespeare's Bawdy* (London: Routledge and Kegan Paul, 1968), p. 91, speculates that the usage of deer as sexual symbol may arise in wordplay. Spenser's spelling of the "gentle deare" in sonnet 67 confirms his opinion.

16. Six is appropriate to the sonnet's patient anticipation of a day that will knit the eternal knot: Cooper, *Illustrated Encyclopedia*, identifies it as a number of equilibrium, and as hermaphroditic.

17. White, *The Bestiary*, p. 39.

18. Plato, *Laws* 8.844.d,e, in *Plato, The Collected Dialogues*, ed. Edith Hamilton and Huntington Cairns, trans. A. E. Taylor (Princeton, N.J.: Bollingen, 1973).

19. I have chosen to quote this time (modernizing slightly) from the Geneva Bible: the *dynamis* of the "water spoutes" in that translation bespeaks an appropriate *energeia*.

MARY I. OATES

Fowre Hymnes:
Spenser's Retractations of Paradise

SPENSER'S *FOWRE HYMNES* (ca. 1590–95) postulate a set of relations among beauty, love, and art and thus have been rightly called
"philosophic poems."[1] It is their character as passionate enactments of such
relationships, however, that gives the great philosophic poems their beauty
and interest. This is as true of the Book of Job, the *Phaedrus,* and the *Symposium* as it is of works actually written in verse like *De rerum natura* and
the *Divine Comedy.* In each case, the poet seizes upon the possibilities of
a genre not usually associated with philosophic discourse to present a fiction that can speak to the reader's experience so that he or she finds the
relational patterns contained in this fiction absorbing and compelling. In
Berel Lang's typology of philosophical styles, *Fowre Hymnes* would be a
variation on the "reflexive mode" which uses a fiction to involve us, together with the author, in a process which promises only that it will "take
us as seriously as we take it, perhaps, finally, to a common point of realization."[2] The poet's energies are thus directed toward "delighting" his readers, then "teaching" them; in their turn, as Sidney said, his readers "shall
use the narration but as an imaginative groundplot of a profitable invention." Such an invention would involve, as Hamilton quotes Sidney to show,
a movement of the "infected will" toward sanity because the images of poetry "strike, pierce, and possess the sight of the soul."[3]

Spenser, however, went farther than his predecessors had done in design-
ing his philosophical poem as a series of lyrics.[4] The fictive hero of the
sequence is a poet-lover, eager to write a song of praise worthy of the object of his love; each poem is, then, like a book of *The Faerie Queene,* with
this hero in simultaneous quest of his love object and his poem. Believing
that if he can attain the one, he will be able to write the other, he assures
the god of love in the *Hymne in Honour of Love:* "If thou wouldst vouchsafe
to overspred / Me with the shadow of thy gentle wing, / I should enabled
be thy actes to sing."[5] Thus the *Hymnes* offer themselves as enactments
of the experience of writing a poem as well as of falling in love.

These hymns emerge from a generic climate in which the sonnet

sequence—itself used by Petrarch and his followers for "philosophic" ends—
was dominant. Like the sonnet sequence, Spenser's series of odes is essentially lyric in its ability to furnish the single voice of the poet with
chameleonlike transformations, epitomizing a succession of attitudes toward
his experience. The sonneteer, however, could carry these transformations
only so far: his attitudes might change, but his object could not. Even when
Petrarch addresses Laura first alive, then dead, she is the same lady. By contrast, a sequence of hymns could celebrate, as Spenser's do, a succession
of objects. Only his impulse to celebrate the object worthily remains the
same. In addition, the ancient hymnic convention that permits the use of
many names for a single object—a way of proclaiming the multifaceted nature of deity and of being sure to call the gods by their "right" names—
affords Spenser a rich resource with which to express the myriad qualities
of an emotion like love that can be in rapid succession an "imperious boy"
(*HL* 120) and "The world's great Parent" (*HL* 156). This multiple naming
where each new name creates a new image for the reader does much to
unify the hymns and adds to the reader's sense of following a single, pro-
gressive experience.

But, although it bears a resemblance to several more familiar genres,
Spenser's sequence of hymns is unlike most epics in that the first-person
narrative is intensely personal, and it is unlike spiritual autobiography in
that the speaker contradicts himself and changes his mind. To make matters even more puzzling, the poems were published with a dedication that
pretends to explain the relationships among the poems, but in fact only
complicates the issue. Because this dedication is crucial to interpretation,
I quote it entire:[6]

To the right honorable and most vertuous ladies
The Ladie Margaret Countesse of Cumberland
and the Ladie Marie
Countesse of Warwicke

HAVING in the greener times of my youth, composed these former
two Hymnes in the praise of Love and beautie, and finding that the
same too much pleased those of like age and disposition, which being too vehemently caried with that kind of affection, do rather sucke
out poyson to their strong passion, then hony to their honest delight, I was moved by the one of you two most excellent Ladies, to
call in the same. But being unable so to doe, by reason that many
copies thereof were formerly scattered abroad, I resolved at least to
amend, and by way of retractation to reforme them, making in stead
of those two Hymnes of earthly or naturall love and beautie, two

others of heavenly and celestiall. The which I doe dedicate ioyntly unto you two honorable sisters, as to the most excellent and rare ornaments of all true love and beautie, both in the one & the other kinde, humbly beseeching you to vouchsafe the patronage of them, and to accept this my humble service, in lieu of the great graces and honourable favours which ye dayly shew vnto me, vntill such time as I may by better meanes yeeld you some more notable testimonie of my thankfull mind and dutifull devotion.

And even so I pray for your happinesse.

Greenwich this first of September.

1596.

Yours Honors most bounden ever

in all humble service.

Ed. Sp.

The dedication has posed problems for admirers of the hymns because Spenser sounds as though he has written two religious hymns to atone for two secular hymns so sensual in nature that they actually corrupted the young. But most readers of the hymns find that the first two express, as Welsford says, "a lofty and spiritual ideal of love between the sexes," that they therefore do not contrast very sharply with the second two, and that furthermore the style is homogeneous throughout.[7] In addition, as Thomas P. Roche has observed in conversation with me, it is certainly odd that, if the second pair were meant as a simple negation of the first, Spenser made so certain by publishing them that the first hymns would receive even wider circulation than before and that he would offend his noble patronesses by proclaiming them "excellent and rare ornaments" of the first kind of love and beauty as well as of the second. One solution sometimes offered to these related dilemmas is simply to dismiss the dedication as conventional palinode, but to do so leaves Roche's objections unanswered and fails to exploit the dedication as a possible guide to meaning.

Believing that the *Hymnes'* best readers are correct in regarding them as essentially unified and are justified in distrusting the dedication if it forces them to regard the second pair as recantations of the first, I will offer additional support for the hymns' unity. I would like to place them in a frame of reference that renders their spirituality psychologically coherent, to relate their structure to the senses of medieval exegesis, and to use their many numerological features to suggest what Spenser wanted their unity to express. The stronger one's sense of the hymns' unity, however, the more painful the "recantatory" clauses of the dedication—indeed, the seemingly recantatory stanzas in the third and fourth hymns—become. The sort of spiritual coherence the poems display gives a clue, I will argue, to the real meaning of this dedication. In addition, the number symbolism in the dedication relates to that in the hymns to qualify even the "recantatory stanzas," making the whole a profound expression of Spenser's capacious and generous understanding of love.

The *Hymnes* resemble *The Faerie Queene* in that an "everyman" figure with whom the reader can readily identify moves through a minefield of emotional experience, stumbling around, mistaking his objects, yet remaining faithful to his ideals and being rewarded at last with a vision that enables him to make sense of his earlier suffering as he comes to understand his youthful follies.[8] Being lyric, however, rather than epic, the *Hymnes* locate their drama in the consciousness of a first-person narrator, a shift that tends to remove the "long ago and far away" quality characteristic of *The Faerie Queene* from much of the hymns, making it easy for the reader who has lived through some of the pains and ecstasies undergone by the narrator to identify with him rather consciously throughout the first two hymns—throughout even the third, if the reader's religious training has been reasonably orthodox. Thus, when arriving at the fourth hymn, readers are more prepared than they would otherwise be to follow in imagination the hero, with whom they have experienced so much, to the contemplation of a final, fully satisfying object of love. This identification enables readers to use the hero's experiences as an "imaginative groundplot" to help them discover their own hope of rest.[9] The paradise that concludes the *Hymne to Heavenly Beauty* is, in its harmony, reminiscent of the first narcissistic paradise of an infant but is richer because it includes dynamic love between subject and object instead of the total identification between subject and object characteristic of the infant's earliest experience.

My argument will suggest, therefore, that the *Hymnes* support what Harold Bloom calls the "qualified Freudian optimism"[10] that one's second (or third or fourth!) chances in love may well be better than the first; the maturing self may actually discover objects of love that improve upon those of the narcissistic, oedipal, or adolescent attachments.

In showing that the hymns form a unified expression of a developing personality, I will draw on the work of object-relations theorists—especially D. W. Winnicott and Ana-Maria Rizzuto.[11] Their studies, which include both the observation of infants and the psychoanalysis of children and adults, give new importance to the preoedipal stages of life, and Rizzuto offers a revision of Freud's location of the religious impulse in mere childish wishing. Her studies suggest that infants begin to form their ideas of God at birth, derive them from a wide variety of objects in their environment (not just from the father, as Freud claimed), revise them throughout life, and "believe" or not "believe" in the objective reality of God, depending on their individual psychic histories. [12]

Rizzuto follows Winnicott in postulating a "transitional space" at the border between subject and object in which the infant appropriates an object which we can see to be at first external to him, but which he so endows with his own fantasy that even to the observer it begins to lose its independent identity and to belong peculiarly to the child. [13] The woolly blanket or plush animal that the child seems to use as a substitute for oral gratification as well as for the cuddling and warmth that he also desires but cannot always command furnishes the data for an "object representation" in the infant's mind, a thought process, not a thing, that mediates between reality and desire. Winnicott believes that such objects inhabit a particular region of psychic "space," the frontier between the "me" and the "not/me," tacitly conceded by the adults around a child, who tend not to question the truth or falsity of the character with which the child endows these belongings. To do so, we might observe, would be analogous to rushing onto the stage to rescue the dying Desdemona, a misunderstanding of genre. For, Winnicott believes, as children grow and learn to play, blocks, dolls, even kitchen utensils become the raw materials out of which they fashion more and more complicated psychic objects—structures that reflect unconscious fantasies and that are thus the precursors of adult works of culture. [14]

Rizzuto, in her turn, considers the idea of God a special sort of "transitional object representation." Fashioned from relationships with family and other close associates, this mental representation of deity is "half-stuffed," as Rizzuto says, with the child's own wishes, needs, and fantasies. [15] This "internal object" may change in response to new needs and new knowledge or may become meaningless and be abandoned as new objects or new capabilities diminish the child's need for an omnipotent, omnipresent "companion" to compensate for the failures of fallible, often absent parents. Most often, Rizzuto says, the child's "god" is relegated to the toy box of unconscious memory with other abandoned playthings, although it may (like the actual dolls and stuffed animals) be brought out in times of joy or sorrow, dusted off, hugged, praised, or mutilated as the occasion demands. [16] Abandoned or denied though it may be, however, the "god idea" cannot be lost to unconscious memory. Thus the feelings once associated with it are latent in every individual.

If these speculations—borne out by Rizzuto's psychoanalytic explorations of patients of many stripes of belief—are correct, the first two hymns can be seen as the progression of a particular sort of soul from infantile narcissism through oedipal frustration through latency to adolescence and young adulthood. The object of praise changes as the persons changes, developing new needs and discovering new objects upon which to bestow devotion. At the end of the second hymn, the poet's disappointment with a haughty lady reduces him to a despair out of which grows fresh aspiration toward new creativity expressed by the third hymn, in which the poet-lover adopts Christ as his hero—a hero who, in his suffering for humanity, has himself endured unrequited love. This adult spirituality longs to share its hero with others, generating the magnificent fourth hymn, in which the soul feels secure enough to risk a "regression" to childlike meekness and thus is rewarded with the astonishing vision of Sapience enthroned in the bosom of God, a revelation that the feminine "goddesses," toward whom so much of the poet's love has gravitated, have their heavenly analogue. In addition, Winnicott's paradoxical observation that the infant "creates the objects he finds and finds the objects he creates" explains why the hymns associate creativity so closely with aspiration toward a love object. "Creating" and "discovering" come closer and closer together in the hymns—reality is seen to conform to imagination—as the self matures spiritually, until at last he "sees" what he was trying all along to "create"—a figure powerful and compassionate, wise and loving, able to satisfy his most seemingly contradictory longings.

In order to examine the way in which Spenser's poet-hero pursues his quest, I will first consider the odes as separate lyrics, focusing, since the quest is the controlling fiction, on their conclusions to show the relations among them. Each hymn ends with the hero contemplating an object of worship enshrined in a "paradise," but his first two objects meet disappointing reverses, contain the seeds of their own decay. At the same time, however, each contains elements out of which the poet's "high-conceipted spright" can create new objects that will be more adequate to the "scope of his desire."[17] Only the last vision, of God with Sapience enshrined in his bosom, is "pretended" as the most satisfying experience available to human beings on earth, itself an imaginative transformation of the first narcissistic identity of subject and object.

On the way to each new image of completion, a series of confusing and demonic parodies of deity is proposed and partly left behind, although Spenser is slow to claim that any dragon is ever finally crushed by the heel of art. The poet, he seems to say, can show that the demonic is ugly, imprisoning, self-defeating (a projection indeed of our own destructive impulses), but that only divine intervention can effect its permanent destruction.

I will trace this pattern of blisses proposed, then abandoned, in the *Hymne in Honour of Love,* then go on to analyze the relation among the first three paradises as resting places on the poet-lover's quest. I will examine, in addition, the relationship the hymns reveal among erotic, religious, and poetic aspiration, especially with respect to the creative process, as Love "creates" the world in the first hymn and the poet-lover feels impelled to create anew in the last hymn, even after enjoying the vision of Sapience.

At the beginning of the *Hymne in Honour of Love*, the poet-lover presents himself as engaged in a self-therapeutic enterprise. Love himself, a "restless" tyrant in lines 1–3, has wasted the lover, but the lover hopes that by finding a formula adequate to express his misery he may somehow ease it, and determines to propitiate Love with a secular hymn (*HL* 9). His constant effort in this first poem is directed toward finding some haven from his grief in order to allow his spirit to revive and reverse its downward emotional spiral toward despair or lust.

In his weakness, the poet-singer imagines himself huddled beneath the wing of Love as a bird sheltered beneath its mother's wing (*HL* 20). This ephemeral fantasy of a simple, protected paradise yields, then, to the first mythic paradise where the Greeks imagined the gods living their domestic lives, supping on nectar and ambrosia. Spenser displays only what interests him in this pagan dream, the natural ("kindly") scene in which Venus, like any human mother, nourishes and dandles her infant, Love.

Although the poet-hero does not seem, himself, to aspire to these "silver bowres," this fiction early in the poem is, as Welsford says,[18] an adumbration of the lovers' paradise at its end (*HL* 280–93). It is a significant "version" of paradise because many poets have thought of this stage of primary narcissism, when the infant experiences no dichotomy between subject and object, as the prototype for later experiences of this sort (or for the longing for them). For example, in *The Prelude* Wordsworth associates the "Babe . . . who with his soul / Drinks in the feelings of his Mother's eye!" with the "one dear Vale" to which he feels he must return in memory before beginning to chart accurately "the growth of the poet's mind."[19]

More recent observers of infants have seen this phase of primary narcissism and the weaning period to which it must yield as the basis for all later creativity. As Winnicott's ingenious paradox has it, the infant "creates" the breast (warm lap, gentle hands) that he "finds" and regards them for some time as part of himself. The processes of thought that "represent" these objects to him purely as sensation constitute "subjective objects" before the infant is physiologically mature or experienced enough to allow the existence of actual objects external to himself. The child's very weakness (from the observer's point of view) creates "omnipotence" from his own standpoint.[20] Like Cupid in Spenser's poem, he is a little god.

During the nursing period, the infant learns, Winnicott claims, to cre-

ate and manipulate "transitional objects"—pieces of cloth, stuffed animals—
to fulfill longings that even the most assiduous parents are sometimes unable to satisfy. As his caretakers disabuse him of his omnipotence during
weaning, he becomes more and more efficient at manipulating such "symbols," the transitional phenomena that, Winnicott and Rizzuto insist, can
remain meaningful only if the child continues to receive "good enough"
care to reinforce the relation between signifier and signified. Creativity,
then, like Love in the myth Spenser uses, is born of penury and plenty.
The need to create symbols is born out of the poverty of reality, a poverty
of which the growing child, learning to moderate his instinctual demands
from parents who gradually withdraw from their first nearly total adaptation to the infant's needs, is painfully aware. The infant's confidence in his
ability to create these symbols is born of his earlier conviction that a world
to meet his needs was created by mere wishing and of the willingness of
his caretakers to provide for him "well enough," thus leaving the symbols
intact.[21] Spenser's decision, then, to present the account of Love's birth and
the scene of nursing at the beginning of the quest for creative energy draws
not only on the familiar analogy between biological and artistic parturi-
tion but also, perhaps, on an insight parallel to Winnicott's that the human
infant is a doughty "creator."

The poet-hero himself, weakened to almost infantile helplessness (having regressed, the psychologist might say), by his frustrating experiences
in love, finds the strength to urge Love to leave his own haven of safety
(in effect, submit to weaning) to "come softly," to "kindle a fire" in the
poet's feeble breast. The myth tells us, then, that the hero is not content
with the regressive solution to his disappointment, but hopes to make con-
tact with his own infantile creative impulses in order to produce a new
level of integration in his personality. But such an ambition (embodied in
the poet's prayer to Love) produces an effect that is more than either poet
or god bargained for. The poet is led, as a result of Love's inspiration, to
ever more strenuous forms of aspiration; in the course of the *Hymnes,* the
god undergoes metamorphoses (renaming, "reformation," in the terms of
Spenser's dedication) into the poet's lady, the infant Christ, the adult Christ
as mangled courtly lover of mankind, and finally Sapience, "the sovereign
dearling of the Deity," who nestles in God's bosom as securely as Cupid
had done in Venus's lap.[22]

But first, like any human infant, Love must sally forth into a dark
world—dark because as yet a blooming, buzzing confusion of sense data.
As he journeys (matures), he learns—by analogy with his first "me/not
me" discriminations at his mother's breast—to organize these impressions
into objects that he eventually will perceive as self-subsistent, independent

of his needs; "the world *was* not," however (and *is* not for any percipient creature), so far as he is concerned, "till he did it make" (*HL* 75).

And so the hymn proper begins with two of the traditional "places" in sixteenth-century elegy: *genus eius* and "acts done."[23] Love is an elderly baby, a miraculous birth of three parents differentiated sexually only to the extent that Venus "bears" him.[24] He sleeps "securely," naked in his mother's lap, until wakened by Clotho, youngest and gentlest of the Fates. Like Artegall, Red Crosse, or Prince Arthur, Love is himself a lover: he is stirred from his "idle seate" by "desire" to seek a heroic destiny. He creates "the world that was not till he did it make" (*HL* 75), and, bringing harmony out of discord, infuses all living creatures with his own fire to "multiply the likeness of their kynd" (*HL* 100) (the creative impulse as it applies to the brute world): the significance of the pun on "kindled," repeated in one of its forms fourteen times in the hymns, and "kind," which appears eight times, is here first apparent. "Kindling" is *natura naturans,* the generative principle in the universe; it is also the source of human creativity of all sorts: the heroic deeds which Love performs (*HL* 65), as Spenser's knights often undertake their own tasks, partly "in the dark," trusting to borrowed light (*HL* 70),[25] and the special vocation toward religious poetry which the poet-lover receives in the last two hymns (*HHL* 6–7). The light for Cupid comes from his mother; the willingness of Spenser's knights to endure — even when bewildered — comes from the fairy queen herself or sometimes from one of her split-off virtues (Una, Belphoebe, or Arthur); and the devotional poet's "pure lampe of light" (*HHL* 43) comes from the Holy Spirit or from the "soveraine light" of Sapience (*HHB* 295). Our first strivings toward maturity are unconscious and can occur only if, like Spenser's figures, we can trust to a figure more powerful than ourselves to guide them. The way in which Love creates the world, bringing order out of chaos, is parallel to the activity of Plato's Demiurge and parallel, too, to Winnicott's account of infant and child play.

It looks in the beginning as though the whole of Love's creation will reflect the harmonious "heaven" from which he came, a world in which all desire can find "kindly" gratification. This world of primary narcissism turns to hell in an instant, however, when man's "deducted spright" (*HL* 106), cut off now from the wholly harmonious world of purely subjective objects, retains yet the memory of that most beautiful first object and is driven by love to recover somehow the primeval unity. As I have said, the weaning child creates endless substitutes, "not," as Spenser says, "for lust's sake," for this activity predates the oedipal period, but out of his aspiration toward the beauty he experienced in his infantile heaven. The infant uses his "transitional objects" to articulate a world that will last, be immortal, will not "die" (as his mother does every time she leaves him for longer than he can summon her image in his short conscious memory.) [26] In lines 113–20, Spenser identifies beauty in general, not the particular beauty of women, as the object of the deepest longings of humankind, and, if we translate the Platonic notion (appropriated by Spenser, Wordsworth, and others) of prenatal existence into the unconscious memories we retain of infantile (even intrauterine) life, we can see why such "immortal longings" are not specifically sexual in nature. They derive from a time when (as Auden says) we did not distinguish between hunger and love. (Spenser very often uses images of nutrition when he describes the soul's longing for beauty or its enjoyment of it.) Even though the period following weaning is full of conflict and generates great creative energy to resolve the conflict, it is still a world in which the child can gain a large degree of parental support for his aspirations; he may feel guilty, as Melanie Klein and her followers believe, over his rejection of his parents as internal to his own psyche or over his projection of his own hostilities onto them, but Love has not yet found his mischievous way to force the child into coveting his nearest neighbor's spouse, that is, the much more dangerous conflict of the oedipal period.

For suddenly the world's "great parent" turns "imperious boy," the pyromaniac who kindles a wasting, destructive flame for which no "kyndly" cure seems available, and the poem shifts the psychological drama to the poet-lover, showing him enduring agonies which correspond equally well to oedipal and early adolescent phases. There is no immediate cure for incestuous longing that either the child or his parents can accept, and the objects of puppy love in Spenser's world and to a very large extent in our own are, if not wholly tabooed, relatively unattainable. (At all points in the *Hymne in Honour of Love* one feels the extraordinary intensity characteristic of the oedipal and adolescent periods, but the emphasis on jealousy (*HL* 266–72) relates it more closely to the former.) The more devoted the hero is to the unattainable object, the more he suffers. He puzzles over this "unfairness" (the child, as Bettelheim reminds us, has a strong sense of justice),[27] and, of course, the oedipal conflict is, for several reasons, quintessentially "unfair." Spenser's hero finds that the more he puzzles, the tighter the emotional noose becomes: he tries to tell himself that, in effect, "whom he [Love] loveth, he chasteneth" (*HL* 162–68) — a way of excusing parental "unfairness"; he idealizes (and excuses) his object by explaining that her very beauty, being spiritual, makes it impossible for her to yield to "kyndly desire" so materially experienced; accordingly, he hopes that when he purges his love of "lust" (*HL* 179) (nearly always in Spenser a name for frustrated, confused love) he will be able to enjoy the felicity of the gentle knight rather than that of the "moldwarpe" (*HL* 182), a vivid figure for the dif-

ference between regressing to the (very infantile) level of a burrowing animal or moving on to latency when, as Erikson says, "the individual [is]
ready to learn quickly and avidly and to become big in the sense of sharing
obligation and performance rather than power; in the sense of making things,
not of 'making' people." [28]

If this section of the poem is read as pertaining to adolescent desire, then
if the adolescent can become the gentle knight, he can entertain not unreal-
istic hopes of winning his lady through achievement. The latent child must,
on the other hand, identify with the parent of his or her own sex and hope
to please both parents with achievements in the outside world, postponing
libidinal ambitions until a more generous array of objects is available. In
this respect, the reader should note the emphasis in the *Hymne in Honour
of Beauty* on the plurality of "deare ornaments" praised by Spenser's hero
before he settles down to the ecstatic contemplation of the beauty of his
single "dame." Some analysts think that oedipal difficulties may be less
acute in societies that permit more freedom of sexual expression among
young children than Spenser's did or than ours usually does; whether or
not this is the case, Bettelheim's suggestion that the "oedipal" child might
actually prefer an age mate for a love object to the parent ought not to
be neglected. [29]

The decision to forswear lust seems momentarily satisfactory as the poet-
hero creates a paradise within, constituting his own mind a temple for the
beauty that seems to him "so heavenly" (*HL* 196). But he cannot sustain
such a level of sublimation, and suspicious images of pleasures grosser than
those of disinterested contemplation recur "to feed his hungrie fantasy"
(*HL* 198). Heaven turns hellish again when the lover, disillusioned, represses his longing for the impossible, claiming now that "nought may
quench his infinite desyre, / Once kindled through that *first conceived* fyre"
(*HL* 202–03, emphasis added). Love—begotten, we recall, of penury and
plenty—condemn his thralls to "pine in most satiety" (*HL* 201). They can
fully imagine perfection, that is, but cannot hope to attain it.

The fixation of this hell mocks the "rest" of heaven mocks even the
"stillness" and "constancy" of line 195); "faine" chimes with "vaine," as
the lover enshrines the image of his "saint" within the frail temple of his
breast. This "felicity" of the "heaven of the mind" is fragile because it depends entirely on the lover's ability to project imaginatively the beauty he
seeks, and we recall that such transitional objects lose their meaning when
real objects are consistently disappointing. Its "fayning" and "counting"
undermine it as they do the fantasies of marrying one's parent characteristic of the oedipal child or the crushes of early adolescence. Experience dis-
illusions both.

The weary lover finds no rest; he must take to the road again, and like any hopeful lover he "faynes" (*HL* 240) "heavens of joy" that he will experience when he wins his lady's "lyking." Such hope is compromised, however, by the craziness and tragic ends of all the lovers of history and legend whom he follows "through heaven and hell" (*HL* 236), and he begins to lose faith in the hope he had originally generated through imaginative exertion: "faine" always, it seems, rhymes with "vaine." The dialectic of frustrated desire crackles faster and faster as each new "heaven" proves unstable and yields him up to ever more intense troublings of a mind by now so perverse that the gifted imagination seems able only to "faine" new torments for itself.

With all love's joys defaced by the "cancker worme" (*HL* 267), jealousy, the god of love appears again, using the lover's sufferings to reenter his own "heaven." Hoping to join him there, the lover now optimistically hopes that the "hell" he has endured will turn out to have been only purgatory, a hedonist's hell meant merely to make heaven seem pleasant by contrast. And this paradise, an insipid sort of Muslim fantasy feebly projected by the exhausted imagination, certainly needs such heightening. Lines 280–86 show the lover longing for the narcissistic joys of the pleasure principle, the heaven from which Love originally emerged. The successful lovers are indeed rewarded with what Cupid himself apparently has to offer: they feed on nectar "heavenly wize," are Venus's "dearlings" lying in ivory beds, covered with the roses and lilies of female and male imagery, and enjoying "joyous, happy rest." Rest is certainly one desideratum after all the lover's suffering, but, since the delight proposed was union with the beloved, we look for signs of "kindly bliss." In the stanza that follows we do find an intimation that something sexual is intended, but it is the ambiguous sexuality of Love's own original appearance as Venus's "dearling," a charming, but infantile, minion. Sexually undifferentiated as they were in lines 31–39, Love's "folke" play at childish sports, "hurtlesse" because preoedipal, retreat to the breast of a maternal figure, Pleasure, then crown her their queen in a little ludic ritual. Unready, like children in latency, to partake of any actual sexual experience, the lover has not himself attained even to this heaven and, as the next stanza makes clear, is vague about what his "wished scope" or "happie port" would really be. He is, perhaps, too worn out with his restless pursuit to remember what his object was, another way of saying that he has repressed his desire for the unattainable.

The paradise of Pleasure is the "happily ever after" of fairy tale which satisfies the child temporarily as he emerges from the acute jealousy of his oedipal phase[30] or as the endings of romantic novels reassure the often frustrated and disappointed adolescent that perseverance will eventually be rewarded. But the infinitude of his hunger keeps pushing the goal just out of reach—even out of sight—at every stage, and although the propitiatory ambition of the poet is frustrated in a way that parallels his erotic disappointment, his determination still to aspire to "an heavenly Hymne such as the Angels sing" suggests that he will not yield to despair or be content to regress to a heaven suitable only for infants. Because of the parallel that Spenser has formulated between the lover's libidinal strivings for the perfect soulmate and for the ideal song, we know that the quest cannot end here, although he and Love must content themselves temporarily with the level of understanding expressed in "this simple song" (*HL* 307).

The terminal paradises of the first three hymns are related to one another as were the first three "senses" of traditional exegesis. The first hymn presents a "literal" sense (as Welsford says, "Spenser . . . makes hardly any use of metaphor"),[31] the second an ethical and the third a theological interpretation of the essential terms, love and beauty. The psychological (literal) experience of frustrated love, which Spenser recounts in terms as familiar to his original readers as Freudian psychology to us, ends, as we have seen, in a wholly imaginary and rather vague idea of what its object ought to be. Despite the idealized picture of the proud beauty which he carries in his heart and whose virtue makes her deaf to his pleas, the queen of the imagined paradise is "pleasure," not evil in herself, of course, but limited in her ability to provide "rest"—lasting satisfaction. This literal level serves as a ground bass for the other hymns and thus takes its place in the powerfully self-conservative economy of the literature of "retractation" in which no experience, no matter how frustrating, humiliating, or painful, is ever wasted, a literature which parallels developmental psychology in denying the possibility—or desirability—of wholly forgetting the past. The purpose of the past in both accounts is to furnish material for re-formation of self, object, or both.

Saint Paul initiated this kind of operation for Christians, and Saint Augustine elaborated it; with the wisdom of retrospection, all one's follies can be seen as manifestations of a providential irony that gives most when it seems most to deny. The experience of jostling aspiration, disappointment, lust, love, desire begetting desire begetting desire, is a paradigm for the whole experience of living—seen by Spenser as by Freud as essentially libidinal. Love is the ravisher that keeps us forever "pregnant," as Donne said, "with the old twins Hope and Fear." It is also the presenter of the opening scenes of plays like *A Midsummer Night's Dream* or *As You Like It* that bring their lovers together in a chaotic, indiscriminate way reminiscent of the heap of elements that Spenser describes (*HL* 76–77) before Love "raunged" them in order. The hell the lover endures in the first hymn seems scarcely compensated by the baby love he might hope to win; the author of the play will eventually deal justly and mercifully with the cruelly tormented lover, but the state of being inside the comedy prevents him from seeing that it is one. The lover in Spenser's hymn calls love by many names, a hymnic convention that does justice to the Protean nature of the emotion he experiences, but the impulse remains somewhat polymorphous; not yet able to direct it toward an attainable object, he, like the child, cannot imagine very clearly what form the "lineaments of gratified desire" would take.

But the *Hymne in Honour of Love* is relatively unconcerned with ethics. It is an account of a painfully paradoxical experience in which one's very virtues lead to torment and where every gain proves a loss. One understands that idleness and "moldwarpism" are both regressions to be avoided, but the poet's aim is not to show the results of wrong choices. Readers are left to make such inferences for themselves. The *Hymne in Honour of Beauty* is much more heavily ethical, perhaps as befits the exegetical sense to which it corresponds, and is less likely to furnish readers with unconscious "solutions" to their own conflicts. The poet does achieve a more mature object, however. In love with love before, we might have said, he now yearns after a single earthly lady. Again, the poet-hero is propitiatory and has an idea that his hymn will so please his actual lady that she will stream "some deaw of grace" into his "withered hart." "Grace" and "deaw" are both punning, pointing to Book VI of *The Faerie Queene* and line 57 of this poem, both of which see the earthly graces of courtesy and art as analogues of heavenly grace.[32]

The hymn praises Venus by describing the descent of the soul into fleshly mold, gathering her beautiful influence as it falls.[33] The "heaven" from which it came is only named, but the initially imagined harmony of beautiful soul with beautiful body seems to create a paradise in exile. Through line 131 the *Hymne in Honour of Beauty* represses any suspicion it might have of this asserted concordance, making the body as fit palace or fit dress (pun on "habit in," *HB* 130) seem cheerily consonant with experience. The concluding couplet, however, is too consonant, and the empirical appeal of the following stanza undermines itself drastically at line 140: "That [beauty] is a signe to know the gentle blood." Spenser did not believe that "signs" were arbitrary any more than psychoanalysis believes that dream images are accidental, but—if his artistic commitment to allegory may be taken as an indication—seems rather to have thought as Launcelot Andrewes, his fellow student at the Merchant Taylor's School and at Cambridge, said in 1617 that grace and virtue accrue only to those who can "read" signs like that of the babe in the manger given the shepherds in the Book of Luke.[34] A sign of this "prophetic" sort is essentially related to its signified (Christ in the manger a sign of divine humility), but the relation is never immediately apparent. So Spenser's lover considers the paradoxical vulnerability of beauty and virtue incarnate: just as the purest lovers suffer most, so the most beautiful objects are most open to temptation and abuse.

His affection for the "faire Dames, the worlds deare ornaments" (*HB* 162), leads him to remind them of their "first countries sight" (*HB* 166), the heaven whence they came, and to encourage them to join in "gentle love"; with the venerable image of double reflection, he shows how love and beauty "kindle" one another and shine in one another's light.[35] The fair dames must not hide their "light" under a bushel; like Britomart and Amoret they must search diligently (even dangerously) for their mates already "known" from their first country, "their heavenly bowres, where they did see / And know ech other here belov'd to bee" (*HB* 202–03).

The advice to the dames (rather comic, as though the speaker had just attained to this sagacity himself) modulates at line 211 into a consideration of the way in which the lover "overvalues," as Freud said, the sexual object,[36] portraying the refinement of the image of the beloved as a projection of the mind's love for itself (*HB* 218). Again, as in the *Hymne in Honour of Love,* we find an internal accommodation and fixation, begotten of "fancies will," and a "felicitie" which the speaker cannot actually evaluate (*HB* 222–29). His beloved is both more and less fair than he "fancies" her: more, because she is real, less, because he cannot love any object so much as one formed by his hungry imagination to its own "proportion." He falls into a rationalizing praise of this "heaven" and devotes himself to a comic parody of disinterested contemplation (*HB* 246–59). As in an ecstasy, he stares, is wounded by the lady's glances, is cured by her compassion, fed by her smiles, soothed by her "cordial" looks, ravished by her voice. As at a masquing, he is entranced by the "thousand graces" dancing on her forehead, the "ten thousand sweet belgards," the "millions of chaste pleasures" on her lips. He "counts" her fairer indeed; his heart, invaded by Venus's handmaids (the lady's beauties), becomes itself the temple where beauty reigns. There is about the *Hymne in Honour of Beauty* a special flavor of adolescent love (as there were about the *Hymne in Honour of Love* intimations of the childlike oedipal fantasy). Like the adolescent with a crush, the lover idealizes the lady extravagantly, counts himself entirely unworthy of her notice, and is more content than an adult would be with mere chaste indications of her regard. And, like the adolescent, he is harshly judgmental; much as he admires his lady, he cannot stop lecturing her on her duties, cannot trust her to live up to the perfection with which he has endowed her.

He grows up a little, however, when in the last two stanzas he struggles loose from infatuated regard to remind himself that his essential misery is only palliated, not really cured, by this charming experience: thus, he asks "dew" from two different sources. From his lady he wants "one drop of grace," permission perhaps, to live as her "thrall." Her coldness and his passivity suggest that this will be at best a long engagement, and he perhaps hopes to sublimate his frustrations into art; thus at the same time he begs Venus for "one drop of dew relief," a covert prayer to beauty's source to cure his heart, to restore him from death, to send, as Hopkins would say, his roots rain. He still does not despair of writing the angelic anthem first proposed; one suspects that writing poetry stands, in these poems, for doing the work of the world. The inspiration for any real work (as for real play) has libidinal sources, as Spenser clearly feels, but here, as at the end of the *Hymne of Heavenly Beauty,* Spenser seems to withdraw from a wholly contemplative attitude to assume an active one. Like the latent child or the young adolescent, he cannot love as actively as he might wish, but he can still work.

This stage of the quest—although it ends with mention of death—still seems a good deal less anguished than the conclusion of the *Hymne in Honour of Love.* It focuses on ethical decisions with respect to discovering worthy objects of desire and to directing pure desire toward them, and, although the lover's "ecstasy" over a creature is rather theatrical, it is presented as an actual experience, not a dream heaven. The "right" lovers have found each other and, purified of their "drosse," have joined "all the world" in understanding themselves as ordained to be Venus's vassals. The ritual element that Welsford notices as characteristic of Spenser's imaginative life is reinforced by the social milieu in which Spenser sees the privacy of love thriving.[37] (Even the couples at the end of the *Hymne in Honour of Love* participate in a common ritual and pursue their individual pleasures in a single place). The lover is more aware of his situation than in the first hymn and thus is in greater control of it.

La commedia é finita, or so it seems. But this is Spenser, so the last prayer to Venus for "grace" results in a new restiveness that leads to the heavenly hymns and to a new round of imagined heavens. His insight into the mind's love for the beauty of its own projected image of desire (*HB* 218) enables him to imagine the heavenly love of the Trinity (*Hymne of Heavenly Love* 29–35) and thus to project a new image of heaven. The divine narcissism ("It lov'd it selfe, because it selfe was faire," *HHL* 29), unlike the human, is free from love's dislike or pride, yet is "restless" in its own way, "pregnant still with powrefull grace, / And full of fruitfull love, that loves to get / Things like himselfe" (*HHL* 50–52). Desire begetting desire begetting desire, originally an image of the lover's frustration and endemic to the human pursuit of pleasure, is now seen as the principle of universal fecundity, identical with "kindling," *natura naturans*. This heaven of God's inner life, however, seems inaccessible to human experience. Indeed, even the angels became, the poet-lover tells us, "impatient of long resting peace," and Satan "degendering to hate fell from above / Through pride" (*HHL* 78, 94–95). Man, created as a mirror in which God "might his mightie selfe behould," degenders too from his earthly paradise to "never dead, yet ever dying paine" (*HHL* 117, 126). The similarity of the fallen state of man and angel alike to the lover's hell expresses Spenser's understanding that it was this fall that caused man's "deducted spright" (*HL* 106) to be forever racked between erected wit and infected will; for him as for Freud, there is something intrinsically unsatisfying about human sexuality itself—and for the same reason: it is the most adequate paradigm of immortal longings and mortal bounds.

The torments of the lover are transfigured, however, when a new divine infant emerges from the "bosome of eternall blisse" (*HHL* 134) making a heaven of a manger and later displaying the wounds that show him to be the most tormented of all "lovers." Lines 156–62 condense the language of courtly love, "loves deepe wound, that pierst the piteous hart . . . to free his foe," to make clear that, however remote God's inner life seems to men, the dynamic of divine love is consonant with that of human passion; both involve torment and suffering. The torments the human lover has experienced make him able to respond to God's love when he is yet incapable of seeing his beauty: "Learne him to love, that loved thee so deare, / And in thy brest his blessed image beare" (HHL 258–59). Enshrining a new "saint" in his bosom, the lover chooses Christ as his love object so that in the marvelous final stanza he is again ravished with the contemplation of beauty and filled with "sweete enragement of celestiall love, / Kindled through sight of those faire things above." The stanza imitates the unimpeded upward progress of aspiration through a series of prepositional phrases that ends with the mock-preposition "above" that, denied an object, becomes the absolute adverb of heavenly locus.

This theological revision of the literal and ethical understandings of love in the first two hymns seems heaven enough, yet Spenser is almost neurotically suspicious of endings. *The Faerie Queene*, originally an ethical poem in twelve books, became an anagogical one in seven, ending in the "great Sabaoth of the Soul." Reluctant to call any man happy, let alone "thrise happy," before the last day when all vestiges of universal evil are destroyed, Spenser allows himself and his heroes little rest, even in the experience of divine love. As we remember from the first two hymns, "rage" in the breast always leads to "aspiration," and the aspiration toward the heavenly song, a leitmotif throughout the first three hymns, becomes central in the last. Even as Christ came in humility to comfort tormented human beings—love was not enough; action was required—so the poet, vouchsafed the beatific vision, wants to make it in some measure available to mortal sight. The final vision of heaven, corresponding to the anagogical sense of exegesis, requires a more generous response to grace than even the third hymn's meditation on Christ's suffering had done: the *Hymne to Heavenly Love* moved the adult sufferer to choose Christ as a hero. The requirement for this new quest, however, is the biblical one that the lover agree to engage in a transcendent regression, must become as a little child, revising the vision of security and rest enjoyed by Cupid to comprehend the astonishing primal Primal Scene of Sapience, the "soveraine dearling of the *Deity*," herself enshrined in the bosom of the eternal god; the Father is himself now revealed as the happy lover of comedy, as in the third hymn the Son was the hero of tragedy: both are courtly lovers. Christ's descent as a lover in torment intimated a degree of consonance between human love and divine; Cupid's ascent from Venus's lap to create the world shadowed forth the reality of divine engendering. But the divine narcissism envisioned at the beginning of the *Hymn to Heavenly Love* is still only part of Spenser's truth. The lover must return cyclically to the image of the infant Cupid at Venus's breast; Sapience offers the same sort of security and forms with the Father an androgynous and thus perfected object for the lover's devotion. That Sapience is God's "dearling" makes the relationship between her and the hero a mirror not only of a courtly love relationship, but of the family romance cleansed of the fear and guilt of oedipal trespass. The hero insisted, we remember, at the beginning of the *Hymne of Heavenly Love* that divine love had nothing in it of pride or jealousy, and thus reality at the end of the *Hymne to Heavenly Beauty* fulfills the hope of paradise at the end of the *Hymne in Honour of Love*. The hero is reassured to find mother and father figures unified in the deity and experiences enormous relief in the vision of a plenitude that provides food, joy, contentment to the "inward ey" (*HHB* 199, 285–87), and that will provide after death, when work and anthems are done, a rest that he will be able to trust.

The hymns, then, present a view of the cosmogony and of human life within it that attempts to meet the polarities of experience—male-female; sacred-profane; earth-heaven—and to resolve the contradictions between them. The structure of the poems—mirroring as they do a Platonic dialectic, but oriented toward non-Platonic objects—as well as the stanzas with their three rhymes—the first two alternating, the third resolving itself in a couplet (rime royal)—express this concern. When a tribe elaborates a myth to deal with its own similarly experienced polarities, it may either produce a new level of integration or regress to its own myth of origins and develop a cult of universal re-creation. Similarly, an individual in crisis may "reform" his sense of himself to accommodate a contradiction between an old sense of self and a new situation in the environment, regress to an earlier stage of adaptation (repetition compulsion), or repress the contradiction. Spenser, whose myth represents the efforts of a lover to free himself from various wasting levels of fixation, allows this lover to regress in the normal human way only once—at the end of the *Hymne in Honour of Love*. Otherwise, he overcomes the temptation to remain content with any "object" or to return to any earlier object until he is sure that he has the true one. Spenser presents this process as a natural ("kindly") effect of the energy that the poet-lover feels constantly kindled within him.

Rizzuto would find, I believe, this representation of God—the "object" whom the lover finds the true aim of all his strivings—the fruit of a psychic history in which oedipal conflict is fully acknowledged but very successfully resolved—due, in part at least, to the imaginative strength gained in early infancy. Since the infant's first representation of God is preoedipal, sexual differentiation is not for him important—hence, perhaps, the sophisticated, late orthodoxy of a god without gender. Understanding that all human beings worship some deity almost from birth, Spenser revises the traditional myth of a patriarchal god to accommodate the development of human consciousness in which the child feels completely cared for by parents of both sexes and loves so-called masculine and feminine qualities of each. The fourth hymn completes imaginatively what the child begins imaginatively: the love that persons of both sexes feel for their first caretakers (male and female alike) finds an ultimate object in the godhead, a powerful interpretation of Augustine's dictum that Welsford quotes with respect to the *Hymnes:* "Thou hast made us for thyself, Lord, and our hearts are restless until they rest in Thee."[38]

But even in the fourth hymn the poet is very reluctant to dismiss "lower beauties" as unworthy of the redeemed soul. Not only does he adjure the pilgrim to rise to the contemplation of heavenly beauty by admiration of earthly loveliness; he still conceives of the starry heavens domestically as the "house of blessed Gods" (*HHB* 52) with its "King and Queene," the sun and moon, thus anticipating the appearance of Sapience and the eternal God. Indeed, it seems that Spenser is not content wholly to relinquish any achieved level of integration. Hans Loewald has suggested that, rather than define the mature consciousness as one that has successfully transcended infantile and adolescent stages, we should look for a flexibility of levels of integration adaptive to various situations.[39] Thus in Spenser's poem the lover does not regress in a negative sense but shows superior strength and a firm grasp of reality when he becomes "as a little child," meek before his origi-

nal Mother and Father. And, similarly, although the rhetoric of the ending
of the *Hymne to Heavenly Beauty* speaks of the relative ugliness of earthly
things to the contemplator of heavenly beauty, the reader does not forget
the beauties exhibited at the beginning of the poem as means to rise to
these heights.

The poet-lover is also slow to end his hymn. As the first hymn re-
counted Love's creative endeavors and the third, those of "the god of Love,"
so the end of the fourth shows the poet feeling that he must emulate them:
after extravagant praise of Sapience, he concludes that, since no mortal poet
or painter could begin to do justice to her beauty, he ought to resign to
the angels themselves his mission to write "an angelic anthem": "Enough
is me t'admyre so heavenly thing, / And being thus with her huge love
possest, / In th'only wonder of her selfe to rest" (*HHB* 236–38). The ca-
dence of "rest" sounds final enough, but he remembers his promise to
"show Some litel beames to mortall eyes below" and ends his poem instead
with an impassioned account not of Sapience herself but of the joys he has
himself experienced as her adorer. Thus he follows the vocation of vatic
poet which has been calling to him from the beginning of the hymns. At
the end of the final hymn, he addresses himself, reminding himself that
to experience again the ecstasy he has described, he must discipline his wandering thoughts, and he reminds them of the "soveraine light" which they
must place above all others. The reward of doing so will provide, he believes, the final "rest" with which the poem ends.

This psychological progression from earth to heaven is mirrored and reinforced by the numerological relations among the hymns. Alastair Fowler
claims numerological design for "all of Spenser's shorter poems," instanc-
ing, in particular, *Daphnaida* with which *Fowre Hymnes* was originally published.[40] After explaining in his first chapter that "the monad — one — related
to god and was both masculine and feminine, [but] the dyad [was] only
feminine," Fowler goes on in his second chapter to show that, for the Py-
thagoreans, "the divisive principle is also the source of the material aspect
of the universe. . . . In medieval and Renaissance thought the principle of
the dyad is regarded as especially manifest in human nature. For man is
a creature of double nature — partly spiritual, part mortally dyadic — so that
the opposed principles find in him a uniquely close confrontation."[41] I do
not claim that the *Hymnes* employ numerology as a structural principle
but rather as a rich store of allusion. The title of the sequence, for example,
refers to "four," the number, as Fowler says, of "cosmic concord":[42] if, in
Pythagorean terms, one were to write hymns praising the fecundity of the
material world, one would write two, whereas if one wanted to show how
the material world harmonized with the rest of creation, one would write

four. In addition, the hymns use the symbolism of numbers in a great many ways. The third hymn, for instance, praises the Trinity, describes the angels ranked in their "trinall triplicities," and emphasizes Christ as mediator between offended heaven and guilty earth while the fourth includes two pair of kings and queens (Sun and Moon, God and Sapience) and adds the beauty of Sapience to the love of the Trinity. Most significant, however, is the progression from one (the Creator) to two (the Creation) to three (the Trinity) to four (cosmic concord): the poems must be four in number, and the two earthly hymns must have been intended to form an essential part of this whole.

The poems do constitute, then, a narrative and structural whole, but there is no reason to deny that the first two might have been written (as the dedication says they were) in the poet's youth. If so, they may have been revised, as Welsford suggests, to make their style harmonize with the latter two. As such, as Terry Comito remarks, they offer a Spenserian *Vita Nuova*.[43] But does the author (as distinct from the speaker in the poems) mean, as the dedication suggests, to recant the first two hymns, replete as they are with lofty (if often frustrated) love? Good readers have been loath to think so, and the dedication is not only ambiguous enough to let them have their way but also actually encourages them.

First of all, it is certainly significant that Spenser does not accept blame for the "abuse" of his poems: defects in the readers caused them, he says, to misunderstand — an unfortunate situation that may well have given rise to the several stanzas in the *Hymne in Honour of Beauty* (155–75) which insist that Beauty in itself should not be blamed for the follies it may occasion. Nor can it be shown conclusively that he recants either the early or the late versions. He says only that "by way of retractation [I resolved] to reforme them." The *OED* offers, in fact, two definitions for *retractation* that may be closer to Spenser's meaning than "recantation" (*OED*, def. 2). One definition, for the plural, is: "The title of a book by St. Augustine containing further treatment and corrections of matters contained in his former writings." Among the citations included to illustrate this use is the following sentence from George Salmon's *The Infallibility of the Church* (1888): "St. Augustine's 'Retractations' does not mean retractations in our modern sense of the word, but a re-handling of things previously treated of." The *OED* also notes of *retractation* that it is "used similarly of other words," although this definition is rare. Here the *OED* cites as an example William Fulke's 1583 reference to "Beda, in his preface vnto his retractation vpon the Acts of the Apostles" *(A defense of the sincere and true translations of the holie scriptures into the English tong)*. Yet another definition (although "obsolete" and "rare") is: "A rejoinder, retort." The citation for this use is taken from George Gillespie, *A dispute against the English-popish ceremonies obtruded upon the church of Scotland* (1637): "If so, my retractation is, that if he be excused in one way, hee must be accused in an other way." Thus "retractation" in Spenser's dedication may look backward to his revisions of the earlier hymns and forward to the "re-handling" of the essential terms in the "heavenly hymns," while the entire project may be a friendly "retort" to the accusation of one of his patronesses. "Recantation" does appear, however, as the second definition for "retractation" and was, apparently, used very widely in that sense. To muddle matters still further, "retraction" was often used (even to refer to Augustine's book!) as a synonym for "retractation," in the second sense, and, since it was the term Chaucer used, would have been especially familiar to Spenser. "Retraction" was not used, however, to mean either "rehandling" or "retort," so that if Spenser had wished to beat his breast unambiguously, he could have done so by using that word.

On *one* reading, then, of the dedication, a misinterpretation of innocent poems leads to a rehandling of the material they contained in the twin forms of revision and addition, a rehandling which, as Roche points out, is dedicated to the critic and her sister and published with hope of their patronage. It is plausible that the entire dedication is meant to guide "reading," a word that turns up in both its literal and figurative senses remarkably often in these hymns. Spenser could not directly accuse his noble patroness of overreacting to whatever she thought young persons found provocative in the hymns to love and beauty, but—reminding her in the elaborate, euphuistic figure of the first sentence that hermeneutics is a moral exercise—could, by praising her and her sister for their excellence "both in the one & the other kinde," encourage her to give the earthly manifestations of love and beauty the due he thinks owing to them.

If we recall the importance of number symbolism in the poems, Spenser's repetition of the word "two" (five times), its synonyms, and homonyms in the dedication can be seen as an additional reminder that earthly love and beauty are—as the praise of both soon to follow will so strongly claim—the kindling elements of *natura naturans*. For two was, we remember, the number of the material world, and it was also the mean between one and four—the numbers, respectively, of perfection and concord. Indeed, the dedication to the "two honorable sisters" as to the "most excellent and rare ornaments of all true love and beauty, both in the one & the other kinde," with "both" meaning "both sisters" and "both kinds," may suggest that the countesses are more than mere exempla, are the "double means" binding earth to heaven.[44] The riddling linguistic quality of the dedication reminds all his readers to be alert to similar ambiguities in the world and in the world of the poem.

For it is in the latter that the question of "recantation" becomes acute. I accept Welsford's emphasis on the fiction of the poem but think she does not go far enough, either in noticing the philosophical genre to which it belongs or in maintaining the fiction of the poet-lover as distinct from the author of the dedication. *Fowre Hymnes,* like a sonnet sequence, pretends to record the artistic creations (in this case, hymns of praise) of a "hero" at different stages of a quest. In that the hero's perspective is trapped in his fiction, it is more like an epistolary novel or a stream of consciousness novel with a first-person narrator than a spiritual autobiography. The spiritual autobiographer knows that his story ends happily, but the speaker in the first two hymns does not. On the contrary—as Welsford observes—both of the first two hymns end with the word "death," and the hero's disappointed aspirations lead, as she says, directly to the "recantatory" stanzas of the *Hymne of Heavenly Love.*[45] If we maintain that the speaker is distinct from Spenser, the "lewd layes" (*HHL* 8) can refer to the oeuvre of the poet-hero who enacts the repentance with which Spenser would identify if he did consider his early work either "unclerkly" or "lascivious." But, as my alternative reading of the dedication shows, there is no definite evidence that he did, and we may wonder at the thoroughness with which that "other Spenser" managed to cover his tracks. Similarly, the last stanzas of each of the second pair of hymns are the fictive "report" of a person who has undergone a profoundly compensatory religious experience after a series of miserable amatory adventures, not the more balanced view of one who, like the "I" of *Epithalamion,* for example, can see the part earthly love plays in the divine dispensation.[46] What this speaker says must be estimated in terms of what he has endured; to identify wholly with him and his enthusiasms would be to err in a different direction, but in the same way as "those of like age and disposition" had done earlier. It is not necessary to convict the poet-lover of sin, as Welsford does, to see why he "recants."[47] That would be necessary only if we had to identify a Spenserian degree of enlightenment with this character who is from any point of view very far from having a clear idea of his own situation. He "recants" because present joy so far exceeds past sorrow. His beliefs and the passion with which he holds them are the result of his psychic history about which we partly know.

But the rewards of such renunciations are, I fully agree with Welsford, far from Platonic. This hero suffers from disappointment with earthly love and beauty, but the second two hymns are so clearly "retractations" of the first two in their rehandling of "love" and "beauty" that the reader can see the poet-lover exploiting his disappointments and the understanding gained from them to generate new hope. The second two "levels of integration" are continuous with the first, and, if there is any ladder here, it is like the rope ladder, symbolic in Eastern religions as the link between heaven and earth: Spenser's hero gathers his rungs as he climbs, using the lower to strengthen the upper. The rungs connect earth and heaven by "means" of language ("love," "dearling," "beauty," "kindled," "fire") that applies (with differences the "good" reader can discern) to both heaven and earth. Thus the reader can be reassured that the feelings by which he himself is driven do have their proper object and that perseverance will find its reward, however unanticipated and unexpected. Love is, finally, as in the myth from *Timaeus* which Spenser uses in his first account of the Creation — and which, according to Fowler,[48] gave such currency in the Renaissance to four as the number of cosmic concord — the force which "tempering goodly well / Their [the elements'] contrary dislikes with loved meanes, / Did place them all in order, and compell / To keepe them selves within their sundrie raines, / Together linkt with Adamantine chaines" (*HL* 85–89).[49] The hymns kindle a new myth assuring us that human beings, who must all suffer poignant libidinal disappointments, can see their efforts to substitute new objects for lost ones as a series of "retractations" or revisions of their psychic lives, one of which may finally provide, as Spenser's does, "rest."

These poems, then, with their dedication, form an artistic and philosophic whole. The vision of Sapience enshrined in God's breast is the "answer" to the hero's "problem." But the poems "show work," make us see how the poet-lover arrived at his answer — they employ, that is, Lang's "reflexive mode."[50] And just as we often do not know how fully we should concur with Socrates in, for example, the *Symposium* or the *Phaedo;* or with Pietro Bembo in the *Courtier;* or with Raphael Hythloday (or More's own persona) in *Utopia,* so we are to bring our own psychic histories to bear on the hymns to decide how far to identify with the poet-hero. Whether we choose to imitate him in whole, in part, or at all, will in turn depend on the invention we nurture in the hymns' "imaginative groundplot" (in Sidney's terms), but the dedication seems to warn against passive identification with any sort of fictional character. After all, Spenser might say, we are told to work out our *own* salvation in fear and trembling, and mere imitation, the Renaissance poets never tired of reminding each other, is not creation. Like the Creator himself — with whom these poets associated themselves so strongly — Spenser leaves us burdened with choice: we may identify with the poet-hero or react against him, but in either case, his fictional experience furnishes us with fresh material — conscious and unconscious — for novel, real-life "retractations" of our own.

Rider College

NOTES

1. Jon A. Quitslund, "Spenser's Image of Sapience," *Studies in the Renaissance* 16 (1969), 210.

2. Berel Lang, "Space, Time and Philosophical Style," *Critical Inquiry* 2 (1975), 273; see also Gary Shapiro, "Reading and Writing in the Text of Hobbes's *Leviathan," Journal of the History of Philosophy* 18, (1980), 147–57.

3. Sir Philip Sidney, *Apology for Poetry,* quoted in A. C. Hamilton, *The Structure of Allegory in "The Faerie Queene"* (Oxford: Clarendon Press, 1961), p. 27. I have modernized Sidney's spelling.

4. Lyric, in the Renaissance sense of a (rather!) short poem with a single voice. Its impulses might range, as Helen Vendler asserts of lyric generally, from reflection to song: "When song and reflection join, lyric is born" ("Sociable Comets," *New York Review of Books* 28 [1981], 24). Spenser's *Hymnes* tend toward the latter, but within his reflections occur exclamations that presage the nineteenth-century notion of lyric as "the spontaneous overflow of powerful feelings."

5. *Hymne in Honour of Love,* 19–21. All quotations from *Fowre Hymnes* are taken from *Spenser: Fowre Hymnes, Epithalamion—A Study of Edmund Spenser's Doctrine of Love,* ed. Enid Welsford (New York: Barnes and Noble, 1967). Subsequent references to this edition appear parenthetically in the text, abbreviated *HL (Hymne in Honour of Love), HB (Hymne in Honour of Beauty), HHL (Hymne of Heavenly Love),* and *HHB (Hymne of Heavenly Beauty).*

6. In *Spenser: Fowre Hymnes,* ed. Welsford, p. 92.

7. Enid Welsford, introduction to *Spenser: Fowre Hymnes,* pp. 36–37.

8. James Nohrnberg, *The Analogy of the Faerie Queene* (Princeton, N.J.: Princeton University Press, 1976) uses a version of developmental psychology—one emphasizing the work of Erik Erikson—to illuminate the quests in *The Faerie Queene.*

9. Bruno Bettelheim argues in a manner reminiscent of Sidney that fairy tales told to children help them to integrate discordant parts of their personalities and to remain hopeful about the rewards for the effort of growing up (*The Uses of Enchantment: The Meaning and Importance of Fairy Tales* [New York: Alfred Knopf, 1977], p. 5).

10. Harold Bloom, *The Anxiety of Influence: A Theory of Poetry* (New York: Oxford University Press, 1973), p. 8.

11. D. W. Winnicott, *Playing and Reality* (London: Tavistock Press, 1971); Ana-Maria Rizzuto, *The Birth of the Living God: A Psychoanalytic Study* (Chicago: University of Chicago Press, 1979). Arthur F. Marotti, "Countertransference, the Communication Process, and the Dimensions of Psychoanalytic Criticism," *Critical Inquiry* 4 (1978), 471–89, of which I learned only when this essay was substantially complete, gives, as well as an admirably clear account of the relevance to the arts of Winnicott's work, a very useful methodology for studies of the sort I have undertaken.

12. Rizzuto, *The Birth of the Living God,* p. 202; she refers to Sigmund Freud, *The Future of an Illusion* (1927).

13. Winnicott, *Playing and Reality,* p. 5.

14. Ibid., pp. 4, 5.

15. Rizzuto, *The Birth of the Living God,* pp. 177, 179.

16. Ibid., p. 179.

17. Many twentieth-century scholars have interested themselves in the widely dispersed human longing for and imagining of "paradise": among psychologists, Freud, Erikson, Melanie Klein, and their followers have seen paradises in art and dreams as regressive wishes for a return to the primary narcissism of early infancy, while historians have shown that

the quest for a heaven-on-earth motivated many of the European explorers in Spenser's Europe; and, as Frank Kermode, *The Sense of an Ending* (Oxford: Oxford University Press, 1968), has argued, these ambitions coalesced with the various millenarian beliefs of the Middle Ages and Renaissance; Mircea Eliade writes too of present-day tribes in Latin America who have been wandering in search of an earthly Land-without-Evil for more than three hundred years (*The Quest: History and Meaning in Religion* [Chicago: University of Chicago Press, 1969], p. 102).

18. Welsford, introduction to *Spenser: Fowre Hymnes*, p. 40.

19. Winnicott's discussion is uncannily close to Wordsworth's understanding of the genesis of creativity; see the passage beginning "Blest the infant babe," *Prelude* 2.233–64.

20. Winnicott, *Playing and Reality*, p. 42.

21. The importance of "mirroring" experience in early infancy is first stressed by Jacques Lacan, "Le Stade du miroir comme formateur de la fonction du Je, telle qu'elle nous est révélée dans l' expérience psychoanalytique," *Revue Française de Psychoanalyse* 13 (1949), 449–55, and cited in Rizzuto, *The Birth of the Living God*, p. 122. It is anticipated not only by Wordsworth but also by many of the reflexive images in Spenser's *Hymnes* (see esp. *HB* 224; *HHL* 29–30; *HHB* 134). With respect to adolescent love, Erik Erikson notes, "To a considerable extent [it] is an attempt to arrive at a definition of one's identity by projecting one's diffused ego image on another and by seeing it thus reflected and gradually clarified" (*Childhood and Society* [New York: Norton, 1956] p. 262).

22. This claim that the god is successively transformed from the externalization or objectification of an emotion to the object of that emotion will be perhaps clearer in the discussion of the fourth hymn. On earth love drives us toward beauty, but in heaven, as Welsford says, love and beauty are the same (introduction to *Spenser: Fowre Hymnes*, p. 50). Or as Donne would say not much later, God is both "the object [thing known] and the wit [way of knowing]"—a more scholastic way of putting the neoplatonic formulation.

23. Richard Rainoldes, *A Boke Called the Foundacion of Rhetoricke*, quoted in Douglas Peterson, *The English Lyric from Wyatt to Donne* (Princeton, N.J.: Princeton University Press, 1967), pp. 55–56.

24. For Welsford the three parents of love posed a problem of consistency. I accept her solution that Plenty and Penury—the suspension between which describes the lover's typical state of soul—form a single masculine parent (notes to *Spenser: Fowre Hymnes*, p. 147), and would add only that the account of Love's parentage (like other details in this poem) is rather charmingly naive and seems to emerge from an infantile point of view in which the exact number of parents that one must have is still a little hazy.

25. Terry Comito, in "A Dialectic of Images in Spenser's *Fowre Hymnes*," *SP* 74 (1977), 303, points out that "wanting" in *HL* 70–71 puns on "lacking" and "desiring."

26. Winnicott, *Playing and Reality*, p. 22.

27. Bettelheim, *The Uses of Enchantment*, p. 9.

28. Erikson, *Childhood and Society*, pp. 86–87.

29. Bruno Bettelheim, *Symbolic Wounds: Puberty Rites and the Envious Male*, rev. ed. (New York: Collier, 1971), p. 64.

30. Bettelheim, *The Uses of Enchantment*, pp. 10–11.

31. Welsford, introduction to *Spenser: Fowre Hymnes*, p. 39.

32. Edward Tayler, *Nature and Art in the English Renaissance* (New York: Columbia University Press, 1968), pp. 115–16.

33. Ben Jonson's poem on Venetia Digby's "Mind" claims similar origin for his mistress: "A Mind so pure, so perfect fine, / As 'tis not radiant, but divine; / And so disclaiming any tryer / 'Tis got where it can try the fire." *Ben Jonson, The Works*, ed. C. H.

Herford, Percy Simpson, and Evelyn Simpson (Oxford: Clarendon Press, 1925–52), vol. 8, p. 279.

34. Launcelot Andrewes, *Ninety-six Sermons* (Oxford: John Henry Parker, 1865), p. 201.

35. See note 21 for the significance of "mirroring."

36. Sigmund Freud, "The Most Prevalent Form of Degradation in Erotic Life," in *On Creativity and the Unconscious: Papers on the Psychology of Art, Literature, Love, Religion,* ed. Benjamin Nelson (New York: Harper & Row, 1958), p. 184.

37. Welsford, introduction to *Spenser: Fowre Hymnes,* p. 38.

38. Welsford, notes to *Spenser: Fowre Hymnes,* p. 172.

39. Hans Loewald, "Ego and Reality," *International Journal of Psychoanalysis* 32 (1951), pt. 1, pp. 10–18: "I mentioned earlier that Freud has raised the problem of psychological survival of earlier ego-stages side by side with later stages of ego-development, a problem which he says has as yet hardly been investigated. If we look closely at people we can see that it is not merely a question of survival of former stages of ego-reality integration, but that people shift considerably, from day to day, at different periods in their lives, in different moods and situations, from one such level to other levels. In fact, it would seem that people are more alive (though not necessarily more 'stable'), the broader their range of ego-reality levels is. Perhaps the so-called fully developed, the mature ego is not one that has become fixated at the presumably highest or latest stage of development having left the others behind it, but is an ego that integrates its reality in such a way that the earlier and deeper levels of ego-reality integration remain alive as dynamic sources of higher organization." Compare Eliade: "The 'sacred' is an element in the structure of consciousness, not a stage in the history of consciousness" (*The Quest,* p. i).

40. Alastair Fowler, *Spenser and the Numbers of Time* (New York: Barnes and Noble, 1964), p. 248.

41. Ibid., pp. 5, 9.

42. Ibid., p. 25.

43. Comito, "A Dialectic of Images," p. 309.

44. Fowler, *Spenser and the Numbers of Time,* p. 25. By Elizabethan standards, such a suggestion was not particularly extravagant, certainly not blasphemous. These ladies, devout, noble, fruitful, could have easily been accorded typological significance.

45. Welsford, introduction to *Spenser: Fowre Hymnes,* p. 48.

46. Ibid., p. 60.

47. Ibid., pp. 61–62.

48. Fowler, *Spenser and the Numbers of Time,* p. 25.

49. See ibid., and Welsford, introduction to *Spenser: Fowre Hymnes,* pp. 149–50, for the punning character of "meanes."

50. Lang, "Space, Time and Philosophical Style," p. 273.